Laurens County South Carolina

WILL BOOK A
VOLUME II

1840–1853

❧

Frances T. Ingmire

Heritage Books
2024

HERITAGE BOOKS

AN IMPRINT OF HERITAGE BOOKS, INC.

Books, CDs, and more—Worldwide

For our listing of thousands of titles see our website
at
www.HeritageBooks.com

Published 2024 by
HERITAGE BOOKS, INC.
Publishing Division
5810 Ruatan Street
Berwyn Heights, MD 20740

International Standard Book Number
Paperbound: 978-0-7884-7757-7

FORWARD

This volume contains verbatum copies of the old wills of Laurens County, South Carolina.

Records have been copied just as they exist, including the duplications, errors in spelling and variations of names-many of which reflected the signatures affixed by the same person.

Some of the entries are illegible to the extent that interpretation cannot be conclusive. Abbrivaiations have been used as in original documents.

Due to the usual corruptions in surnames and questionable legibility of many records, it is suggested that researchers consider all known variations and phonetic spelling in using this material.

WILL OF ROBERT MCNEES

South Carolina Laurens District. In the name of God, Amen. I Robert MCNEES of the state of South Carolina and District of Laurens considering the uncertainty of this mortal life and being of sound mind, blessed be the almighty God for the same, do hereby make and ordain this my last will and testament in manner and form following to wit. I give and bequeath unto my wife Sarah MCNEES one bed, bedsted, and furniture. Secondly, my will and desire is that the whole of the remainder of my estate both real and personal be sold by my executors hereing after named within one year after my decease on a suitable credit and out of the proceeds of said sale, all my just debts and funeral expenses to be paid. And the balance to be divided into seven shares and paid as follows to wit. One share to be paid to my son Samuel. One share to my daughter Susannah, the wife of John MILNER. One share to the children or child of my deceased daughter Margarett BABB. One share to my son Richard. And one share to the children of my deceased son James MCNEES the survivor or survivors of them. One share to my daughter Agnes, wife of Joshua TEAGUE, to her and the heirs of her body. And to my daughter Sabra WHITE, one share. And I do hereby appoint my friend Joseph BABB and John S. JAMES executors of this my last will and testament, hereby revoking all former wills be me here to fore made. Signed, sealed, and declared by the said Robert as his last will and testament. In the premise of us, who at his request and in his presence and in the presence of each other have subscribed our names as witnesses to the due executors of the same this 30th March, Anno Domine, 1833.

David Dorroh   Robert McNees (SEAL)
John Phillips
Elijah Saunders
Recorded in Will Book A, Page 1. Recorded date not available.
Proven Jan. 23, 1840. W. D. Watts, Ordy. Original will not in file of Probates.

WILL OF WILLIAM THOMPSON

South Carolina Laurens District. In the name of God, Amen. I William THOMPSON being of sound and disposing mind and memory and calling to mind the uncertainty of life, and knowing that it is appointed unto all men once to die, and not knowing how soon I shall be called, do ordain and institute this my last will and testament. Revoking all other here to fore made. First, I bequeath my soul to God, who gave it to me, and my body to the dust from whence it sprang to be buried in a christian like manner. Secondly, after paying all my just debts and funeral expenses I desire that my executors herein after named may sell any of my personal porperty that they think they have no particular use for on the farm. The balance of my property I wish to remain on the place during the term of the natural life or widowhood of my beloved wife Jane THOMPSON to be managed to the best

1

advantage by my executors for the use and benefit of my family. If any other of my children should marry before the death of my wife, Jane THOMPSON or a final division, I wish them to be made equal to them who are married, Viz, as much in property and one hundred dollars which will make them equal. If my beloved wife Jane THOMPSON should marry, I give her a child part of my estate both real and personal to dispose of as she may think proper. And the balance both real and personal to be equally divided amongst all my children Viz.; Sarah Ann, Isabella, Elizabeth D., Nancy, Jane, and Mary. I hereby nominate constitute and appoint my wife Jane THOMPSON and John W. PERRY my sole executors to this my last will and testament. In testemony where of I have hereunto affixed my hand and seal this the twenty third day of September, one thousand eight hundred and thirty six. Signed, sealed, published, and declared as and for the last will and testament of the above named William THOMPSON in the presence of.

John H. Coleman   William Thompson (SEAL)
Allen Coleman
William G. Coleman
Proven date June 18, 1840. Recorded in Book A, Page 2. Recorded date not available. W. D. Watts Ordy. Original will not in files of Probate Judge.

WILL OF AMBROSE GARRETT

In the name of God, Amen. I Ambors GARRETT of the destrict of Laurens in the State of South Carolina, being of sound and disposing mind and memory, but weak and afflicted in body. And calling to mind the uncertainty of life, and being desirious to dispose of all such worldly estate as it has been pleas God to bless me with, do make and ordain this my last will in manner following, that is to say. I desire my black smith tools together with a part of my stock of cattle, and if any think more that my wife thinks proper to spare be immediately sold after my decease, and out of the money arising there from, all my just debts and funeral expenses be paid. After my debts and funeral expences is paid, I give to my wife Nancy GARRETT all the balance of my estate, both real and personal during her natural life or widow hood, in order that she may be able to raise and school my children. And give to each of them at their becoming of age, or day of marriage, equal to what I have given the rest of my children, that has left me. And after her death, I give the same to my children and direct my executor to sell the same and make equal destribution among them , having respect to what has or may be given out. And I give the same to them, their heirs, executors, administrators and assigns forever. Provided never the less if my said wife Nancey GARRETT should marry, then and in that case my will is that my executor expose all my estate both real and personal to sale and make destribution as above directed, giving to her one third part. And lastly, I do constitute my said wife Executrix and my friend Fountain MARTIN executor of this my last will and testament. Hereby revokeing

2

all other and former wills and testaments by me heretofore made. In testamony I have here unto set my hand and affixed my seal this 9th day of May, 1840. Signed, sealed, published, and declared as and for the last will and testament of the above named Ambrose GARRETT in the presents of us.

Stephen Garrett   Ambrose Garrett (SEAL)
Jepe Davis
Bresden Davis
Proven date July 9, 1840. W. D. Watts Ordy. Original will page 3, Book A, Bundle 83, Package 10.

WILL OF RACHEL OWINGS

State of South Carolina Laurens District. This the 17th day of June, 1840. In the name of God, Amen. Of being of sound and disposing mind and memory, but weak in body, and calling to mind the uncertainty of life and being desirous to dispose of all such worldly estate as it hath pleased God to bless me with, do make and ordain this my last will in manner following. I this day am in my mind and I will to sister Nancy CHILDS and her son Richard a negro boy named Ben, and also one fether bed, and two sheets and one blanket, and one quilt, and also my cloke to sister Nancy. And also my bonet to sister Nancy, and also all of my cloth, 1 half to sister Nancy and the other half to broth er William OWING, Nancy and also 1 lady saddle to brother William OWING, Nancy and all my cows and calf to brother Will OWING and $14 to brother William OWINGS which is in the hands of Granberry WILLIS and also $69 which is in the hands of John GARRETT Junr. to be equally divided between my four brothers, namely; Wm. OWINGS and Richd OWINGS and Archd OWINGS and John OWINGS. Signed sealed in the present of us. Test.

                                                         her
B. K. Owings   Rachel X Owings
James Owings   mark
H. E. Owings
Recorded in Will Book A, Page 4. Recorded date not available. Proven July 12, 1840. W. D. Watts, Ordy. Bundle 89, Pkge. 10.

WILL OF MARTHA BOLEN

South Carolina Laurens District. In the name of God, Amen. I Martha BOLEN of the District aforesaid, being of perfect mind and memory. Calling unto mind the mortallity of my body, and knowing it is appointed for all men onst to die, and being desireous of disposing of all such worldly estate as it hath pleased God to bless me with, do make and ordain this my last will and testament. Item first. I give and bequeath to my two sons William H. BOLEN and Albert D. BOLEN the hole of my real estate to be equally divided between them. If either of them should die and the other live, I will that the serviveing brother shall pofsefsn the deceasd. brothers part unless death shall not take place untill they have legal heirs of their own . In that case,

I wish it to go to their legal heirs. Also my will is that my two sons before mentioned shall have each a horse, and bridle, and saddle out of my personal estate in lieu of all other claims therein. My will is that my single daughters that is to say, Elizabeth, Patsa, and Mitilda, shall remain together with their brothers as long as they live single and during that term, for them to have an interest in common with there brothers in the real estate, so far as it regards a home and the produce of the soil for their support. But as they marry, this interest abates to them that do marry. After my debts and buryal expences are paid out of my chattle estate, I will that the remainder continue undevided, and continue on the premices for the joint use of all my children which are single untill my daughters marry. And as they marry, I wish them to receave an amounte equal to the amount which have been recvd. by my two daughters which are now marryed. And after my daughters which are now single are all marryed, and have recvd. an amount out of my chattle estate as before doscribed, I desire that the refsedue be devided equeilly between all my daughters, that is to say; Nancy, Polly, Elizabeth, Patsy, and Metilda. One lastly, I do hereby appoint my son William H. BOLEN and my brother William GREEN executors of this my last will and testament. And I do hearby uterly disalow revoke and disanul all and every other testaments, wills, legacies, bequests, and executors by me in any wise before made, willed and bequeathed. Ratifying and confirming this and no other to be my last will and testament. In witnefs where of have hear unto set my hand and seal on this the 25th day of August in the year of our Lord, one thousand eight hundred and thirty four. Signed, sealed, published, pronounced, and declared by the said Martha BOWLEN as her last will and testament in the presents of us, who in her presents and in the presents of each other have hearunto subscirbed our names.

	her
Elisha Watkins	Marha X Bolen (SL)
Franklin Glen	mark
John C. Watkins	

Recorded in Will Book A, Page 4, Bdl. 83, Pkg. 14. Recorded date not available. W. D. Watts Ordy. Laurens District. Proven date not available.

WILL OF JOSEPH GOODGOINS

South Carolina Laurens District. In the name of God, Amen. This I affirm this evening that I am now in my right mind and that this is my last will and testament. I do will and bequeath this tract of land I now live on to my wife and children. And the small interest which William ALLEN has now in said land, is left in the care of William F. DOWNS his agent to be signd over when called on the deed, then to be proved and recorded. All my other to be absolutely thears during her lifetime or widowhood, or if practicable sell the whole. All the improvement made by cultivation or otherwise of said property to go them or the use of the children, that they should be well edcated. I wish my wife to appoint Micajah BERRY together with her self or any other person who she may think proper to appoint to adjust said business. It is my request that all my book accounts should be carefully examined and collected. Given under my hand and seal this 4th day of August, Ano Domino, 1837.

Attest Garlend Lewis   J. Goodgoins (SEAL)
Attest Thomas Pedero
Attest Jonathan Downs
Recorded in Will Book A., Page 5. Original will not in files of Probate Judge. W. D. Watts Ordy., Laurens Dist. Proven December 7, 1840.

WILL OF JANE HAMILTON

State of South Carolina. In the name of God, Amen. I Jane HAMILTON of Laurens District and State aforesaid, being of sound and disposing mind and memory. And calling to mind the uncertainty of life and being deserous to dispose of all such worldly estate as it hath pleased God to bless me with, do make and ordain this my last will in manner following, that is to say. I give to my daughter Elizabeth TAYLOR one negro girl named Edith and boy Henry, one small waggon and one cloth loom. I give to my son in law William MILLS and my daughter Margrett MILLS one negro boy named Jobe and one cow and calf. I give to my daughter Nancy MCCLINTOCK one negro woman named Mary and her increase and one child called Emily, one sorrel mare and colt, all my house hold and kitchen furniture, not otherwise mentioned, all my plantation tools, namely; ploughs, hoes, axes, mattock, and one half of all my stock of hogs. I give to my son John MCCLINTOCK one negro man named John and boy named Andrew, and all the crop and provision that I may have on hands, only so much as may be necesary for a support for Nancy MCCLINTICK and her negroes till she can make a crop, also our hulf of my hogs. I give to my grand daughter Jane TAYLOR our clay or creamed colored colt. I give to my grand daughter Elizabeth TAYLOR one bed and furniture. I give to my grandaughter Mary Julia MILLS one sorrel horse, known by the name of Tom. I give to my grand daughter Jane MCCLINTICK one hundred and fifty dollars. It is my will that if I have any lawful claim to the negroes or any part of them that have been distributed among my children, that they keep them as they got them, that is to say. Elizabeth TAYLOR to keep the bcy Solomon. Margarett MILLS to keep the boy Joe. And firt Caroline Nancy MCCLINTICK to keep the boy Sie and girl Mary Ann. And John MCCLINTICK to keep the bcy Cemp. I give to my daughter Nancy MCCLINTICK all that tract or parcel of land whereon I now live to a line running to a stack corner worth spring to a stake corner on John Deam MCCLINTICK line near the scool house spring to have and to hold during her life time. After her death to be equally divided between all my grand children. I give to my son John MCCLINTICK and his heirs forever all the balance of (Illegeable)   The above line and more particularly disignated made by me to hime some years since and witnefsed by William BONAR Esqr. and Mayante MCCLINTICK. All the rest of my

5

estate both real and personal not herein disposed of I desire
may be given to my son John, out of which his to pay all my just
debts and funeral expences. And also to pay the above named
legacy of one hundred and fifty dollars to my grand daughter
Jane or in line thareof to give the said Jane, one negro girl
named Matildia. And lastly, I do constitute my said son John
MCCLINTICK sole executor of this my last will and testament. In
testimony whereof I have bin unto set my hand and affixed my seal
this 19th, May, 1834. Signed, sealed, published, and declared
as and for the last will and testament of the above named Jane
HAMILTON, in the presence of us.

	her
John Deam	Jane X Hamilton
Jurbert Hutchenson	mark
T. Deam	

Recorded in Will Book A, Page 5. Recorded date not available.
Proven April 16, 1839. W. D. Watts, Ordy. Original will not in
file of Probates.

WILL OF THOMAS MCCARLEY

I Thomas MCCARLEY do constitute this my last will and testament,
to wit. First, I give and bequeath to my wife Martha MCCARLEY
one bed, bed stead, and furniture, one iron grey horse and her
saddle and bridle to be hers absolutely. Also the sum of one
hundred dollars to be annually paid to her for her support during her natural life, the first of every year by my executor
Alexander MCCARLEY. Second, I give to my grand son Thomas Augustus MCCARLEY my saddle and bridle and watch. Third, I give
and bequeath to my son Alexander MCCARLEY all the balance of my
property, to wit, my negroes, Spence, Charlotte, Sam, Henry,
Mose, Leah, Downs, and Nancy, all my stock of horses, cows, hogs
and sheep, all my cotton, corn fadder wheat, oats, flour and
bacon, which may be on hand at the time of my death. My waggon
and gears and farming tools of every sort, all my house hold and
kitchen furniture, and my books. Together with all monies on
hand and all due to me and every other article of property belonging to me not here, in other wise disposed of. Out of which
said Alexander is to pay my debts and the fore going annuity to
my wife. Fourth, I appoint my son Alexander MCCARLEY sole executor of this my will. In testimony whereof I hereunto set my
hand and affix my seal this thirteeth day of December, in the
year, 1839. Signed, sealed, published, and declared as and for
the last will and testament of Thomas MCCARLEY in presence of.

C. Williams	Thomas McCarley (SEAL)
William Power	
Alexander Power	

Proven date March 23, 1840. Recorded date not available.
Recorded in Book A, Page 7, Bundle 83, Package 11. W. D. Watts
Ordy.

WILL OF WILLIAM SULA

State of South Carolina Laurens District. I William SULA of the district and state aforesaid, do make and publish this my last will and testament hereby revcking and making void all former wills by me at anytime heretofore made. And as to such worldly estate as it hath pleased God to intrust me with, I dispose of the same as follows. First, I give and bequeath to my beloved wife Sarah E. SULA during her widowhood one yellow girl share about twelve or thirteen years of age. And after her marriage or in the event of her marring, I will and bequeath said share and her future in cream to John GARLINGTON in trust for the use and benefit of my said wife during her natural life. And at her death I give and bequeath said named Louisa and all her previous and future increase, absolutely to my children or to such of them as may survive, their said mother to be equally divided amongst them, shair and shair alike. Or should any of my said children die previous to their mother leaving a child or children, then and in that event said child or children shall be in- tilted to the shair which thair father or mother if living would be intitled to. Secondly, I give and bequeath all my other goods and chattels and closes in action to my said wife Sarah E. SULA absolutely, except my watch, which I give to my son George Moore SULA. And lastly, I do hereby make and ordain my beloved wife Sarah E. SULA executrix of this my last will and testament. In witnefs whereof I William SULA the testator have to this my last will written on one sheet of paper. Set my hand and seal this the fifth day of August in the year of our Lord, one thousand eight hundred and forty. Signed, sealed, and delivered in the presence of us. Also have subscribed in the presence of each other.

John Wm. Simpson   William Sula (SEAL)
Wm. M. Garlington
Richard Denten
Recorded in Will Book A, Page 7. Recorded date not available.
(Illegeable)

WILL OF ROBERT R. HAND

South Carolina Laurens District. In the name of God, Amen. I Robert HAND of the state and district aforesaid, being weak in body, but of sound and disposing mind and memory, and calling to mind the uncertainty of life, and being desirous to dispose cf such worldly wealth, as it has pleased God to bless me with, do make and constitute this my last will in manner following, that is to say. I desire that immediately after my decease, my execu- tors to be hereafter named do sell at publick auction, and to the highest bidder the whole of my estate both real and personal of every description whatever on a credit of twelve months. And after paying my funeral expences, and all my just debts, that the net proceeds of my estate be divided as follows, that is to say. I give to my dearly beloved wife Elizabeth HAND one tenth part

of the neat proceeds of my estate to her use and benefit forever
solely and absolutely that she may dispose of in any way or
maner she pleases. It is my will and desire that the remaining
nine thenths of my estate be equally divided between my nine
children or their legal representatives, share and share alike,
to that each may have an equal dividend of my estate. It is my
express will and desire, that, that portion of my estate which
by this will, goes to the children of my daughter Polly (to wit)
Sally, Polly, and Nancy THOMASON the daughters of Robert THOMAS-
ON be retained in the hands of my son Robert HAND, in trust for
the said children, and that he put the money to interest for
their benefit, and as they come of age or marry that he pay to
them their equal distributive share. It is also my desire that
my negroe man Lewis and his wife Faney be sold in a lot together
so that they be not separated or divided in the sale. Lastly, I
do nominate, constitute, ordain, and appoint my trust friend
Reuben BURDITT and my son Robert HAND my sole executors of this
my last will and testament, hereby revoking, disannulling and
disallowing all other wills and testament by me heretofore made.
or executed. In testemony whereof I have hereunto set my hand
and seal the ninth day of November, in the year of our Lord, one
thousand eight hundred and twenty seven. Signed, sealed, pronounced published, and declared to be his last will and testament
by Robert HAND in the presence of us.

	HIS
Archd. Young	Robert R. Hand (SEAL)
Thos. Wright	mark
E. Young	

Recorded in Will Book A, Page 8, Bdl. 90, Pkg. 1. Proven 24th
of July, 1840. Recorded date not available. W. D. Watts Ordy.,
Laurens Dist.
Whereas I Robert HAND Sen. of Laurens District have made and
duly executed my last will and testament in writing bearing date
the ninth day of November, one thousand eight hundred and twenty
seven, and thereby did nominate, constitute, ordain and appoint
Reuben BURDITT one of the executors of my said last will and
testament. Now, I do hereby revoke and make void the said nom-
ination and appointment and do hereby nominate constitute, ordain and appoint my beloved wife Elizabeth HAND executirx of my
alst will and testament in substitution of the said Reuben BUR-
DETT. Signed, sealed, published, and declared by the sd. Robert
HAND, as and for a codicil to his last will and testament, to be
taken as part thereof in the presence of us the 8th day of October, 1838.

	his
John N. Young	Robert R. Hand (L.S.)
Arch. Young	mark
Thos. Wright	

WILL OF AVENT FULLER

South Carolina Laurence District. In the naem of God, Amen. I
Avent FULLER of the state and district aforesaid, being of

perfect mind and disposing memory, and calling to mind the uncertainty of life and being desirous to dispose of what property it hath been please God to bless me with, do make and ordain this my last will and tesment. Revoking and anuling all others in manner and form following, that is to say. I desire that all my just debts be paid and I will to my niece Rebecca A. FULLER one bed and furniture. I give to John Twisvan FULLER son of my nice Delphy FULLER, one hundred dollars and that he have schooling to the amount of fifty dollars. I give to my niece Delphy FULLER the tract of land where on I now live containing one hundred and forty acres, more or lefs, together with all my household and kitchen furniture. And I give her also all my stock of all kinds, horses, hogs, and cows, with all the crop of corn and fadder, wheat, and oats, together with all my plantation tools, and every other article not mentioned, that I may have at my decease, after so much of the perishable property being sold as to pay all my just debts and the above bequss to be hers forever. I give to my niece Delphy FULLER my negro man Charles to be hers and her heirs forever. And I do hereby appoint my niece Delphy FULLER executrise and my friend Henry one all my lawful executor of this my last will and testament. In witnefs where of I here unto set my hand and seal this 31 August, one thousand eight hundred and thirty eight. Signed, sealed, and declared in the presence of us.

Justiman Henderson   Avent Fuller (SEAL)
James Leamon
James P Perry
Proven date Sept. 6, 1841. Recorded date not available. Recorded in Book A, Page 9, Bundle 92, Package 13. W. D. Watts Ordy.

WILL OF MARY VANCE

South Carolina Laurens District. In the name of God, Amen. I Mary VANCE of district and state aforesaid, being of disposing mind and memory calling to mind the uncertainty of life, and certainly of death, and being desirous of making a distribution of such worldly estate as it hath pleased heaven to bless me with in this life, do make and ordain this my last will and testament, the manner and form following, (Viz). First, It is my will and desire that my executor hereinafter named do as early as practicable after my decease pay all my just debts and funeral expences. Secondly, I then give and bequeath to my son John VANCE a negro boy named Nelson now in his pofsefsion. Thildly, I give and bequeath to my son James W. VANCE a negro boy named Hilman. Fourthly, I give and bequeath to my son Joseph H. VANCE a negro boy named San, and six hundred and fifty dollars in cast out of the ballance of the proceeds of my estate. Fifthly, It is my will and desire that the above named negroes given to my three sons as above named and the six hundred and fifty dollars given to my son I. H. VANCE in the fourth clause of this my last will and testament, be given extra over and above my other children, then to have an equal share of the ballance of my estate

with my other children. Sixthly, It is my will and desire that
the ballance of my property not otherwise disposed of, both real
and personal, be sold by my executor and equally divided amongst
my children that is Samuel Nathaniel Allen David John, James
Washington Joseph H. VANCE, Frances GREEN and my deceased son
William VANCE's children they drawing the portion their father
if a living would have been intitled to. And should either of
his the deceased children die before marriage or coming of age,
its portion to be equally divided amongst its sisters and brother then living. Seventhly, It is further my will and desire and
so I direct that the amount coming from and left by me to my
daughter Frances GREEN to be for her sole use and benefit during
her life and then to her bodily heirs forever. And I do order a
and direct that my sons David and Allen VANCE do as trustees lay
out the amount of money coming to my daughter Frances GREEN in
the purchase of one or more negro girls and hold them in trust
for the use and benefit of my daughter Frances GREEN during her
natural life. And at her death to make such disposition of them
as in their judgement may best comport with the interest of her
surviving children. Appointing David and Allen VANCE trustees
with fule power to act in the above case. Eight and lastly, I
do nominate, constitute, and appoint my son Joseph H. VANCE my
executor to this my last will and testament. Revoking all others
in testimony whereof I have hereunto set my hand and affixed my
seal this the   day of   Annon Domine, 1840. Signed, sealed, published, and declared by the said Mary VANCE for her last
will and testament in the presence of.

                                              her
Jno. Watts   Mary X Vance
Elihu Attom   mark
J. W. Watts
Recorded in Will Book A, Page 9. Recorded date not available.
Proven Nov. 16, 1841. W. D. Watts Ordy. Bundle 89, Pkge. 12.

WILL OF SARAH DOLLER

South Carolina Laurens District. In the name of God, Amen. I
Sarah DOLLER of the district and state aforesaid, being aged and
infirm in body, but of sound memory and understanding and being
desirous to make a disposition of my little worldly property, do
make and ordain this my last will and testament Viz. 1st, I
give to my daughter Susan COLEY my interest in a tract of land
belonging to my husband named DOLLER decend of Laurens District
whereon my son William DOLLER now lives to her and her heirs forever. Also one fsided no horn cow, calf and yearlin, also two
jars, one pot and one oven. 2nd, The balance of my property to
be sold and equally divided among the rest of my children, Viz.
Reuben DOLLER, William DOLLER, Rhoda BIGLES, Elizabeth BAKER,
and the heirs of John DOLLER deceased. And lastly, I do constitute and appoint Charles G. FRANKS executor of this my last will
and testament by me heretofore made. In testimony whereof I
have hereunto set my hand and affixed my seal this the twenty-
sixth day of October, eighteen hundred and forty one. Signed,

sealed, and declared in the presence of us, who at the request of the testatrix and in her presence subscribed the same as witnefs.

J. D. Hopper
Joshua Burns
Thos. Luvens

her
Sarah X Doller (LS)
mark

Recorded in Will Book A, Page 11. Original will not in files of Probate Judge. Proven and recorded date not available. W. D. Watts. O. L. D.

WILL OF JAMES DARROH

In the name of God, Amen. I James DARROH of the State of South Carolina and District of Laurens, being weak in body, but of sound and disposing mind, memory, and understanding praised be to God, for the same, do make and declare this my last will and testament in manner and form following, that is say. I give and devise all that plantation or tract of land containing one hundred and fifty acres (more or lefs) whereon I now live, in the District and State aforesaid, together with the rights members hindtaments, and appurtences to the said primses belonging as in any wise appertainice unto my son James DARROH Junr. to have and to hold the same his heirs and afsigns forever. Also, I give grant and devise unto my said son James DARROH Junr. one negro wench named Fanny, twenty fur years old, with her increase, that she may hereafter have, also one negro boy named Frederick about seventeen or eighteen years old, and one negro boy named Franc about five years old, also one negro boy named Tom about two years old to have and to hold the said negroes his heirs and afsigns forever. Also I do further give and bequeath all the residue and remainder of my personal estate of what nature or kind soever unto my said son James DARROH to have and to hold the same his heirs and afsigns forever. Saving and reserving out of the above willed property a sufficeicy for the complete maintenance of my wife Jane DARROH. And I do hereby nominate and appoint my said son James DARROH Junr. executor of this my last will and testament, hereby revoking and making void all former wills and testaments at any time heretofore by me made, and do declare this to be my last will and testament. In witnefs where of I have at the bottom of this my will (the whole whereof a coutained, on this, and the other side of this leaf) subscribed my hand and seal this 23 day of April, in the year of our Lord, one thousand eight hundred and ten. Signed, sealed, declared, and published by the above named James Senr. as and for his last will and testament in the presence of us, who at his request and in his presence have subscribed our names as witnefs thereto.

John Taylor
A. Downs
George Perace

James (X) Darroh (SEAL)

Proven date Oct. 2, 1820. David Anderson Ordy. Recorded date not available. Recorded in Book A, Page 11, Bundle 21, Package 13.

WILL OF NATHAN BRAMLETT

Know all men by these present that I Nathan BRAMLET of the state of South Carolina and District of Laurens, being of sound mind and memory, and mindful of the uncertainty of life, do publish and declare the following as my last will and testament. Item 1. I give and bequeath my body to decent burial and my soul into the hands of its merciful authro. Item 2. I give and bequeath to my beloved wife Elizabeth BRAMLETT all and singular my estate both real and personal of whatever the same amy consist be the same, lands, negros, tenements, heredtaments, chattels, real and personals, or chores in action to have, hold and enjoy the same during her natural life time. And after her death I make the following desposition of the said property to wit. Item 3. I give and bequeath unto William M. KENNEDY, Henery BAFS, David DERRICK trustees (appointed in the manner herein with the author-ity and continued as herein after specified) and their succefsors in office the land on which I now live. Negroes and stock of every kind household and kitchen furniture, Blacksmith tools, farming tools, waggon, and riding carriage. In trust, that they will duly apprepsiate the same to the use, benefit, and behalf of the mifsionary Society of the South Carolina Conference, Auxiliary to the Mifsionary Society of the Methodist Episcopal Church, provided always and be it exprefsly understood that this direction and appointment, and within the limits of the South Carolina Annual Conference of Ministers and Preachers. Item 4. I give and bequeath unto the said William M. KENNEDY, Henry BAFS David DERRICK trustees and their sucefsors in office the land on which I now live negroes and stock of every kind, household and kitchen furniture, Blacksmith tools, farming tools, waggon, and riding carriage, intrust, that they will immediately convey the same to the trustees of that institution of the South Carolina Annual Conference known by the name of the Fund of Special Relief for the uses and purposes specified and directed by the consti-tution of said institution. Item 5. I give and bequeath unto the said William M. KENNEDY, Henry BAFS, D. DERRECK, trustees and their succefsor in office the land on which I now live negros and stock of every kind, household and kitchen furniture, Black-smith tools, farming tools, waggon, and riding carriage, in trust that they duly and faithfully and as soon as the same shall by the provisions of this will be brought with their control, convey the same to the trustees of the trust, for the Relief of the Superannuated or worn out preachers, and the widows and or-phans of Preachers, of the South Carolina Annual Conference, in trust that they appropriate the same according to the consti-tution of the said institution of the said South Carolina Annual Conference. Item 6th. I give and bequeath unto the said William M. KENNEDY, H. BAFS, D. DERRICK trustees and their succefsors in office the land on which I now live negroes and stock of every kind, household and kitchen furniture, Blacksmith tools, farming tools, waggon, and riding carriage, in trust that they duly and faithfully convey the same as soon as it may come under their control by the provisions of this will herein before mentioned

to the Society of the South Carolina Conference for the Relief
of the Children of its members, to be appropriated and managed
by the officers and managers of said Society according to the
provisions of the Constitution of said Society. Item 7th. It
is my further will that when any one or more of the said trustees
shall die or a vacancy be caused in their body by death, or
otherwise, that said vacancy or vancancies shall be filled by
the South Carolina Annual Conference until such time as the several trusts for which they were appointed shall be fully executed.
Item 8. I give and bequeath unto the said William M. KENNEDY,
Hennery BAFS, David DERRICK trustees and their succefsors in
office the property before mentioned. In trust to be appropriated by them for the human support and maintenance of James and
Billy, or as many of them as may be alive after the death of my
wife or as much thereof as may necefsary for said purpose and
the ballance if any, to be conveyed to the four Societies of the
South Carolina Conference herein before mentioned to be equally
divided by the same. Item 9. I hereby nominate, constitute,
and appoint Thomas BROWNLEA, and William HENDERSON my executors
of this my last will and testament. In testimony whereof I here
unto set my hand and seal this 11th day of March, 1839. In
presence of. Interlined 1st. Item before Signed. Also "annual"
in 5th Item.

D. Higgins   Nathan Bramlett (SEAL)
Jas French
James B. Higgins
Recorded in Will Book A, Page 12, Bdl. 90, Pkg. 5. Proven and
recorded date not available. W. D. Watts Ordy., Laurens Dist.
For as much as nothing was said in the forepart of my will of my
beloved wife having any authority to dispose of any of the property in her hands after my death should she survive me, I would
here observe that I give her power and authority to give as much
of the household furniture as she pleases, likewise to sell any
of the stock of horses, cows, or hogs. Should she have more
than she needs for the support of her family, and to purchase
with the money any thing she needs. It is my will that the executors of my will should give Billy leave to choose his master and
to take what he is willing to give. Witnefs my hand and seal
this 11th day of March, 1839.

D. Higgins   Nathan Bramlett (SEAL)
Jas. French
James B. Higgins

WILL OF ALEXANDER FILLSON

South Carolina Laurens District. In the name of God, Amen. I
Alexander FILLSON of Laurens District S. Carolina, being of sound
and disposing mind and memory, but weak in body, and calling to
mind the uncertainty of life, and being desirous to dispose of
all such worldly estate as it hath pleased God to bless me with,
do make and ordain this my last will and testament in manner

following, that is to say. I desire first, that all my just
debts and funeral expenses be paid by my executors out of the
money on hand at my death if sufficeint. And if not, it is my
wish that my executor sell such of my personal estate as can be
best spared to enable him to pay the same. After payment of my
debts and funeral expenses, I give and bequeath to my beloved
relation FILLSON (whom christian named I do not know), being the
eldest son living at this time of my cousin Robert FILLSON of
the State of Penseyvania, all the residue and remainder of my
estate of every description counting of lands, negroes and other
personal property to be held by him during his life. And at his
death to be equally divided amoungst his children. If he should
die leaving any, and if not to go to his next legal heir of the
name of FILLSON, provided that the above property is willed to
the said FILLSON upon the condition that he remaines to the lands
bequeathed to him in Laurens District, and resides therein or in
the neighberhood. If not, it is my will that the property go to
his next oldest brother living on the same conditions. And lastly I do constitute and appoint my friend Henry C. YOUNG executor
to this my last will and testament. Sgined, sealed, published,
and declared as and for the last will and testament of the above
named Alex FILLSON in presence of.

Wm. Leak   Alexander Fillson (SEAL)
Milton Pyles
M. I. Lockhart
Proven date Oct. 8, 1842. W. D. Watts, Ordy. Recorded date not
available. Recorded in Book A, Page 14, Bundle 101, Package 18.

WILL OF HEWLET PYLES

South Carolina Laurens District. I Hewlet PYLES of the State
and District aforesaid, knowing that I have to die, and being in
a low state of health, but sound of mind, do constitute this my
last will and testament in the following manner. First on my
decease, I do commend my soul to God, and wish for my friend to
decently bury my body. Secondly, I wish my executors in the
first place to pay my funeral expenses, and also my just debts
out of my personal property. Thirdly, I wish my real estate
consisting of one hundred and eleven acres of land to be disposed of in the following manner and for the following use and
purposes (Viz). I set it apart for a home for my wife and children to live on untill my youngest child may become of age. And
then I direct that my executors do proceed to sell the land and
divide the proceed equally between my loving wife Nancy PYLES
and my two children Diadama and Elsa and as there is a prospect
of my wife being delivered of an other heir soon, and should it
be raised, in that event, I wish it to share equally in my estate with my wife and my other two children, that is for the
proceeds of my land and my personal property to be so divided
that my wife is to have just the same proportion that each of my
children may have, that is share and share alike. Fourthly, In
the event of my wife marring and undertaking to waste the property

or let my children suffer, I wish and authorize my executors to
rent out the land from year to year for the support of the children. And also in that event for my executors to take my children and raise them or live then out to some proper persons to
raise and educate untile they become of age. And also should
they have to take the children to make a sale and sell my personal property that is left after paying my debts and give my wife
one third or fourth part, in propertion to the children. Lastly
I do constitute and appoint my father John PYLES and my brother
Nathanal PYLES my executors to carry this my will into effect
and wish them to manage the estate without going to any expence
in the court of Ordinary, as I have full confidence in them, and
know they want rong my wife nor children out of anything. Witnefs my hand and seal this 10th May, 1834. Hewbet PYLES. Signed
sealed and published in the presence of.

Joseph Sullivan   Hewlet Pyles (SEAL)
Charles H. Simmons
William Simmons
Proven date Sept. 6, 1842. W. D. Watts Ordy. Recorded date not
available. Original will not in files of Probate Judge.

WILL OF SAMUEL TAYLOR

South Carolina Laurens District. In the name of God, Amen. I
Samuel TAYLOR, Sr. of the State and District aforesaid, being
weak in body, and knowing that it is appointed unto all men once
to die, but being of sound and disposing mind and memory, thanks
be to God for his mercies, and desirius to settle and arrange my
worldly affairs. Touching the substance with which it has pleased God to bless me, do ordain and declare my last will and testament in manner and form following, that is to say. 1st. It is
my will and desire that all my just debts and funeral expenses
be paid by my exeuctors herein after to be named immediately
after my decease, or as soon there after as practicable. 2nd.
It is my will and desire that the homestead and plantation on
which I now reside, together with a tract of land which I lately
purchased from James TEMPLETON shall continue to be occupied by
my beloved wife Jane together with my two daughters Martha and
Margaret, and my two sons Andrews and Kennedy, and remain as a
home for them for and during their natural lives, or the survivors or survivor of them, provided however, if either or both of
my said sons To wit, Andrew and Kennedy should choose to marry
or live apart to themselves, they are to have the priviledge of
selecting out of the tracts of land above mentioned one hundred
and fifty acres of land each, but such selection not to be made
in detached parcels, nor in such manner as to include my dwelling house in which I now live. It is further my will and desire
that after the decease of my wife Jane and my two daughters Martha and Margaret (excluding my two sons Kennedy and Andrew,
should they choose to live seperate by selecting land in pur-
suance of the priviledge above given them) or the survivors or
survivor of them, the said homestead and tracts of land, or the

15

residue thereof should my said sons select land as provided for, be sold by my executors and the proceeds thereof be equally divided amongst my surviving children, share and share alike. The lawful ifsue of any of them who may be deceased taking amongst them the share to which their father or mother would have been respectively entitled to if living. 3d. I give to my daughter Martha a negro girl named Becca to her and her heirs forever. Also her bed, bedding and clothing, and this bequest is intended to be exclusive of her distributive share of my estate not other wise disposed of and which may be sold by my executors. 4th. I give to my friend and nephew David C. TEMPLETON in trust for the use and benefit of my daughter Margaret the sum of five hundred dollars exclusive of her distributive share of my estate, not otherwise disposed of and which may be sold by my executors, which distributive share I also give to David E. TEMPLETON in trust for the use and benefit of my said daughter Margaret. 5th. I give to my sons Kennedy and Andrew, a bed and bedding each, and also a horse, saddle, and bridle each the later to be valued to them when received and any inequality in the amount thus received to be accounted for in the division of the resideue of my estate not otherwise disposed of and this clause is intended to apply to all and each of my children who may have been heretofore advanced by me. 6th. I give to my beloved wife Jane the residue of my beds, bedding, household and kitchen furniture and my books to be at her disposal after her decease. I give to my wife a horse, saddle and bridle such as she may choose. I also give to my wife the following negroes, to wit, Allen, Matilda, and Dill for and during her natural life and after her decease the said negroes to be sold and the proceeds divided as provided for and directed in the second clause of my will. 7th. It is my will and desire that after my decease no portion of my estate be sold until a new crop shall have been made and gathered in, out of which one years provisions are to be reserved. The balance to be sold together with any surplus which may be on hand of the stock of provisions at the time of my decease. It is further my will and desire that my wife have reserved to her for the use of the plantation the customary farming implements, (Illegeable)   and loom. 8th, I give to my son John the tract of land on which he now lives which together with other property I have given him, I value to him at seven hundred dollars to be considered and so much received by him and accounted for on a final division of my estate not otherwise disposed of. 9th. I give to my son David the tract of land on which he now lives valued to him at six hundred dollars which together with a horse to be valued to him and a saddle and blanket at fourteen dollars is to be considered as so much received by him and accounted for on a final division of my estate not otherwise disposed of. 10th. I give to David C. TEMPLETON in trust for the sole and seperate use of my daughter Katharine wife of Robert TAYLOR, and the heirs of her body that portion of the tract of land on which the said Robert H. now lives as laid off to him by myself in presence of his brother Charles TAYLOR. This land I value at seven hundred and fifty dollars which together with

twenty one dollars advanced by me for a cow and a saddle as to
be considered as so much of the trust property received. It is
further my will and I do hereby give to said David E. TEMPLETON
in trust for the sole and seperate use of my said daughter Katharine and the heirs of her body, whatever distributive share may
be coming to her on a final division of my estate not otherwise
disposed of. 11th. I give to my friend and relative Robert
GILLILAND in trust for the sole and seperate use and benefit of
my daughter Mary Ann, wife of Joseph MCCULLUM and the heirs of
her body whatever sum may be coming to her on a final division
of my estate not otherwise disposed of. The sum of thirty two
dollars to be accounted for on said division which has been
already received by my said daughter Mary Ann. But should she
depart this life without heirs of her body, then and in that
event her share is to revert to my estate and be divided as provided for and directed in the second clause of my will. 12th. I
give to David C. TEMPLETON in trust for the sole and seperate
use of my daughter Elizabeth wife of John TEMPLETON and the heirs
of her body, the distributive share which amy be coming to her
on a final division of my estate not otherwise disposed of,
which said share I direct to be laid by the said trustee D. C.
TEMPLETON in the purchase of a tract of land for the benefit of
my daughter Elizabeth and the heirs of her body as above mentioned. I desire that this purchase be made as early as practicable
after my decease either with money or sale notes equivalent
thereto. It is provided nowever, that from the distributive
share of my said daughter Elizabeth, there be deducted as so
much already advanced, the amount of judgment discharged by me
for said John TEMPLETON without calculating interest from the
date of the payments by me so made, and also the sum of twenty
five dollars advanced for a cow and a saddle. 13th. My daughter Nancy having received the sum of one hundred and twenty one
dollars, she and her husband William ?. TAYLOR will account for
this sum on receiving her distributive share of my estate. 14th
My daughter Jane having received forty six dollars and fifty
cents, this amount to be accounted on receiving her distributive
share of my estate. 15th. My son William now deceased, having
received in value the amount of seven hundred and thirty dollars
this sum to be deducted from the distributive share that would
be coming to him and my son Henry, having received in value the
sum of eight hundred dollars, this account is to be deducted from
his distributive part of my estate. 16th. As my son James holds
judgments on Charles LITTLE obtained on notes which I pofsed to
my son James, it is my desire that he have his choice either to
take said judgments as worth the sum of one hundred and sixty
seven dollars as so much received or to surrender said judgments
to my executors and take his regular distributive part of my
estate, but as he has received in cash and property to the value
of five hundred and sixteen dollars this sum is to be accounted
for as so much received, but a not which I hold on him is not to
be accounted for nor collected. I direct that the residue of my
estate both real and personal not with the directions given in
the seventh clause of this my will and the proceeds thereof

distributive as directed in the second clause of my will each legatee accounting for advancements in the division so that all may be equal. 16th. I do hereby nominate and appoint my beloved wife Jane and my son David executrix and executor of this my last will and testament hereby revoking and annulling all other wills and testaments by me heretofore made. In testimony where of I have hereunto set my hand and seal this third day of January in the year of our Lord, one thousand eight hundred and forty two. Signed, sealed, published, and declared as and for the last will and testament of Samuel Taylor Sr. in presence of us.

Andrew Kennedy   Samuel Taylor (SEAL)
Feril Milam
Thos. Milam
Recorded in Will Book A, Page 15, Bd. 110, Pkg. 14. Proven November 3, 1843. Recorded not available. W. D. Watts. O. L. D.

WILL OF ABRAHAM COOK

South Carolina Laurens District. In the name of God, Amen. I Abraham COOK of the District and State aforesaid, being of sound and disposing mind and memory, but weak in body, and calling to mind the uncertainty of life and being desirous of disposing of all such worldly estate as it has pleased God to blefs me with, do make and ordain this my last will and testament in manner following Viz. 1st, I commend by soul to the all mighty God, and my body to the dust. 2ndly. It is my will and desire that all my just debts and funeral expences be paid as early as may be convenent after my decease. 3rdly. I will and bequeath to my beloved wife Henrietta COOK all that tract or lot of land, purchased of Jno W. SIMPSON, called the vilage place, to her during her natural life or widowhood. And then to the trustee herein after appointed of my three daughters Martha E. COOK, Henreitta Frances COOK, and Mary Louisa COOK, in trust to and for the use and benifit of my said daughters and their heirs forever. But should my wife become dissattisfied with the vilage place, and be desirous to change her residence, my executor hereinafter named shall be at liverty to sell said lot and lay out the proceeds, in purchase of another tract of land that may suit her better. But the tract of land so purchased shall be held in the same manner and pofsed the vilage lot under my will to my said daughters. And it is further my will and desire that my children continue with their mother untill they become of age or marry, should they desire to do so. I also give and bequeath to my beloved wife, all my household and kitchin furniture during her natural life or widowhood, and to be divided among my children equally as they may marry, giving to them such articles as she can convenuently spare. And at there death or marriage to be equally divided among all my living children each accounting to the other for any advancements before receved. 4thly. I will and devise to my executor herein after named all that plantation or tract of land containing eleven hundred acres, more or lefs lying on Little River in the District and State aforesaid composed of three tracts, called the James, Power and Caldwell tracts to be sold by my said executor, in one or more lots or parcels as he may think most advantageous to the estate, on a credit of one and two years, taking bond with approved security for the purchase money in every instance. 5thly. I will and bequeath to my said executor the whole of my personal estate not before dispoased of (the negroes excepted) to be sold by him on a credit of one year taking bond and sufficent security for the payment, except the cotton crop on hand, which I desire to be sent to market and sold for cash and applied to the payment of my debts. 6thly. I will and bequeath to my executor aforesaid, all my negroes (except such and so many as may be nesfsacy for the support and comfort of my family) to be hired by him annually except such as he cannot hire who are to live at the vilage place, if my wife should continue there, and be supported by my executor as herein after prescribed. 7thly. I will and desire that my executor hire out the negroes above mentioned, and out of the proceeds to give my daughters a liveral english education, decently cloths and support my wife and children and maintain such negroes that cannot be hired. And if necefsasy draw upon the funds of the whole estate, until my son William COOK arrives to the age of twenty one years, or any of my daughters marry. But should not my daughter Mary Louisa COOK have completed her education at the time of the general division, my executor to retain funds sufficent for that purpose. Then it is my will and desire that my executor make a correct and full inventory of my whole estate not hereto fore disposed of including negroes, notes, monies, goods and chattels and all other claims, and distribute the same as follow Viz. One fifth to my beloved wife Henrietta COOK during her natural life or widowhood, and at her death or marriage to be equally divided among my son and daughters share and share alike, to them and their heirs forever. One fifth to my son William COOK, also my silver watch and gold chain, and one hundred dollars in cash to him and his heirs forever. (Illegeable)   district and state aforesaid, in trust for the use and benefit of my daughter Martha E. COOK during her natural life. And after her death to the heirs of her body forever. One fifth to the said Alsy FULLER in trust for the use and benifit of my daughter Henrietta Frances COOK during her natural life, and after her death to the heirs of her body for ever. The remaining one fifth to the said Alsey FULLER in trust for the use and benefit of my daughter Mary Louisa COOK during her natural life and after her death to the heirs of body forever. 8thly. It is my will and desire should any of my children die without issue, or before the payment or delivery of their respective legacies, then their share or shares to be equally divided among their brother and sisters living at the time, the child or children of any deceased parent, to receive the distributive share that the parent would have been intitled to if living, to have and to hold the same to them and their heirs respectively forever. 9thly. I will and desire after the general division of my estate is made, according to this seventh clause of this my will, that the trustee of my daughters herein named, take charge of their respective shares, and clothe, educate and support each of them as he would if they were his own children out of their shares respectively until they arrive of age or marry. At which time they may if they desire it, take pofsefsion of their respective legacies, receive, use and enjoy the events profits and emoluments arising from the use of the same without the right of transfering or changing the wrights of said property, and subject to the countract and management at all times of the trustee and such regulations as he may deen necefsacy for the protection and safe of the trust property. 10thly. Should the trustee of my daughters hereun appointed fail to act from death or any other cause, it is my will and desire that the court of equity appoint a trustee or trustets reserving the right of choosing to such of my daughters that have arrived to the age of choice, and also reserving the right to such that have not, when they arrive to the age of choice should they be dissattisfied with the appointement made by the court, and such trustee or trustees so appointed shall take charge of the trust property, be visted with same powers, and for the same purposed as the trustee appointed by myself, but to give bond and security for any trust funds that may pass into their pofsifsion. Lastly, I do nominate, constitute and appoint my friend Alsy FULLER executor of this my last will and testament, hereby revoking all other and former wills by me heretofore made. In testimony whereof I have hereunto set my hand and seal this 30th day of May, one thousand eight hundred and forty three. Signed sealed and acknowleged in presence of.

John Young   Aberham Cook (SEAL)
Silas M Bailey
Henry Miller
Proven date Oct. 11, 1843. W. D. Watts Ordy. Recorded date not available. Recorded in Book A, Page 19, Bundle 123, Package 11.

WILL OF JOHN COOK

South Carolina Laurens District. I John COOK of the aforesaid State and District, being weak in body, but of sound and disposing mind and memory, and calling to mind the uncertainty of life, and being desirous of disposing of all such worldly estate as it has pleased God to bless me with, do make and ordain this my last will and testament in manner following. 1st. It is my will and desire that as soon after my death as may be convenient that all my stock of goods or merchandise now on hand together with all such other articles as my beloved wife can conveniently spare shall be sold on a credit of twelve months, and all the funds arising therefrom, together with all outstanding debts except such debts as are owing by any of my children, which they shall be at liverty of using and enjoying until the decease of my beloved wife, by securing said debts and paying annually to the interest of the same to her if she should desire it. And all my cash on hand except what is hereinafter excepted, and after paying all my just debts and funeral expenses to be equally

divided among all my children share and share alike, except my
son James COOK share, which is in every instance to pafs first
into the hands of Alsey FULLER as trustee for him, and be paid
over to him in such manner as said trustee may deem best for his
interest. It is further my will and desire that my daughter
Mary Ann BABB shall use and enjoy all the profits and emoluments
arising from her share of my estate. And after her death to be
equally divided among the heirs of her body to them and the heirs
forever, her part to be funded for that purpose. It is further
my will and desire, that the share of my deceased daughter Edny
LIGON shall be equally divided among all her living children,
but to remain in the hands of Alsey FULLER for them use and benefit and to be paid over to them when they arrive of age or marry,
with such interest as may accrue thereon after deducting expences
The tract of land on which my son James COOK now resides is to
pafs into the hands of Alsey FULLER as trustee for the said
James COOK, together with the rights of said land, and to be at
his disposal for the use and benefit of my son James COOK and
children, valued at four hundred dollars in the settlement of
his share. I have already given unto my son William COOK the
tract of land sold to Nancy OWEN valued at four hundred dollars
and to be settled in his share accordingly. I give unto my son
Willis COOK two tracts of land, the on one which he now resides,
and the tract of land I purchased of Jasiah CASON including a
small piece of land purchased of Mary STILL valued at seven hundred dollars and to be settled in his share of my estate. I give
unto my son Franklin COOK two tracts of land the one on which he
now resides and the tract of land purchased of Elizabeth OWENS
valued at seven hundred dollars and to be settled as so much of
his share of my estate. It is further my will that my tract of
land in Arkansas be left to the disposal of my executors herein
after named as they may think best. I have given unto my four
daughters a negro each or money in liew thereof valued at four
hundred dollars each, and to be settled as so much of their distributive share of my estate. I give unto my beloved wife
Catharine COOK all my estate, both real and personal, of whatever
nature or quality so ever not herein before disposed of including a certain purse of silver containing three hundred dollars
to her during her natural life for her sole use and benefit.
And after her death to be sold the real estate on a credit of
one, two and three years interest from the date, the personal
property on a credit of twelve months and to be equally divided
share and share alike among all my children and their heirs forever in manner above mentioned and disposed of according. It is
also my will and desire that after my death, that my body be
decently buried without any ceremonies. It's further my will
and desire that you my children should treat your dear mother in
her declining years with the tenderest affection and honor her
gray hairs that she may descend to the grave in peace. Lastly,
I constitute and appoint my son in law Alsey FULLER and my son
Willis COOK executors of this my last will and testament, hereby
revoking all other and former wills by me heretofore made. In
witnefs whereof I hereunto set my hand and seal this 16th day of

July, one thousand eight hundred and thirty five.   In presence of.

David Owen   John Cook (SEAL)
John Hitt
A. Griffin
Recorded in Will Book A, Page 19. Original will not in files of Probate Judge. Proven June 24, 1844.

WILL OF WILLIAM LOWE

In the name of God, Amen. I William LOWE Senior of Laurens District in the State of South Carolina, being weak and infirm of body, but of sound and disposing mind and memory, being desirous of making some disposition of such worldly estate as it hath pleased God to blefs me with, do make constitute, and ordain this my last will and testament in manner and form following, that is to say. First, I will and desire that my funeral expenses, the expenses of my last illnefs, and all my just debts be paid. Second, I give and bequeath unto my son James LOWE the tract of land whereon I now live containing two hundred acres more or lefs, bounded by lands of D. John NICKELS, Wiley WILL, Henry FULLER, and Alsy FULLER, and a negro woman named Sarah and her child Rosetta and their future increase in trust for the sole and separate use of my daughter Martha C. CRYMES during her natural life and at her death to be equally divided amongst the children of my said daughter neither the said property or the rents profits or income thereof in any event to be liable for any debts or contracts of her present or any future husbands. And should my daughter Martha C. CRYMES die without leaving a child or children, thn it is my will and desire that the land and negroes above mentioned and the increase of the negroes be equally divided amongst the children of my son James LOWE. Third, I give to my son James LOWE the sum of five hundred dollars in trust for the use and benefit of my grandson James YOUNG, son of John YOUNG, untill he arrives to the age of twenty one years, when the said sum of five hundred dollars with the interest that my (illegeable) thereon is to belong to my said grandson and be paid over to him by the said trustee. But should my grandson James YOUNG die before he arrives at the age of twenty one years leaving no child or children, then it is my will that the said sum of five hundred dollars and the interest be equally divided amongst the children of my son James LOWE. Fourth, I give to my son James LOWE one hundred and fifty dollars and one feather bed in trust for the sole and separate use and benefit of my son All Allen LOWE the interest of the said sum of one hundred and fifty dollars to be applied to the support and maintenance of my said son Allen LOWE as it may be needed during her natural life. And at his death, the said sum of one hundred and fifty dollars with the unexpended interest and the feather bed to be equally divided amongst the children of my son James LOWE. Fifth, I give to my son James LOWE a negro man named Adolphus and one feather bed in trust for the use and benefit of my son Pleasand LOWE during his natural life. And at his death, I give the said negroe and bed to the children of my son James LOWE to be equally divided amongst them. Sixth, I give and bequeath to my son James LOWE two negroes Risidy and Lemon and their future increase in trust for the sole and separate use and benefit of my daughter Elizabeth YOUNG, wife of John YOUNG, during her natural life. Only should she die before the said John YOUNG, her husband, neither the said negroes or their hire or labour to be subject to the control or disposition of the said John YOUNG or liable to his debts or contracts and at the death of my daughter Elizabeth YOUNG if before the death of her husband, I give the said negroe and their increase to the children of my son James LOWE to be equally divided amongst them. But should my daughter Elizabeth survive her husband John YOUNG, at his death it is my will that the said negroes Randy and Simon and the increase belong absolutely to my said daughter Elizabeth YOUNG. Seventh, I give and bequeath to my son James LOWE one share in the Louisville, Cincinnate, and Charleston Rail Road Company, my silver wath, and the feather bed, which I now use and lie on in trust for my grandson William LOWE, son James untill he arrives at the age of twenty one years when the said property si to be paid over and delivered to the said William and become his absolutely. But should the said William die before he arrives at the age of twenty one years then the said property to be equally divided amongst his brothers and sisters. Eighth, I give unto my son James the following negroes, to wit, Judy, Bill, Henry, Mary, Perry, and Jane to him and his heirs forever. Ninth, I will and desire that all the balance of my estate be sold by my executors on such credit as they may think most advisable and the proceeds of said sale be applied to the payment of my debts and the legacies above given and whatever of my estate that remains, I give to my John James LOWE. Tenth, As my son William LOWE is indebted to me in the sum of two hundred dollars with interest for mony loaned and advanced to him, it is my will that he be released and discharged from the payment of said money and interest which is in full of all that he is to receive of my estate. And I appoint my sons James and Pleasant LOWE my executors. Witnefs my hand and seal this twentieth day of January, one thousand eight hundred and forty four. Signed, sealed, published, and declared as the last will of William LOWE in presence of interlined before signing.

H. C. Young   Wm. Lowe (SEAL)
James C. Bailey
      his
Henry ll Fuller
      mark
Recorded in Will Book A, Page 20. Recorded date not available. Proven July 23, 1844. W. D. Watts, Ordy. Bdle. 93, Pkge. 9.

WILL OF JOHN FARROW

In the name of God, Amen. I John FARROW Senr. of Laurens District

23

and State of South Carolina, being weak of body, but of sound and disposing mind and memory, do make, constitute and ordain this my last will and testament in manner and form following, to wit. First, It is my will and desire that all my just debts and funeral expences be paid. Secondly, I will and bequeath to Euphemia BROWN the following negros to wit, Harry, Simeon, Leah, Marish, Keziah, Lid, Isaac, Mary, Nancy, Ralf, Frank, Daniel, Peter, Sam, and Nelson, also Willis and Pat, with their future increase and all the land that I own lying and adjoining the flat shauls on Enoree River in Laurens District containing about five hundred acres with all the cash that may be on hand at my death, together with all my household furniture, stock and other property of every description, to be held and enjoyed by the said Euphamia BROWN during her natural life. And at her death I will and bequeath all the said negroes with their increase, the land and cash and other property above mentioned unto William Winder HITCH his heirs and afsigns forever. Lastly, I do nomin-ate, constitute and appoint Joshua SAXON, William C. BYRD, and Dr. James H. DILLARD executors of this my last will and testament by me heretofore made. In testimony whereof I have hereunto set my hand and seal this 23rd day of July, 1841. Signed, sealed, published, and declared as and for the last will and testament of the said John FARROW in presence of interlined before signed.

Joshua Saxon   John Farrow (SEAL)
Isaac B. Henry
James J. Newman

CODICIL

Whereas I John FARROW Senr. of Laurens District and State of South Carolina have made my last will and testament in writing bearing date the 23rd July, 1841, and have thereby given to W. W. HITCH after the death of Euphanial BROWN all my estate both real and personal. Now I do by this my writing **which I here**by declare to be a codicil to (Illegeable)   I will and direct that upon the promise or condition that the before named W. W. HITCH cannot hold by law the before specified properties together with all of my cash on hand note and bonds for the pay-ment of money that may be owing to me at my death. Then my will and desire is that after the death of Euphamil BROWN all of my estate both real and personal, be equally divided among my child-ren or their legal representatives. And lastly, it is my desire that this my present codicil be annexed to and made a part of my last will and testament to all intents and purposes. In witnefs whereof I have hereunto set my hand and seal this the 5th day of Sept., 1843. Signed, sealed, published, and declared by the above named John FARROW as a codicil to be annexed to his said will and testament, in presence of. Test

Z. D. Bragg   John Farrow (SEAL)
T. F. Murphy
Joshua Saxon

Recorded in Will Book A, Page 21. Original will not in files of Probate Judge. Proven Jan. 22, 1844. W. D. Watts O.L.D. Recorded

Continued on page 25

Continued from page 24
date not available.

WILL OF JOHN DALRYMPLE

South Carolina Laurens District. In the name of God, Amen. I
John G. DALRYMPLE, being of sund mind, memory, and understanding
but weak in body, do make and ordain this as my last will and
testament in manner and forn following, Viz. First, It is my
desire that my friend's Dr. Jas. DILLARD, Joshua SAXON, George
BYRD, John CRAIG, John F. KERN, John HENDERSON, and W. D. BYRD
examine my papers and assertain my liabilities and assist my
wife Sarah DALRYMPLE in selecting property to dispose of to satisfy all my just and legal debts. Then it is my desire that
they value the residue or remainder of my whole estate, after
thus satisfying my just debts. I give and bequeath unto my wife
Sarah DALRYMPLE the whole cf my property, both real and personal
so long as she lives. Should she, the sd. Sarah DALRYMPLE, die
having no heirs or increase, then it is my desire that one half
the amount of the property thus valued as afforesaid after my
death be equally divided between my brothers and sisters or
their heirs or representatives, but should my wife Sarah DALRY-
MPLE die leaving heirs or issue, then it is my desire that she
the said Sarah DALRYMPLE have the whole of my estate to do and
dispose of as she may think proper or desire. Should she die
leaving no increase or heir, it is my will and desire that she
have the full controle and disposition of the residue of my estate at her death after paying as above stated the one half of
the amount of the value of my estate at my death when all the
legal clames an satisfy over to my brothers and sisters or their
legal representives. I do hereby ratify and confirm this as my
last will and testament hereby revoking all other will by me
made or constituted. Given under my hand and seal this 22nd day
of Sept., one thousand eight hundred and forty three. Signed,
sealed, and acknowledged in the presence of us.

David Templeton Senr.   John G. Dalrymple (SEAL)
Berry C. Beasly
W. D. Bryd
Proven date Nov. 6, 1843. Recorded in Book A, Page 22. Package
14, Bundle 93. Recorded date not available. W. D. Watts, Ordy.

WILL OF ANDREW TODD

In the name of God, Amen. I Andrew TODD of Laurens District
South Carolina, being of sound and disposing mind and memory.
Calling to mind the uncertainty of life and desiring to dispose
of my worldly estate, do make and ordain this my last will in
the manner following Viz. I give to my beloved wife two negro
women, one named Ruth and the other Lucy, all my stock of horses,
pigg, cows, hogs, and sheep, (except one mare, one cow, and calf)
my waggon, carding machine, wheat, flour, bacon, 1 doz. plain
chairs, three beds, and bedsteads, together with their furniture,
two small tables together with all the balance of the furniture

not mentioned below. I give to my daughter Lititia one negro
boy named William, 1 child chair, half a dozen windsor chairs,
1 folding leaf table, 1 large looking flap. I give to my daughter Margret 1 big high post bedstead, 1 bed, and furniture, 1
block, 1 large looking glass and bay mare, one negro girl named
Licey, together with her child, and cow and calf. The above
named property left to my wife as above named if she should
marry is to be sold at publick auction and the proceeds thereof
to be equally divided among my two daughters Viz; Letitia and
Margret by paying my wife twenty dollars and bed. And lastly, I
do constitute and appoint my friends Saml. B. LEWERS, and my son
in law Enock EGNEW sole executors of this my last will and testament. In witnefs whereof I have hereunto set my hand and affixed my seal dated Aug. 6th, 1835. Witnefs present.

Joseph Cooper   Andrew Todd (SEAL)
James Dorrah
Charles Smith
Proven date Dec. 4, 1843. W. D. Watts, Ordy. Recorded date not
available. Recorded in Book A, Page 23. Bundle 93, Package 15.
To my wife all my part of judgements debts which are in my
brother John's hand or any of theirs.

WILL OF WILLIAM GILBERT

South Carolina Laurens District. In the name of God, Amen. I
William GILBERT of State and District aforesaid, do make and
publish this my last will and testament. I give unto my son
William H. GILBERT all my tract of land and premises four hundred
acres more or lefs. I also give unto him a note of hand which I
hold against him, it being given for money loaned to him and his
heirs forever. The ballance remainder and residue of my estate
shall be sold on twelve months credit and be equally divided
among my other four heirs, viz; Matilda AUSTIN, she being dead,
the heirs of her body shall have one fourthe part. Lucinda
AKINS if she be alive she shall have one fourth part, but if she
be dead the heirs of her body shall have one foruth part. Nancy
COOPER, she being dead, the heirs of her body, shall have one
fourth part. Edward GILBERT if he be alive, shall have one
fourth part, but if he being dead, the heirs of his body shall
have one fourth part with the exception of one hundred dollar
note that I hold against him which he give to me for loaned
money, the principal and interest shall be deducted out of his
part. I do appoint William H. GILBERT my whole sole executor
and he shall act and do all my businefs without any commifsion
for I considered that I have willed him enough to do my businefs
without any commifsions. I publish this my last will and testament as witnefs my hand and seal this the thirtieth day of April
in the year of our Lord and Saviour, one thousand eight hundred
and forty two, and sixty sixth year of the Independence of the
United State of America. Signed, sealed in the presence of.

G. B. Teague   William Gilbert (L. S.)
Continued on page 27

Continued from page 26
W. H. Hughes
J. P. Garett
Recorded in Will Book A, Page 23. Recorded date not available.
Proven March 21, 1843. W. D. Watts, Ordy. Original will not in
files of Probates.

WILL OF MARTHA ABRUMS

In the name of God, Amen. I Martha ABRUMS of Laurens District,
being of sound and disposing mind and memory, but weak in body,
and calling to mind the uncertainty of life, and being diserious
to dispose of all such worldly estate as it haith pleased God,
to bless me with, do make and ordain this my last will in manner
following, that is to say. First, I desire that all my personal
estate emideately be sold after my death and out of the money
arising there from all my just debts and funeral expenses be paid
and if they should be as much as fifty dollars over and above
paying my just debts, I desire the fifty dollars may be divided
equel between my children Thomas, Joseph, James, George, William
and John ABRUMS transions the heirs of Mary MUNGUMORY, Elizabeth
JONES. 2 And I further desire that my real estate may emedeately
be sold on a credit of one and two years credit with interest
from the sole imediately after my death and the monies arising
there from to be equally devided between my four daughters, Mar-
git, Siddar, Anna and Lookey. And if this is more then fifty
dollars left of the personal estate, the over must be divided
between my last four daughters named last in number two. 3, and
lastly, I do appoint my friend John WHITMORE executor of this my
last will and testament. In testamoney whereof I have here unto
set my hand and seal and affixed my seal this 4 of April, 1840.
Signed, sealed, published, and declared as and for the last will
and testament of the above named Martha ABRUMS in the presents
of us.

Thos. Whitmore   Martha (X) Abrums (SEAL)
Gio Young Jur.
Byrd B. Allen
Proven date Nov. 8, 1842. Recorded date not available. Record-
ed in Book A, Page 24, Bundle 108, Package 27. W. D. Watts Ordy.

WILL OF JANE WILLIAMSON

State of South Carolina Laurens District. In the name of God,
Amen. I Jane WILLIAMSON of the State and District aforesaid,
being of sound disposing mind and memory, but weak in body, and
calling to mind the uncertainty of life, and being desirous to
dispose of all such worldly estate as it hath pleased God to
bless me with, do make and ordain this my last will in manner
following, that is to say. I desire that my executors herein
after named pay out of the estate given them all my just debts
and funeral expenses. And after the payment of my just debts
and funeral expences, I give to my son Sanders WILLIAMSON a
negro boy about seventeen years old named Isaac and Tilda a negro

girl about twelve years old, together with her future increase to him and his heirs, executors, administrators or afsigns forever. I also give my son Sanders WILLIAMSON half the tract of land I now live on to be divided in equal shares according to quantity and quality, and a bed to him and his heirs forever. I give unto my daughter Mary GAMBRELL two negroes, Peter, a negro boy about sixteen years of age, and Clary, a negro girl about fourteen years old with her future increase (if any) to her the said Mary GAMBRELL and the heirs of her body forever. And also, I give my daughter Mary GAMBRELL the other half of the tract of two hundred and twelve acres to be divided share and share alike between Sanders WILLIAMSON and two beds and same furniture, one roan horse, two cows and calves, one cupboard, and my household and kitchen furniture to her during her natural life, and then to the heirs ifsue of her body forever. And lastly, I constitute and appoint Sanders WILLIAMSON and Ira GAMBRELL executors of this my last will and testament. In testimony whereof I have hereunto set my hand and affixed my seal this 29th, April, 1840. Signed, sealed, published, and declared as and for the last will and testament of the above named Jane WILLIAMSON. In the presence of us.

	her
Benj. Arnold	Jane X Williamson (LS)
Joel Stone	mark
Stephen Stone	

Recorded in Will Book A, Page 24. Original will not in files of Probate Judge. Proven Oct. 8, 1842. Box 97, Pkg. 2. W. D. Watts, O. L. D.

WILL OF JOHN FULLER

In the name of God, Amen. I John FULLER of the State of South Carolina Laurens District, being of sound and disposing mind and memory, but weak in body, and calling to mind the uncertainty of life, and being desirous to dispose of all such worldly estate as it hath pleased God to blefs me with, do make and ordain this my last will in manner following, that is to say. I desire that immediately after my decease or as soon after as may be convenient that so much of my estate as may be desired necefsary be sold, and out of the monies arising there from all my just debts and funeral expences be paid. I will and bequeath to my dearly beloved wife Elizabeth G. FULLER all of my estate of what kind or quality soever, consisting of stock of all kinds, household and kitchen furniture will all monies, notes, bonds, or accounts that may be in my pofsefsion or due me, together with every and all such goods and clothes and may die pofsefsed of. I also, give and bequeath my negro boy Tom to my aforesaid wife Elizabeth G. FULLER which said negro boy was omitted to be named in the second clause of this instrument. I desire futher that my wife Elizabeth G. FULLER is to have and to hold all and singular the above mentioned estate hereby bequeathed to her, to her heirs, and afsigns forever. And lastly, I do constitute and appoint my beloved wife Elizabeth G. FULLER executrix of this my last will

and testament by me heretofore made. In testimony where of I
have hereunto set my hand and affixed my seal this 12th day of
September, one thousand eight hundred and forty two, and the
sixty sixth year of American Independence. Signed, sealed, published, as and for the last will and testament of the above named John FULLER in the presence of us.

Anthony F. Golding   John Fuller (SEAL)
Abraham Thompson
I. I. Brownlee
Recorded in Book A, Page 25. Proven date Oct. 29, 1842. W. D.
Watts, Ordy. Original will not in files of Probate Judge.

WILL OF PAUL FINLEY

South Carolina Laurens District. In the name of God, Amen. I
Paul FINLEY of the State and District aforesaid, being of sound
and disposing mind and memory, but weak in body, and calling to
mind the uncertainty of life, and being desirous of disposing of
all such wordly estate as it has pleased God to blefs me with,
do make and ordain this my last will and testament in manner
following, viz. 1st. It is my will and desire that I may be
buried in a decent christian like manner, and as soon after my
death as may be convenient, all my just debts and funeral expenses be paid, out of any monies, notes, or accounts on hand or
sales hereinafter directed to be made. 2ndly. I give unto my
beloved wife Mary FINLEY, the plantation or tract of land on
which I now live, it being the tract I purchased of my son Hampton FINLEY, my two negro girls, including any children said girl
may have at the time of choosing. One years provisions, two
horses, and as much of every other kind of stock, household and
kitchen furniture, and plantations tools as she may deem necefsary for her support to her during her natural life. And after
her death to be disposed of as herein after directed. 3rdly. I
give unto my daughter Margaret M. FINLEY two hundred and fifty
dollars. To my daughters Nancy RANK, Anne COLEMAN, Lettice
COLEMAN, and Jane HOULDETCH two hundred dollars each. And I also
give unto the children of my deceased daughter Elizabeth CARGIL
two hundred dollars to be equally divided among them and to be
paid over to them by my executor when they become of age or marry.
But should any of said children die without ifsue, before receiving the legacies herein willed to the, then and in that case
their respective shares to be equally divided among the survivors.
4thly. I give and bequeath to Sarah WAITS, daughter of Nancy
ARNOLD deceased, three hundred dollars to her and her heirs forever. (Illegeable)   all my estate both real and
personal of whatever nature or quality soever, not herein before
disposed of, be immediately sold after my death by my executor.
The land on a credit of one and two years, the personal property
on a credit of one year, and (after paying the aforesaid legacies)
the monies arising there from to be equally divided among all my
children, share and share alike viz; John FINLEY, Hampton FINLEY
Nancy HANK, Anne COLEMAN, Lettice COLEMAN, Margaret M. FINLEY,

29

Jane HOULDITCH, and the children of my deceased daughter Elizabeth CARGIL, the children receiving the distributant share their
mother would have been entitled to if living, to them and their
heirs forever. 6thly, It is further my will and desire that all
the property real and personal, willed to my wife during her
natural life, be immediately sold after her death by my executor
on the same credits and to be disposed of in the same manner and
to the same persons as above directed in clause the fifth of this
my will. Lastly, I constitute and appoint my son Hampton FINLEY
sole executor of this my last will and testament, hereby revoking all other and former wills by me heretofore made. In witnefs
whereof I have hereunto affixed my hand and seal. This 15th day
of June, one thousand eight hundred and forty three. Interlina-
tions made before signed. In presence of.

Larkin Coleman   Paul Finley (SEAL)
F. G. Fuller
Alsey Fuller
Recorded in Will Book A, Page 25. Bundle 92, Package 10. Proven
date Sept. 12, 1843. Recorded date not available. J. W. D.
Watts, Ordy. Laurens County Laurens District.

WILL OF WILLIAM CARGILE

State of So. Carolina Laurens District. In the name of God,
Amen. I William CARGILE ina and of the district aforesaid,
being in bodily health, but of sound mind memory and understanding, praised be God for the same, do make this my last will and
testament in manner following. To my ever kind tender and affectionate mather Salley CARGILE, I give and bequeath the whole
of my ready money, my notes, books of ac't, and each and every
of my goods and chattles of every kind and description to have,
hold use and enjoy in way and manner herein after prescribed.
My will and wish are that my death mather the above Salley CAR-
GILE use and enjoy from time to time and at all times so much of
my aforesd. estate and effects as she may please to use for her
own comfort and benefit, and for the benefit of my two sisters,
Elvira and Rebecca CARGILE in the way of proper apparel or other
necessary expenditures consistant with their circumstances and
condition. Always confident of my mother the afores'd Salley
CARGILE's discretion and predence, in due I hereby vest solely
and exclusively all my estate, goods, and effects of whatever
kind to be by her used and enjoyed so far as she for her comfort
may need during her natural life. And if after such pofsession
use and enjoyment by my mother the afores'd Sally any part or
portion of the above devised estate as affects remain afrom her
demise. My will is that any and all remainder be equally divided
amongst my four sisters (Viz.) Rachel, Nancy, Elvira, and Rebecca
or their representatives N. B. First, I desire and will that
all my just debts my funeral expences my medical accounts, the
probate of this my will be paid and settled to this end and for
the effutration of what is above written. I do make, nominate,
constitute and appoint M. T. EVINS Esqu. my sole executor of

this my last will and testament hereby revoking and making void all and every other will and wills at any time heretofore be me made, and do declare this to be my last will and testament. In witnefs whereof I have hereunto set my hand and seal the 20th day of January, in the year of our Lord, 1844. Signed, sealed, declared and published by the above named William CARGILE as and for his last will and testament. In the presence of us, who at his request and at his presence have subscribed our names as witnefses thereunto.

Arch L. Owings   William Cargile (SEAL)
Amelia Owings
N. P. Evins
Recorded in Will Book A, Page 26. Recorded date not available.
Proven June 27, 1844. W. D. Watts, Ordy. Bundle 96, Package 15.

WILL OF JAMES WATTS

In the name of God, Amen. I James WATTS of Laurens District and State of South Carolina, do call to mind the certainty of death and uncertainty of life, and being of sound mind and memory, do make this my last will and testament in manner and form to wit. First, I commend my soul to God who gave it me. Secondly, I wish all my just debts well and truly paid. Thirdly, I leave it in the power of my executors at my death to sell all my estate both real and personal, except two tracts of land nemely, the woods and the wheeler land. I will that Elihue C. WATTS have the land known by the name of woods land at eight hundred dollar. I will also that Priscilla GRIFFIN have the land known by the name of Wheeler's land at eight hundred (dollars) and two dollars for which Elihue C. WATTS and Priscilla GRIFFIN shall account to my executors for at the division of my estate. I will that my son James WATTS children and also that Marcifsa GOODMAN's children have a part equal to one of my children. I will that my son John WATTS have one bed and furniture and one cow and calf, over and then one equal part with the rest of my children, above the rest of my children, after which I will that the ballance of my estate be sold and an equal division be made amongst all my children; Betsey CHAPMAN is to account to my executors for seventy five dollars at the division of my estate. I do hereby appoint Elihue C. WATTS, William D. WATTS, and John WATTS executors of this my last will and testament, hereby revoking all wills by me heretofore made. Given under my hand and seal this the second day of October, one thousand eight hundred and thirty nine. Signed, sealed, and delivered as and for the last will and testament of the above James WATTS, who have and at his request and in the presence of each other subscribed our names as witnefses to the same.

W. B. Merriwether   James Watts (S. L.)
Hazle Smith
Elizabeth H. Smith
Recorded in Will Book A, Page 27. Original will not in file of
Continued on page 32
31

Continued from page 31
Probate Judge. June 7, 1843 proven date. Recorded date not available. W. D. Watts, Ordy. Laurens District, Laurens County.

CODICIL OF JAMES WATTS

I James WATTS do make the following codicil as a part of my will, to wit. All advancements are to be accounted for, and my old negro woman Ginny, I give to Betsey CHAPMAN, if she will go with her, if not she is to choose where she will go and Betsey CHAPMAN is to have what she is valued to extra. I give Tibitha, to Emily SPEARMAN with her children that she may have at my death at valuation. I give Margarett and her children to John WATTS at valuation. I give Arch to E. C. WATTS at valuation. I give Willis to W. D. WATTS at valuation. I give William, Jeffrey, Jane, and Hannah to the children of James WATTS at valuation and desire that they be not sold for division amongst them. Be it understood that Fammy SPROUL is to have Harriet and Wyat, Allen, and Bob, at my death at valuation. And that nothing herein is intended or to be construed so as to divide my estate otherwise, then equal between my children. The children of a deceased child taking the share of their parent. Witnefs my hand and seal January 4th, 1843.

W. B. Merriwether   James Watts (SEAL)
Marcus Dendy
Martha Walker

WILL OF MARTIN DIAL

State of South Carolina Laurens District. In the name of God, Amen. I Martin DIAL and of the plan aforesaid, being weak of body, but of sound mind and memory, and knowing that all flesh must die sooner or later, do make and ordain this my last will and testament, hearby revoking all other will or wills by me previously made and C., and this alone to remain in force in manner following Viz. And first, I bequeath my soul to God, who gave it in earnest asurence of the resurection of the dead and eternal slavation through Jesus Chris my Saviour. 2ndly, I will that all my just and lawful debts be paid by my executor here after appointed. 3rdly, I gave and bequeath unto my son Jonathan DIAL the following property Viz. The tract of land I now live on and one negro man by the name of Cary, also one negro woman by the name of Estre and wagon and gears and all my working tools, also all my stock of cattle, cows, hogs, and sheep, and two feather beds and furniture with all other household and kitchen furniture. 4dly, I will that my wife Hannah DIAL shall have a jenteel mentainance her life time out of the above mentioned property. And I hearby appoint my sd. son Jonathan DIAL my sole executor to carry into affect the above will acording to the true intent and meaning of the same. In witnefs whereof I have here unto set my hand and seal this 30, June, 1827. Signed and sealed in the presents of us. Test:

Eliher Abercrombie   Martin Dial (SEAL)
Jonathan Abercrombie
Continued on page 33

32

Continued from page 32
J. G. Sims
Recorded in Book A, Page 14, Bundle 95, Package 28. Proven date
Feb. 5, 1844. Recorded date not available. W. D. Watts, Ordy.

WILL OF WILLIAM NUGENT

The State of South Carolina. In the name of God, Amen. I William NUGENT of the District of Laurens, being of sound and disposing mind and memory, and calling to mind the uncertainty of life
and being desirous to dispose of all such worldly estate as it
hath pleased God to blefs me with, do make and ordain this my
last will in manner following. I desire after my decease that
all my just debts be punctually paid. I give and bequeath to my
three daughters and grand daughters namely; Jane NUGENT, Martha
NUGENT, Elizabeth NUGENT, and Emily F. OWENS, the plantation and
tract of land whereon I now live containing by a late resumery
two hundred and one acres, together with all my personal property
of every description. And should either of my daughters or
grand daughters die, it is my wish that all my estate above described be and the same is hereby given to them that may survive.
And I do hereby constitute and appoint William BLAKELY Junr.
executor of this my last will and testament. In testimony where
of I have hereunto set my hand and affixed my seal this fifteenth
day of September, in the year of our Lord, one thousand eight
hundred and thirty six. Signed, sealed, published, and declared
as and for the last will and testament of the above named William
NUGENT. In the presence of us.

Nancy Day   William Nugent (S. L.)
Willis Hill
Nathaniel Day
Recorded in Will Book A, Page 28, Bdl. 97, Pkg. 11. Proven
March 9, 1844. Recorded date not available. W. D. Watts O. L. D.

WILL OF MARTHA TAYLOR

The State of South Carolina Laurens District. In the name of
God, Amen. I Martha TAYLOR of the District and State aforesaid,
being of sound and disposing mind and memory, and calling to
mind the uncertainty of life and being deserous to dispose of
all such worldly estate as it hath pleased God to blefs me with,
do make and ordain this my last will in manner following, that
is to say. I desire in the first place that all my just debts
(should I owe any) and my funeral expences be paid. I give to
my following named children Viz; Robert TAYLOR, John TAYLOR,
Samuel TAYLOR, Elizabeth SPEERS, Jane GOODWIN, and Mary WORKMAN
each the sum of twenty dollars to be paid to each of them after
my decease, provided that I should be unable to pay the money in
my life time. I give to my son James TAYLOR the remainder of my
estate consisting of the following property to wit, the tract of
land whereon I now live containing by the last resuvey about two
hundred and one acres, seven negroes named Sambo, Fillis, Ritty,
Sylvia, and her child named Caroline, Stephen, and Thomas,

together with their increase, to him his heirs or afsigns forever. Also my horses, cattle, and stock of every kind together
with all my household and kitchen furniture, plantation tools
and that may be in my pofsefsion at the time of my death. And
lastly, I constitute and appoint my friend Samuel TAYLOR Senr.
executor of this my last will and testament, hereby revoking all
wills formerly be my made. In testimony whereof I have hereunto
set my hand and affixed my seal this fourteenth day of February,
in the year of our Lord, one thousand eight hundred and thirty
one. Signed, sealed, published, and declared as and for the last
will and testament of the above named Martha TAYLOR in the
presence of us.

	her
Nathaniel Day	Martha X Taylor (SEAL)
John Taylor	mark
Henry S. Taylor	

Recorded in Will Book A, Page 29. Recorded date not available.
(Illegeable).

WILL OF JAMES TAYLOR

South Carolina Laurens District. Know all men by thest presents
that I James TAYLOR of the District and State aforesaid in con-
sideration of the natural love and affection which I bear to
Samuel TAYLOR, (my brother), Mary WORKMAN, Jane GOODWIN, Robert
TAYLOR, Elizabeth SPEERS, and the children of my brother John
TAYLOR deed, as well as the consideration that my mothers will
is not protested have bargained sold and conveyed unto the said
Samuel TAYLOR, Mary WORKMAN, wife of Hugh WORKMAN, Jane GOODWIN
Robert TAYLOR, Elizabeth SPEARS, wife of Wm. SPEARS, and the
children of my deceased brother John TAYLOR. The said children
jointly only to take the share that each of others receive, all
that plantation or tract of land containing two hundred acres
more or lefs adjoining lands of Lewell BEASLEY, Andrew SPEARS,
C. C. TEMPLETON et, al. It being the tract of land whereon my
mother Martha TAYLOR lived and died to them and their heirs forever. Together with all and singular the rights, members, hered
tanants, and apputenances thereunto belonging or in any wise
appertaining and I do hereby bind myself my heirs, executors,
and administrators to depend all and singular the premises afore
said unto the grantees aforesaid against myself and my heirs and
against all legal claims whatever made through me. Reserving to
myself the use and accupation of the said tract of land during
my natural life. Witnefs my hand and seal this 19, Oct. 1843.
Signed, sealed and delivered in presence of.

	his
J. C. Wright	James (X) Taylor (SEAL)
J. H. Irby	mark

South Carolina Laurens. Personally came before me J. D. WRIGHT
who made oath that he saw the above named James TAYLOR sign seal
and deliver the aforegoing deed as his act by makin his mark for
the purposes and uses therein mentioned, and that he together
with J. H. IRBY witnefs the due execution of the same. Sworn to

and subscribed before me this 27th Oct. 1843.

J. W. Simpson   J. D. Wright
(Illegeable)

Whereas Martha TAYLOR late of the District of Laurens departed
this life after having executed a paper as her last will and
testament wherein the said Martha TAYLOR devised and bequeathed
to her son James TAYLOR, the tract of land whereon she lived
adjoining lands of Andrew SPEARS, Samuel BEASELEY, and others
with all her personal estate except a legacy of twenty dollars
to her other children each to wit: John TAYLOR, children, Mary
WORKMAN, Jane GOODWIN, Robert TAYLOR, Samuel TAYLOR, and Elizabeth SPEARS. And whereas the said pecuinary legatees last above
mentioned are about to enter a protest against the validity of
the said last will and testament of the said Martha TAYLOR. Now
in consideration that the said John TAYLORS children, Mary WORK-
MAN, Samuel TAYLOR, Jane GOODWIN, Robert TAYLRO, and Elizabeth
SPEARS with draw all defence against the probating of the said
will of Martha TAYLOR. I do hereby bind myself, my heirs, executors, or administrators, and afsigns that all there person estate
of the said Martha TAYLOR of every description whatever shall be
sold either by the executor named in said or an administrator
with the will annexed and the proceeds thereof equally divided
unto seven shares. One of which is to be paid to myself, one
share to Samuel TAYLOR, one share Robert TAYLOR, one share Hugh
WORKMAN, in right of his wife Mary, one share to John TAYLORS
children, one share to William SPEARS, in right of his wife
Elizabeth, one share to Jane GOODWIN. And I do hereby in consideration of the premises aforesaid bind myself my heirs, exts.
and admors., in the sum of one thousand dollars each of the afor-
said parties to abide by and fulfil the provisions of this con-
cenant. In witnefs whereof I have here unto set my hand and
seal Oct. 19, 1843. Witnefs:

J. D. Wright   James (X) Taylor (SEAL)
J. H. Irby

Recorded in Book A, Page 30. Proven date Nov. 13, 1843. Recorded date not available. Original will not in files of Probate
Judge. W. D. Watts, Ordy.

WILL OF JOHN CRAIG

In the name of God, Amen. I John CRAIG of Laurence District and
State aforesaid being of sound and disposing mind and memory,
but weak in body, and calling to mind the uncertainty of life,
and being desirous to dispose of all such wordly estate as it
has pleased God to blefs me with, do make and ordain this my last
will in manner following, that is to say. Item ls. I will and
desire that all my just debts be paid. Item 2d. I will and
desire that my niece Jane HARLAND, daughter of Joseph HARLAND
receive out of my estate four thousand dollars in money. Item
3d. I will and desire that George CRAIG my nephew do take at
valuation the following negroes viz., Lewis, Lucinda, Nat, Geines

Jerry, Anna, James, and Clark. Item 4h. I will that William Perry CRAIG take my negroes named as follows at valuation viz., Isaac and his wife Caroline. Item 5h. I will that Thomas LITTLE takes the following negroes at valuation viz., Lewis, Jones and his wife Eliza. Item 6h. I will that Samuel J. CRAIG takes Scintha and her three children at valuation. Item 7h. I will that the heirs of William CRAIG named Jane E. CRAIG and John B. CRAIG have their fathers part of my estate and to remain in the hands of my exeuctors untill the become twenty one years of age free of interest. Item 8h. I give to W. D. BIRD in trust for Elizabeth inlew the following tract of land commencing at the draw bars, thence to N. C. VANCES corner at stake, thence down said Vances line, thence down Foster line untill it intersects Andersons fence thence up said fence to draw bars for his use and benefit. Item 9h. I will and desire that the balance of my property not heretofore specified be sold at public auction, both real and personal by my exeuctors and the proceeds to be equally divided between Thomas CRAIG, Robert CRAIG, and the heirs of William CRAIG or their legal representatives the part the heirs of William CRAIG is entitled to under this change to remain in the hands of my (Illegeable)   Thomas CRAIG and Robert CRAIG executors of this my last will and testament. In testimony whereof I set my hand and affixed my seal this the 18th day of October, 1843. Signed, sealed, published, and declared as and for the last will and testament of the above named John CRAIG in the presence of us.

Thomas B. Rutherford   John Craig (LS)
N. C. Nance
W. D. Byrd
Samuel H. Murell
REcorded in Will Book A, Page 31, Bundle 112, Pkge. 4. Proven date Oct. 30, 1843. Recorded date not available. W. D. Watts, Ordy. Laurens District, Laurens County.

WILL OF SARAH HOLT

South Carolina Laurens District. In the name of God, Amen. I Sarah HOLT of the aforesaid State and Dist., being of sound disposing mind and memory, but weak in body, and calling to mind the uncertainty of life, and being disirous of disposing of all such worldly effects as it has pleased God to blefs me with, to make and ordain this my last will and testament in manner following Viz. 1st, I bequeath my body to the dust from which it came and my soul to God that gave it. 2nd, It is my will and desire that I be buried in a decent christian like manner, and as early after my decease as may be convenient all my just debts and funeral expences be paid. 3rd, I give unto my daughters Elizabeth ROBERTSON, Gilley BRADEN, Charlotte NELSON, and Deboraham BAILEY, one feather bed and furniture each or the value of a bed and furniture in mony should their not be beds sufficent for all of them. 5thly, It is further my will and desire that all my estate of whatever nature or quality not herein before disposed

of be sold my executor herein after named. And the proceeds to
be equally devided among all my children, share and share alike,
Viz.; Larkin COLEMAN, Alfred COLEMAN, Alsey COLEMAN, Elizabeth
ROBERTSON, Gilley BRADEN, Charlotte NELSON, and Deboraham BAILEY
to them and their heirs forever (except the part going to my
daughter Gilley BRADEN) which shall be equally divided between
herself and all his children by Josiah NELSON and Mabra HUNTER
share and share alike to them and their heirs forever. Lastly,
I constitute and appoint my son Larkin COLEMEN, executor of this
my last will and testament, hereby revoking all other and former
wills by me heretofore made. In witnefs where of I have hereunto set my hand seal this 17th day of October, one thousand
eight hundred and forty three. 4th Clause erazed before her
signed.

	her
Jones Miller	Sarah X Holt
Illegeable	mark

Recorded in Will Book A, Page 31, Bdle. 94, Pkge. 8.
(Illegeable)

WILL OF JESSE E. CLARDY

South Carolina Laurens District. In the name of God, Amen. I
Jefse E. CLARDY of the District and State aforesaid, being of
sound disposing mind and calling to mind the uncertainty of life,
and being deserous to dispose of all such worldly estate as it
haith pleased God to blefs me with, do make and ordain this my
last will and testament in manner following, that is to say. I
give to my beloved wife, Rachel CLARDY during her life or widowhood, a tract of land where on my dwelling house now stands containing two hundred and fifty acres more or lefs which is known
by the name of the Pugh tract, one negro boy named William, two
beds and furniture, two work horses, two cows, and calves and one
year provision for her famaly, and stock at the death of my wife
or her marriage again. My will is that all the aforesaid property both real and personal shall be sold by me executors herein after named and the proceeds thereof equally divided amongst
all my children which is hereinafter named. And my will is that
all the refidue of my estate both real and personal be sold by
me executors and all my just debts paid out of the proceeds
thereof and the remainder equally divided amonst all of my children which are named Michiel, William, Caty, Sarah, Mahaby, Jefse,
Elles, James, Andrew, Tackson, Zachariah, Derrack, Smith, John,
Wesley, and Zedakiah Henery, to them and their heirs forever.
And lastly, I do constitute and appoint my brothers James CLARDY
and Michiel CLARDY executors of this my last will and testament
by me heretofore made. In testimony whereof I have hereunto set
my hand and affixed my seal on this the 29th day of July, in the
year of our Lord, 1832. Signed, sealed, published, and declared
as and for the last will and testament of the above named Jefse
Elles CLARDY. In presents of us.

Philips Wait Snr.   Jesse E. Clardy
Continued on page 38

Continued from page 37
John C. Wait
William P. Delph
Recorded in Will Book A, Page 32. Bdle. 94, Pkg. 14. Proven
date Sept. 17, 1843. Recorded date not available. W. D. Watts
Ordy. Laurens District, Laurens County.

WILL OF CASSE HALCOMB

State of South Carolina. In the name of God, Amen. I Cassey
HOLCOMB of the District of Laurens and State aforesaid, being of
sound and disposing mind and memory, and being desirous of disposing of such worldly estate as it hath pleased God to bless me
with, do make, ordain, and constitute this my last will and testament in manner and form following, Viz. First. It is my will
and desire that all my just debts and funeral expences be paid.
Secondly. I give and bequeath all the estate both real and personal of which I may be possessed after paying my debts, to my
beloved sister Pheby HOLCOMB, to belong to her absolutely, and
unconditionally, and to be disposed of as she may think proper.
Lastly, I nominate, constitute, and appoint Pheby HOLCOMB executrix of this my last will and testament. Signed, sealed, published and acknowledged, as and for the last will and testament
of Cassey HOLCOMB this first day of April, one thousand eight
hundred and thirty five, in the presence of. Test:

Emmanuel Lyon   Cassey Holcomb (LS)
Nathaniel D. Thankston
Peter Simpson

Codicil

Whereas I Cassea HOLCOMBE of the State and District above mentioned have made and duly executed my last will and testament bearing
date the 1st day of April, 1835 and thereby giving and bequeathing to my sister Phebe HALCOMBE the whole of my estate both real
and personal. And whereas since the execution of the said will
I have purchased a negro girl named Margret about seven years
old. Now it is further my will and desire, and I do hereby give
and bequeath the said negro girl Margret to my beloved neice,
Cassandra HOLCOMBE, the daughter of my brother John HOLCOMBE,
the said negro girl and her encrease to belong to her and her
(Illegeable)   lawfull ifsue after my death provided neverthe
less. Should my neice Cassandra die leaving no ifsue, then and
in that case it is my will that should my sister Phebe HOLCOMBE
beliving that the said girl Margret and her ifsue remain or go
to her as her property and be disposed of as she may think proper. But should my sister Phebe not be living, then it is my
will that the said girl Marget and her ifsue of any be sold and
the proseeds thereof equally divided between the brothers of my
said neice (Viz) Martral HOLCOMBE, Alfred HOLCOMBE and Kivil
HOLCOMBE, share and share alike. Signed, sealed, published and
declared by the said Cassea HOLCOMBE as and for a Codicil to her
last will and testament and to be taken as part thereof in the
presence of us this 26th day of November, 1842.

Continued on page 39

Continued from page 38
Thos. Wright   Cassea Holcombe (LS)
Lacy H. Griffith
Stephen Griffeth
Recorded in Will Book A, Page 33, Bdl. 96, Pkg. 10. Proven July
10, 1843. Recorded date not available. W. D. Watts, O. L. D.

WILL OF IABEY W. JOHNSON

In the name of God, Amen. I Iabez W. JOHNSON of Laurens District
State of South Carolina, watch and clock mader, being of sound
and disposing mind and memory, and calling to mind the uncearty
of life, with the sure and no distant approach of death, feel
desirous to dispose of all such worldly estate as it has pleased
God to blefs me with. Do make and ordain this my last will and
testament in manner following, that is to say. First, I desire
that my body be committed to the earth in a reasonable time
after my decease in a plain unostentatious manner. Second, I
desire and direct my executortrix here after named to pay my
physicians bill, funeral expences and all my just debts out of
any money I may leave on hand, or from the proceeds of my property hereafter directed to be sold. Third, I give to my daughter Ann W. JOHNSON (my only stay and helf in these my declining
years) my negro man Jim and my two boys Lasan and Hardtimes, my
negro woman Hannah and her two children Amorintha and Bet together with their future issue and increase. And I futher give unto
my said daughter Ann all my beading steads and furniture. Also
my library of books of every kind, also a small clock made by
myself and bearing my name, also my brafs case watch. And I
further give unto my sd. daughter Ann my five shares of Rail
road stock in the Cinnata Louisville and Charleston Rail Road
Company with their corrisponding shares in the bank. Fourthly,
I do hereby direct and require my executors hereafter named to
sell by private contract on otherwise as to her may sum best my
plantation or tract of land whereon I now reside containing three
hundred thirty five and pr acres, more or lefs, and to exeucte
titles to the same or any part thereof. And also to sell or
public auction on the usual terms all the remaining portion of my
property of whatsoever nature or kind not hereto fore disposed
of. And after discharging all my legal liavitites it is my wish
and desire that the next proceed of my land and other property
named in this clause be equally divided between my three children
Ann, William, and Jubez. Lastly, I do hereby nominate and appoint my daughter Ann W. JOHNSON executor (Illegeable)hereunto
set my hand and seal this sixth day of July, eighteen hundred and
forty two. Signed in presence of.

Wm. W. Donan   Jubez W. Johnson (SEAL)
Achilles Dendy
Jno. Godfrey
Recorded in Book A, Page 33, Bundle 107, Package 17. Recorded
date not available. W. D. Watts, Ordy. Proven date June 29,
1843.

WILL OF HENRY MERDITH

Be it rememberd that I Henry MEREDITH considerning the uncertinty of this mortal life, and being of sound mind and memory, thanks be to God for his great goodnefs and his wonderful mercies unto me, I do make and ordain this my last will and testament in manner and form following (Lem). First, I give unto my son Samuel MERDITH all my lands. 2. I give unto my daughter Nancy ARNOLD one dollar. 3. I give unto Fleming MOFLEY one dollar. 4. I give unto Thomas WARTERS one dollar and Boadwin WARTERS one dollar and Permealey WARTERS one dollar. And after my debts and funeral expences are paid all my property excepting my lands and that is given to Samuel MEREDITH and Nelson MEREDITH and Sally MARTIN the wife of Benjamin MARTIN, and Jane BOWN, the wife Wm. BOWAN, and James MEREDITHS, two children Amealey and Henry MEREDITH the both recive as much as Nelson MEREDITH between them both. That is one share to be divided between them both. And after my death all my estate to be sold and divided as above directed. And I hereby appoint my son Samuel MEREDITH my sole executor of this my last will and testament, revoking all other wills made by me this the 15th day of December, 1842. Signed, sealed, published, and declared by me Henry MEREDITH to be my last will and testament. In the presences of us, who at his request and in his presenfs have hereunto subscribed our names as witnefs to the same. Test

William Robertson   Henry Meredith (SEAL)
John H. Templeton
I. F. Dean
Recorded win Will Book A, Page 34, Bundle 96, Pkg. 22. Proven date 3 of Feb. 1843. Recorded date not available.

WILL OF ELIZABETH M. WALKER

South Carolina Laurens District. Jany, 18th, 1842. In the name of God, Amen. I E. M. WALKER being weak in body, but of sound and perfect mind and memory and considering the uncertainty of this mortal life, do make and publish this my last will and testament in the manner and form following. First, I give and bequeath unto my beloved little niece Theadana daughter of G. W. YOUNG the sum of seventy dollars to be appropriated to her education. I do also give and bequeath to my eldest brother John L. YOUNG my house and lot lying in union Village and the sum of four thousand dollars. I do also place the sum of five thousand dollars in my brother John hands to hold so long as my beloved mother in law Mrs. Susannah WALKER lives and pay her annually the lawful interest of the above mentioned sum to be equally divided between her surviving children. I do also give and bequeath unto my beloved brother James four thousand dollars. I do also place the sum of one thousand dollars in his hands to hold so long as my dear sister Eliza GAREY lives and pay her annually the lawful interest of the above mentioned sum. And at her death if she has no children he is to take the sum and appropriate them to his own use. I also give to my sister Eliza GAREY my gold watch and all my jewellry as long as she lives. And lastly, as to all the rest and remainder of my personal estate goods and chattels of what kind and nature so ever, I wish my brothers to sell and appropriate the money to fixing my grave and Amos C. WALKERS. I hereby appoint my brothers John and James as my sole executors of this my last will and testament and hereby revoking all former wills by me made. In witnefs whereof, I hereunto set my hand and seal this 18th day of Jany, one thousand eight hundred and forty two. Signed, sealed, published, and declared by the above named E. M. WALKER to be her last will and testament in the presence of us the testator.

Test-Wm. Young   Elizabeth M. Walker (SEAL)
    W. W. TEmpleton
    John H. Dendy

REcorded in Will Book A, Page 35. Original will not in files of Probate. Proven date Aug. 11, 1842. W. D. Watts, Ordy. State of South Carolina Laurens District. Whereas I Elizabeth M. WALKER of the State and District aforesaid have by my last will and testament in writing duly executed, bearing date the eighteenth day of January, 1842, given and bequeathed to Mrs. Susannah WALKER of Hartford, Connecticut the sum of five thousand dollars and to my brother John L. and James YOUNG the sum of four thousand dollars and to my sister Louisa GARY the sum of one thousand dollars. Now I the said Eliz. M. WALKER, being desirous of altering my said will in respect to the said legacies do therefore make this present writing which I will and direct to be annexed as a codicil to my said will and taken as a part thereof. And I do hereby revoke the said legacies given by my said will to Mrs. S. WALKER and to my brothers John L. and James C. YOUNG and to my sister Louisa GAREY. And I do give to Mrs. Susannah WALKER three thousand dollars only and to my brothers John L. and James C. YOUNG and to my sister (Garey) Louisa GAREY equal shares. And I do hereby notify and confirm my said will in everthing except where the sum is hereby revoked and altered as aforesaid. In witnefs whereof I have hereunto set my hand and seal this the twenty second day of July, 1842.

Samuel Neill   E. M. Walker (L.S.)
W. L. Templeton

WILL OF JOHN BOYCE

South Carolina Laurens District. I John BOYCE of the district and state aforesaid do make, ordain, and constitute this my last will and testament, viz. 1st. I direct that all my debts, if any, be paid. 2nd. I bequeath and desire to my beloved wife Nancy E. BOYCE during her widowhood or life time, if she so long remain a widow, the plantation whereon I now live or may live at the time of my death, except that the said plantation shall not be leased or rented either in whole or in part and the following slaves and other personal property, viz. One negro woman named Tamer and her two children, Margarett, a girl and George, a boy,

and her ifsue she may have hereafter. One negro woman named
Mira and her two children, Essex a boy, Elick a boy, and her
ifsue she may have hereafter. Also one negro man named Washington, three feather beds and furniture belonging to them, also
five hundred dollars in cash to purchase such neccefsaries as
she may need for housekeeping. And at the death of my wife, or
when she may again marry, I direct that the property above devised and bequeathed to her shall return to my estate and be
divided as the rest and residue of my estate hereinafter disposed
of. 3d. I give and bequeath to each of my children which my
present wife Nancy E. BOYCE may have by me a sum equal to that
which each of my other children may receive from the estate of
their deceased grandfather John ROBERTSON. 4th. I direct that
all the rest and residue of my estate both real and personal
(except Bank and Rail Road Stock) be sold and that a credit of
twelve months be allowed with interest from date. 5th. I desire
and direct that the rest and residue of my estate both real and
personal and of whatever nature be equally divided between all
my children. I desire that out of my estate that my grand children, Sarah I. CRAIG and John B. CRAIG children of my daughter
Elizabeth decd. shall have five hundred dollars each as their
share of my whole estate. And if either of my children should
die without ifsue his or her part to return to my estate (Illegeable). 6th. I direct that S. J. CRAIG and J. B. CRAIG shoud
die without ifsue that their part return to my estate and be
divided between my children equally. 7th. In dividing the rest
and residue of my estate I direct that a sum equal to that advanced by me in my lifetime (and for which I hold receipts) to
a part of my children, be paid to the rest, and in case of fail-
ure of my estate, my children so advanced to shall refund as to
make the shares received by each of my children equal. 8th. I
direct that all the Bank and Railroad Stock which I may hold or
be entitled to at the time of my death be not sold but continue
in stock until the charter under which it is held expires. And
if the charter is received during its time and then sold and the
proceeds divided equally between my children as the rest and residue of my estate is disposed of. And in the mean time the profits arising from said stock shall be divided between my children
in like manner. In testimony whereof I have hereunto set my hand
and seal this 8th of Sept. one thousand eight hundred and forty
one.

Rowland Jennings   John Boyce L. S.
John F. Kern
A. R. Boyce
Recorded in Will Book A, Page 36. Original will not in files of
Probate Judge. Proven Aug. 7, 1843. Recorded date not avail-
able. W. D. Watts, O. L. D.

WILL OF GEORGE FUNK

In the name of God, Amen. I George FUNK of the State of South
Carolina Laurens District, being weak in body, but of sound and

disposing mind and memory, and knowing that it is appointed unto all men once to die, and not knowing how soon I shall be called and being desirous to dispose of all such worldly estate as it hath pleased God to blefs me with, do ordain, make and institute this my last will and testament, revoking all others hithertc made. First, I bequeath my soul to God who gave it to me, and my body to the dust from whence it sprang, to be buried in a decent and christian like manner. After paying all my just debts and funeral expenses, I give, demise, and dispose of my property in the following manner, that is to say. I give to my beloved wife Mancy FUNK one third of my estate both real and personal to be her freely pofsefsed and enjoyed forever. The ballance of my estate both real and personal to be equally divided among all my children Viz., Hanpton FUNK, Elizabeth Ann WATSON, Albert W. FUNK, Wade A. FUNK, and Anne WOOD. After making those of my children equal in property or money with them that I have advanced to Viz. I have advanced to Hampton FUNK in property one horse at fifty 5 dollars, one bed stead, and furniture, one sow, and in money sixty two dollars. I have advanced to Elizabeth Ann WATSON one hundred and fifty dollars for the line of my negro girl Eliot, one bed stead, and furniture, and one cow and calf. I have advanced to Wade A. FUNK one colt at fifty five dollars. I have advanced to Anne WOOD one bed stead, and furniture, and one cow and calf, all of the above must be accounted for according to each childs advancement. It is furthermore my desire that the whole of my property be sold both real and personal and that my executors hereinafter named are fully authorized to make good and lawful titles to my land. And lastly, I do hereby constitute and appoint my beloved sons Albert W. FUNK and Wade A. FUNK my executors to this my last will and testament (illegeable) heretofore make. In testimony whereof I have here unto set my hand and affixed my seal this 17th day of Dec. 1842. Signed, sealed, published, and delivered as and for the last will and testament of the above named George FUNK, in presence of us.

J. H. Coleman   George Funk (SEAL)
John Wood
Robert Brady
REcorded in Will Book A, Page 37. Proven Jan. 7, 1843. Recorded date not available. W. D. Watts, Ordy. Laurens District, Laurens County.

WILL OF JAMES CLARDY

South Carolina Laurens District. Know all men by these presents that I James CLARDY laurens District, calling to mind that I am born to die, and being desirous to dispose of all such worldly estate as it hath pleased God to blefs me with. First, I desire to be buried in decent christian form at the discretion of my executors. Secondly, that my just debts and funeral expenses be paid. Thirdly, I lend to my wife Sarah CLARDY all of my real estate during her natural life not otherwise disposed of. Also the negroes which I now name, that is to say: Peggy, George, Isaac, and Hariett, also all my household and kitchen furniture my road waggon, and pleasure carriage with all the aperatus belonging to them. Also two or three of my horses that she may choose, all such plantation tools, as she may wish to keep, as much provisions of all kinds found on the promises at my decease as will be required for her family and stock of one year. At the death of my wife, I wish all the property so lent to my wife to be equally divided between my three sons, Jefse E. CLARDY, James CLARDY, and Michael CLARDY. I give to my three sons before mentioned the tracts of land which I settled them on. I also give them the three negroes which they have now in their pofsefsion. And whereas I have given to the heirs of my son William CLARDY dec'd. the portion of my estate which I alloted them, and whereas I have left one thousanddollars by a deed of trust to my daughter Nancy RIGHT, and also one thousand dollars by a deed of trust to Suckey TIERCE. I do hereby order the said two thousand dollars to be raised out of my estate and applied by my executors hereinafter mentioned as required and provided in said deeds of trust. All the residue of my estate I give to my three sons above named to them and their heirs forever. And lastly, I here by appoint and ordain my three sons above named the execrs. of this my last will and testament. And I do hereby revoke and disannul all other wills by me made, ratifying and confirming this my last will and testament. In testimony thereof I have here unto set my hand and affixed my seal on this the 22d day of September (Illegeable) Seven. Signed, sealed, published, and declared as and for the last will and testament of the above named James CLARDY in presence of us.

John Hall   James Clardy Sen. (LS)
Philip Waite
   his
Wm. x Franklin
   mark

Codicil

Whereas I James CLARDY Senr. of Laurens District South Carolina have made and duly executed my last will and testament in writing bearing date the 22d day of September, one thousand eight hundred and thirty seven. And thereby loaned to my beloved wife Sarah CLARDY for and during her natural life four negroes which are named and whereas one of the said negroes named Isaac have since died. I do hereby loan to my wife Sarah CLARDY two negroes, one named Moses and the other named Unity in lieu of said Isaac which have died, during her natural life. And at her death to be disposed of as directed for the other property so loaned to her. Signed, sealed, published, and declared by the said James CLARDY as and for a codicil to be annexed to his last will and testament and to be taken as part thereof in presence of.

Philip Waite   James Clardy Senr. (LS)
Jeremiah BAiley
James Daniel
Continued on page 45

Continued from page 44
Recorded in Will Book A, Page 37, Bdl. 94, Pkg. 15. W. D. Watts
O. L. D. Recorded date not available. Proven Oct. 14, 1846.

WILL OF WILLIAM SOUTH

In the name of God, Amen. I William SOUTH of the State of South
Carolina Laurens District, being of sound mind, and disposing
memory, and calling to mind the uncertainty of life, and being
desireous to dispose of all such worldly estate as it hath pleased God to blefs me with, do make and ordain this my last will
and testament in manner following, that is to say. Item 1st, I
wish my funeral expences and just debts to be paid out of my
estate. Item 2nd, I give to my beloved wife Eaty SOUTH for and
during her natural life, one hundred acres of land including the
dwelling house where we now lives and all the rest of the nesary
buildings the lines then to be laid out according with her
desire. I also leave to her during her life the property following that is to say. My negroe man named Willis, also my negro
woman named Servina, and as many horred cattle, and hogs, as she
wishes for her use. One horse, sadle, and bridle, all my house
hold and kitchen furniture if she may wish so much as much corn,
wheat, and ment and other provisions as she may need. At the
death of my wife, I wish all the said property which I have left
to her to be sold by me exetrs. hereinafter named at public
autery on such credit as they may think proper. And the proceeds
of said sale to be equally divided amoungst all my children here
in after named, excepting my daughter Nancy HALL, she being
other wise seperatly provide for. Item 3rd, I wish my exors. to
raise from my estate the sum of five hundred dollars. And I
wish my son Gavriel SOUTH to put the said five hundred dollars
out on interest during the life of my daughter Nancy HALL and to
pay over to her anually the amount of interest ariseing from
said five hundred dollars. (At the death of said Nancy, I wish
two hundred and fifty dollars of the said five hundred dollars)
to be put to interest untell William HALL Junr. the sone of my
daughter Nancy HALL attains the age of twenty one years. Then
the said two hundred and fifty dollars with the interest which
may have arisen from it to be deliverd to said William HALL Junr.
in his own right. The remaining two hundred and fifty dollars,
of the above five hundred dollars, I wish put to interest and
the anual proceeds paid into the hand of Patsy ROBERT, the daughter of said Nancy HALL for her own personal use. And if the
presant husband of the said Patsy ROBERTSON should die before
the said Patsy, in that case I wish the said two hundred and
fifty dollars to be put in the hand of the said Patsy in her own
right. And I wish my daughter Nancy HALL or her heirs to have
none other interest in my estate, either real or personal. Item
4th, The residue of my estate real and personal, I wish to be
sold by me exors. and the proceeds arising there from I wish to
be equally devided amoungst my children Viz: Daniel SOUTH, Rachel CLARDY, William SOUTH, John SOUTH, Gavriel SOUTH, Haner NOR-
ROD, Sarah HALL, James SOUTH, and whereas my son Zedekiah SOUTH
have departed this life, and have left a widow and children, I

wish that equal part, that would have gone to my son Zedekiah if
alive, to go to his widow Ruth SOUTH, and her children, and to
be equally devided amoungst them all. And lastly, I do constitute
and appoint my son Gavriel and my son in law Sesse E. CLARDY
exors. of this my last will and testament by me heretofore made.
In testamoney whereof I have hereunto set my hand and affixed my
seal this the second day of September, in the year of our Lord,
one thousand eight hundred and forty two. Signed, sealed, published, and declared, as and for the last will and testament of
the above named William WOUTH in the presence of us.

Philip Waist Snr.   William South (SEAL)
John C. ?ail
R. L. Wait
Recorded in Book A, Page 38, Bundle 122, Package 13. Recorded
date not available. Proven date Aug. 5, 1844. W. D. Watts, Ordy.

WILL OF JOHN ARMSTRONG

The State of South Carolina Laurens District. I John ARMSTRONG
of the District of Laurens in the State aforesaid, do make, publish and declare this as my last will and testament, hereby revoking and making null and void all former wills by me at any
time here tofore made. And as to such wordly estate as it has
pleased God to blefs me with, I hereby dispose of the same as
follows. I desire that all my just debts and funeral expences
be paid out of the first monies coming into the hands of my
executrix. I give and bequeath unto my beloved wife Elizabeth
ARMSTRONG all of my estate both real and personal for and during the term of her natural life or widowhood, with this exception that she is not to give, loan or hire, any of the property
to my daughter Elizabeth, not is she to give or loan her any
money, nor is my said wife to give, loan, or hire any of the
property to my daughter Artemensen, so long as she may continue
the wife of Samuel AUSTIN, nor is she to give or loan her any
money. Also with the exception of the tract of land, now in the
pofsefsion of my daughter Cresy Ann, the wife of William OWENS,
containing one hundred and ninety two and a half acres more or
lefs, known as the ligon tract. Also forty acres of land being
that portion hereafter to be excepted out of the bequest to my
daughter Artemesen of the Samuel AUSTIN land. And also eleven
acres and 3/4 of land excepted in the tract hereafter bequeathed
to my daughter Syntha HOLINSWORTH known as the Moore tract,
which tract of land I give and bequeath to my daughter Cresey
Ann the wife of the said William OWENS, for and during the term
of her natural life. And at her death to the lawful ifsue of
her body. And in the event of her leaving no ifsue of her body,
the said tract of land is to revent back to my estate. At the
death of my wife, I give and bequeath unto Edmond MARTIN and
William OWENS in trust for the sole use and benefit of my daughter Artemesen the wife of Samuel AUSTIN, all that plantation of
tract of land containing two hundred and two ½ acres, more or
lefs with the exception of forty acres to be laid off and run

46

parallel with the line adjoining Elizabeth REED from a stake
corner near the mill pond to another stake corner at the corner
of my field, so as to include the old mill place. It is my will
and desire that the trustees are to account for (Illegeable).
This trust is only to continue so long as my said daughter is
the wife of the said Samuel AUSTIN, or in other words so long as
the said Austin may live during the life of my said daughter.
And should my said daughter dec. leaving no lawfull ifsue of her
body, it is my will and desire that the said tract of land and
the profits arising therefrom if any suplis is to revert back to
my estate. At the death of my wife, I give and bequeath unto my
daughter Suntha, the widow of Isaac WHINTWORTH, all that plantation or tract of land containing one hundred and sixty one ½
acres more or lefs, known as the Haney AUSTIN land, and lying on
the north side of Mudlick Creek, also one other tract of land
containing one hundred and one acres more or lefs known as the
More tract with the exception of eleven and 3/4 acres as will
appear by a plot of the same made by Alsey FULLER. At the death
of my said daughter the said land is to decend to the lawful
ifsue of her body, and in the event of leaving more, it is to
revert back to my estate. At the death of my wife, I give and
bequeath unto my daughter Mary, the wife of Edmond MARTIN, all
that plantation or tract of land containing one hundred and
seventy acres more or lefs known by the Nickels tract adjoining
lands of J. W. WILLIAMS, Elizabeth REED, T. H. RUDD, and of
Nickels and at her death to the lawful ifsue of her body, and
should she leave more the same is to revert back to my estate.
At the death of my wife, I give and bequeath to my daughter
Haney and the lawful ifsue of her body, all that plantation or
tract of land containing five hundred and fifty four acres more
or lefs adjoining lands of J. D. Williams, T. A. Rudd, the estate
of James Word, John Cook, Sally Atwood, and James Leak, being
the place whereon I now live on the expefs condition that she
does not marry a certain John R. FULLER son of Solomon and Febey
FULLER, and in the event of such marriage, I hereby remark the
said bequeath and in lien thereof I give and bequeath unto my
said daughter Haney five dollars which is to be her portion of
my estate both real and personal. I give and bequeath unto my
daughter Elizabeth, the widow of John FULLER or the wife of Dr.
Robert AUSTIN, five dollars which I desire to be her portion of
my estate real and personal. (Illegeable) give and bequeath unto Edmond MARTIN and William OWENS, the following negores Viz.
Sam and Jincy his wife, Brach, Matts, and her child or children,
in trust for the sole, sparate use and benefit of my daughter
Antenesen, the wife of Sameul AUSTIN, with this understanding
that the trustees are to account for the annual line or rents
and profits of the said negroes and at no time to place the same
in the pofsefsion of the cestue give trust during the marriage
or life time of the said Sameul AUSTIN. And at his death the
the trust is to cease and my said daughter put in pofesfion of
the same. And should my said daughter die leaving no lawful
issue of her body, the aforesaid property and increase if any,
is to revent back to my estate. At the death of my wife, it is

47

my will and pleasure that all the balance of my negro property
be equally divided between my four daughters, Cyntha, Mary,
Haney, and Creasy Ann by ballat in the following manner viz. My
executors will select five disinterested freeholders, who will
arrange them by families as near as possible in to form lots
valueing the same and divide the same among my daughters afore
said so as to make them shares of equal value by ballot aforesaid.
Should all or any of my daughters decd. without lawful ifsue of
their bodies, the said negroes and increase are to revert back
to my estate. All the rest residue and remainder of my estate
may be so divided if found practicable, or otherwise sold and
divided among my said daughters. On further reflection should
my wife marry, in that event I give and bequeath unto her three
hundred and seven acres of land, which will appear by a plat and
grant for the same, being part of the tract on which I now reside
and the following negroes viz., Tom and Cherry his wife, Meaky,
Clerv, Esther, Mike, Miney, Arch, and little Sam, the same to
have and pofsefs during her natural life. And at her death to
be equally divided among the past four named daughters by valuation and lot as aforesaid. I nominate, constitute and appoint
my beloved wife executrix of this my last will and testament,
for and during the term of her widowhood, who is fully authorized
to take charge of my whole estate prove the will, take charge of
the estate and amnage the same at discretion, after making an
inventory and return of the estate, I desire that she may not be
troubled in making annual returns. I further nominate and appoint and constitute my trusty and worthy friends John BURTON,
Henry BURTON, and Travis HILL executors of this my last will and
testament to act as such after the death or marriage of my said
wife. Signed, sealed, published, and declared as and for the
last will and testament of John ARMSTRONG who has subscribed the
same in the presence of each other and the testator at his request.

R. Campbell   John Armstrong (SEAL)
W. D. Watts
R. Thompson
A. C. Garlington
John Garlington
Recorded in Will Book A, Page 39. Original will not in files of
Probate Judge. Proven April 26, 1845. Recorded date not avail-
able. W. D. Watts, O. L. D.

WILL OF JANE HAMILTON

In the name of God, Amen. I Jane HAMILTON of the District of
Laurens and State of South Carolina, being of sound and dispos-
ing mind and memory, do make and ordain this my last will and
testament in manner and form following, that is to say. First,
I will and bequeath unto my son Smuel the tract of land whereon
I now live, and also the tract of land I purchased from James
DORRAH and Alexander CULBERTSON, provided however, that if Alex-
ander HAMILTON my son, and my son in law James COLES should come

to this country, he is to furnish them with a place to settle and live on until they can have the opportunity to procure a place for themselves. I also give to my son Samuel a negro man named Edwin and a girl named Nancy, a bed and bedding, to have and to hold said land and negroes and other property during his natural life. And at his death to be equally divided amoungst his children, should he have he die leaving children, but should he die without a child or children living them, it is my will and desire that the said property be equally divided amongst my other children. Second, I give and bequeath to my son John HAMILTON a negro boy named George until his daughter Jane HAMILTON arrives at age or marries, and then I give the said negro George to his daughter Jane HAMILTON. Third, I give to my son Andrew HAMILTON a negro boy named Tom and a negro boy named William, one bed and bedding, and one cow, and calf, and four hundred dollars. 4th, I give to my son Alexander HAMILTON a negro girl named Betsey and four hundred dollars in money. 5th, I give to my daughter Martha DORRAH two hundred dollars. 6th, I give to my daughter Mary COWNS a negro girl named Milly and a negro boy named Lewis and four hundred dollars during her natural life, and at her death to be divided amongst her children. 7th, I give to my daughter Eliza SCOLDS a negro woman named Mary and a boy named Archy, and four hundred dollars during her natural life and at her death to be divided amongst her children, also a bed and bedding. 8th, I give to my grand daughter Eliza DOWNS a negro girl named Martha, bed and bedding during her natural life and at her death to her children. But should she die without a child or children, then the said property to return to my estate and be divided amongst my children. I also give her a horse and saddle upon the same terms. 9th, I give to my four children; Alexander, Andrew, Mary, and Eliza, all the monies due me in judgments to be equally divided amongst them. 10th, I give to my son Samuel all the ballance of my estate after paying my debts and the legacies above mentioned. Lastly, I appoint my two sons Samuel and Andrew executors of this my last will and testament, hereby revoking all other wills by me heretofore made. Witnefs my hand and seal this sixth day of October, 1842. Signed, sealed acknowledged and published in presence of.

H. C. Young   Jane Hamilton (SEAL)
Charles Smith
J. I. Culbertson
Recorded in Will Book A, Page 41, Bundle 189, Pkg. 10. Proven date July 30, 1844. Recorded date not avialable. W. D. Watts, Ordy. Laurens District, Laurens County.

WILL OF ELIZABETH BYRD

The State of South Carolina Laurens District. In the name of God, Amen. I Elizabeth BYRD of the State and District aforesaid, being of sound mind but in bad health, do constitute and ordain this my last will and testament in the manner following to wit. It is my will and desire that after my decease my property of

every kind both real and personal be sold by me executor (here
after named) as they may deem most profitable for all the legatees and the proceeds arising therefrom to be equally divided
between my children in the following manner. The part or portion of my estate that shall go to James C. LASLEY, I place in
the hands of my executors for them to manage in the most profitable manner, for the use of his family, and for the secruity to
the property, either by loaning the money and furnishing the
said family with the interest from time to time, if they shall
think it best or by purchasing negroes or other property for the
use of said family. Retaining however, the management of the
same in their hands so that it may eventually go into the hands
of his children after his decease. Out of James C. LASLEYS portion there is to be deducted thirty dollars, which I have already
paid him and do authorize my exeuctors to make this deduction in
the settlement of my estate. The part or portion of my estate
going to my daughter Hannah H. COOK is conditional Viz, That
whereas my son Austin is security for Daniel COOK to Jesse GARY
or has given his note to the said Gary for the said Cook for a
considerable amount and which my son Austin is likely to have
the same to pay out of his estate. If so it is my desire that
Austin be made whole out of Hannah's portion if sufficient to
pay the same, or so much of it as will make him whole. If on
the contrary David COOK, his heirs, executors or any other person shall pay the said debt or cause the same to be paid, and
make the said Austin whole and safe. Then the protion of my
estate going to Hannah H. COOK shall be given to her, her life
time, then to the heirs of her body. But to be under the control
of my executors. (Illegeable) give to Henry W. LESLAYS, I
give and bequeath unto him his natural life and then to his heirs
forever. The part or portion of my estate going to Austin LAS-
LAYS, I give and bequeath unto him his natural life, and then
unto his heirs forever. The part or portion of my estate going
to Edmound T. LASLAY, I give and bequeath unto him, his natural
life and then to his heirs forever. The part or portion of my
estate going to Eliza COLEMAN, I give and bequeath unto her, her
natural life, and then to the heirs of her body, but the said
part or portion is to be entirely under the management of my
executors. The part or portion of my estate going to Dorthy BLUM
I give and bequeath unto her during her natural life, and then to
the heirs of her body forever. I also give and bequeath to Elizabeth I. LASLAY, daughter of James C. LASLAY, for her kind atten-
tion and services rendered while living with me a horse, and
saddle, which together are to be worth fifty or sixty dollars,
also a feather bed and its furniture, also fifty dollars in
money. Unto Martha MITCHELL, I give and bequeath an equal share
with the rest of my children and then to her heirs forever. I
nominate with full confidence my three sons Henry W. LASLAY, Austin LASLAY, Edmond T. LASLAY, as my lawful executors to execute
and carry into effect this my last will. Signed, with my hand
and seal this the ninth day of December, in the year of our Lord
one thousan eight hundred and forty four.

Continued on page 51

Continued from page 50
Test: Wm. Cook   Elizabeth Byrd (SEAL)
      Jerimma Cook
      DAneil Carter
Recorded in Book A, Page 42. Proven date Jany, 9, 1845. W. D.
Watts, Ordy. Recorded date not available. Original will not in
files of Probate Judge.

WILL OF SARAH DOWNS

South Carolina Laurens District. I Sarah DOWNS of the State and
District aforesaid, being of sound mind and memory, but calling
to mind the uncertainty of life and being desirous to dispose of
what it hath pleased God to blefs me with in this world or part
of it, do make this my last will and testament in the manner following viz. 1st, Whereas I have obtained a decree from the court
of Equity against William F. DOWNS and where as said decree is
contested by the crediters of the said heir of DOWNS, now if
said decree should be confined, I direct my executors to pay all
my just debts out of it. But if said decree should not be confined by the court of Equity, then I direct my executors to sell
my negro woman Molly and her child Sam, and my negro girl Dicy
for the purpose of paying my debts. But if my debts should be
paid out of the decree, then I give and bequeath said negro woman Molly and her child Sam and Dicy and my negro woman Sylva
and her future increase to Wm. D. BYRD in trust for my daughter
Phebe BREWSTER, but not to be liable for any of the debts of
James BRESTER, but to be held by W. B. BYRD as trustee for the
said Phebe BREWSTER during her life with power to will them to
whom she pleases at her death. 2nd, I give and bequeath to William D. BYRD for the sole and separate use of my grand son Jonathan D. BREWSTER my two negro girls Lucy and Parthena and their
increase to be held in trust by said Wm. D. BYRD during the natural life of said Jonathan D. BREWSTER and at his death to be
divided among his legal children if he should have any, but if
the said Jonathan D. BREWSTER should die leaving no legal children, then in that case I give the said negro Lucy and Parthena
and their increase to the children of Wm. D. BYRD to be divided
among them, share and share alike. 3d, I give and bequeath unto
Wm. D. BYRD as trustee for the sole and separate use of my grand
daughter Claracy BREWSTER my two negro girls Ellen and Charlotte
and their increase during her natural life and then to be divided
amoungst her children if she should have any, but if she should
die leaving no children, then I give the (illegeable) and their
increase to the children of Wm. D. BYRD to be divided among them
share and share alike. 4th, Whereas there is certain negroes
namely; Davis Patrick (little) Truna, Leroy, and Emaline, now in
the pofesion of Phebe BREWSTER which negores she the said Phebe
BREWSTER raised but the legal title being in Wm. F. DOWNS, I do
hereby direct my executors to have the said negroes Davis, Patrick, Truno, Leroy, and Emaline, leverid on by the sheriff by
virtue of an execution in the care I have against Wm. F. DOWNS
and have them sold and purchase them and have the title made to
Wm. C. BYRD as trustee for my daughter Phebe BREWSTER to be held

51

in trust the said negroes Davis, Patrick(Little), Truno, Leroy, and Emaline for the sole and separate use of Phebe BREWSTER during her natural life. But should it be thought advisable to all part of said negroes to buy a tract of land, I do hereby authorize Wm. B. BYRD by and with the consent of Phebe BREWSTER to sell such of said negroes as she the said Phebe may set apart, and with the proceeds thereof buy a tract of land and hold the same in trust for the said Phebe BREWSTER, but not to be liable for James BREWSTER debts, she the said Phebe BREWSTER is authorized to will at her death such of said negroes and their increase and land if any should be purchased to any one she may choose. I also direct my executors to have said execution levied on a negro man named Truno and have him sold and purchased him and have the titles made to Wm. R. FARLEY and Dr. Hugh SAXON as trustees to hold said negro Truno in trust for the use and benefit of the family of Wm. F. DOWNS. In order that the foregoing will may be cained into execution, I do constitute and appoint Wm. D. BRYD and Allen BARKSDALE my execution to this my last will and testament. In testimony whereof I have hereunto set my hand and affixed my seal this 17th day of August, in the year of our Lord, one thousand eight hundred and forty two in presents of.

N. Barksdale   Sarah (S) Downs (SEAL)
D. Barksdale
C. Barksdale
Recorded date not available. Proven date Dec. 27, 1844. W. D. Watts, Ordy. Original will not in files of Probate Judge.
                          Codicil
South Carolina Laurens District. 14 Feby, 1844. I Sarah DOWNS yet being of sound and disposing mind and memory, do make this codicil to my above last will and testament; whereas since the above will was executed by me, my grandson Jonathan D. BREWSTER has decd., now I give the two negroes Lucy and Parthena and their increase (that was bequeathed to Jonathan D. BREWSTER) to Wm. D. BYRD trust for the sale and separate use of my daughter Phebe BREWSTER with power to dispose of them at her death as she may choose or desire. I also give my boy Marie to W. D. BYRD in trust for my daughter Phebe BREWSTER with request that she give the colt to my grand daughter Clmasa BREWSTER. Signed, sealed in presence of the day and date above mentioned.
                                          her
Downs Barksdale   Sarah (S) Downs (SEAL)
Elizabeth L. Downs   mark
Cardin Gary

                    WILL OF EASTER DEAN

In the name of God, Amen. I Easter DEAN of Laurens District in the State of South Carolina, being of a sound and of a disposing mind, but calling together the uncertaintes of life, and being in pofsefsion of such worldly estate as it hath pleased God to blefs me with, do make and ordain this my last will and testament.

                          52

First, It is my will after I die, that all my just debts shall be paid by my executors hereinafter mentioned together with my funeral expenses out of my estate though my estate if but little but what there is I have a preference who shall have it. My estate consisting of one half of eighty acres of land more or lefs lying on the waters of Indian Creek bounded by lands of John MASON, David MARTIN, and others together with one beadstead and furniture with my wearing apparel. Also my claim to the kitchen furniture and moreover my claim to the stock of swin cattle and poultry all of which I want sister Polly DEAN to have as long as she lives. Alfter she dies then I want my brother Isaam DEAN, William DEAM's heirs and Sarah DALRYMPOLES heirs all to have three dollars a piece no their children, three a piece but my brothers and sister which I just give three dollars a piece. The balance of my estate after my sister Polly death, I want my brothers Thomas DEAN (senr.) and Job DEAN (senr.) to have it, but they must not give it at their death to noen of the entestien no way it can be fixed. This reason that I give all my estate after my sister Polly's death to Job DEAN (Senior) and Thomas DEAN Senior is this that them two has lived with as near us and has seen to us in our old and last days. And I do not give this preference in this my last will through any impose motives against my sister which is dead, nor against her heirs nor either against my brother William DEAN which is dead nor against his heirs, nor against my brother Issam DEAN who is living, nor against heirs, but I wont it just so. My friend John MASON I appoint executor of this my last will and testament. In witnefs of I have hereunto set my hand and seal this 28th day of March, in the year of our Lord, one thousand eight hundred and fourty four. Signed, sealed, declared and published by the above named Easter DEAN as and for her last will and testament in the presence of us, who at her request and in her presence have subscribed our names.

H. R. Metts
William Hutchison
Caste James

her
Easter X Dean (L.S.)
mark

Recorded in Will Book A, Page 44, Bdl. 96, Pkge. 9. Proven June 7, 1844. Recorded date not available. W. D. Watts, Ordy. Laurens District, Laurens County.

WILL OF GEORGE MCKITRICK

South Carolina Laurens District. In the name of God, Amen. I George MCKITRICK Senr., being of sound and disposing mind and memory, but weak in body, and calling to mind the uncertainty of life, and being desirous to dispose of all such worldly estate as it hath pleased God to blefs me with, do make and ordain this my last will in manner following, that is to say. I desire in the first place that as soon as pofsible after my death all my just debts and funeral expence be paid and should there not be sufficient funds on hand at my death to pay the same, it is my desire that my executor sell enough of such property as can be

53

most conveniently spared to enable him to do the same. It is my will that the remainder of my property real and personal except such as may hereafter be disposed of remain in the pofsifsion of my wife. Should she survive me during her life or widowhood, to be used and enjoyed by her, and at her death to be disposed of as hereafter directed. I give and bequeath to my son Samuel fifty acres of land absolutely and unconditionally forever upon his paying fifty dollars in discharging my present debts. It is my will and desire that at the death of my wife that my son James should pofsefs the balance of the land absolutely and uncondition-ally upon his paying one hundred dollars to my daughters Isabella and Jane, dividing the same equally between them. It is my will and desire that at the death of my wife the balance of the per-sonal property not heretofore disposed of be equally divided be-tween my two daughters Sarah and Elizabeth. It is likewise my will and desire that if either of my single daughter should die without ifsue that the surviving one should pofsefs her distri-butive part of my estate. Further more it is my will and desire that if my son James should die without ifsue that my son Samuel shall pofsefs his share of the land upon his paying the hereto-fore named hundred dollars to (Illegeable). I give and bequeath to my son John one dollars, believing that I have heretofore made his equal with the rest of my children in educating him. And lastly, I do hereby constitute and appoint my son Samuel to be the executor of this my last will and testament. In testimony whereof I have hereunto set my hand and seal this 19th day of October, in the year of our Lord, one thousand eight hundred and forty four. Signed, sealed, published, and declared as and for the last will and testament of the above named George MCKITRICK. In the presence of us.

James F. Blakely III   George McKitrick (L.S.)
Wm. Blakely S. J.
William C. Leak
Recorded in Will Book A. Page 44, Bdle, 97, Pkge. 1?. Proven date Nov. 1?, 1844. Recorded date not available. W. D. Watts, Ordy. Laurens District, Laurens County.

WILL OF S. T. H. TODD

The State of South Carolina Laurens District. In the name of God, Amen. I S. T. H. TODD of the district and state aforesaid, being of sound and disposing mind and memory, but calling to mind the uncertainty of life, and being desirous to dispose of all such worldly estate as it has pleased God to blefs me with, do make and ordain this my last will in manner following, that is to say. First, I desire that all my just debts and funeral expenses be paid out of my estate not hereinafter specifically bequeathed. Secondly, After payment of my debts and funeral expenses as aforesaid, I give and bequeath to my brother Robert E. TODD three thousand dollars, all my negroes, household and kitchen furniture and the unexpired portion of the leave of the house and lot, in the village of Laurens, which I occupy. Thirdly,

54

I discharge and release my brother William A. TODD from the payment of a note I hold on him for eight hundred and fifteen dollars seventy three cents. Fourthly, I give and bequeath to my brother James R. TODD my horse and saddle. Fifthly, I give and bequeath all the rest and residue of my estate in equal shares to my beloved mother and all my brothers and sisters, except Robert E. TODD who is provided for as above stated. I include the children in this clause, of my deceased sister Mary W. HIGGINS who are to take the share their mother would have been entitled to under this clause of my will, even she now living. Sixthly and lastly, I hereby appoint my brother Robert E. TODD sole executor of this my last will and testament. In testimony whereof, I have hereunto set my hand and affixed my seal this 6th day of August, Anno Domini, one thousand eight hundred and forty three. Signed, sealed, published, and declared as and for the last will and testament of the above named S. T. H. TODD, in the presence of us.

Illegeable   S. T. H. Todd (L.S.)
Illegeable
Illegeable
Recorded in Will Book A, Page 45, Bdle. 109, Pkge. 1. Proven Dec. 30, 1844. Recorded date not available. W. D. Watts, Ordy.

WILL OF MARY WOLFF

State of South Carolina Laurens District. I Mary WOLFF being of sound and disposing mind and memory but weak in body, and being desirous of disposing of such worldly estate as it hath pleased almighty God to blefs me with, do make and ordain this as my last will and testament as follows Viz. 1st, I give and bequeath to my grandson John F. SAXON my negro woman Dinah about sixty years and her daughter Betsy eighteen years of age upon condition that he pays the sum of forty dollars for each of the five children of my son George F. WOLFF, Viz. John S., Melton Y., Charles S. James R., and Mary R. WOLFF at such times and in such sums as may be required to give the said five children a ordinary english education. 2nd, I give to my grand sons Lewis SAXON and John F. W. SAXON my negro man George about twenty seven years of age and my negro man Osiswile about twenty five years of age in trust for the use and benefit of my son George F. WOLFF during his natural life and at his death to be sold and the proceeds of sale to be equally divided between his five children mentioned above Viz., John S., Melton Y., Charles S., James R., and Mary R. WOLFF. But should my son George F. WOLFF die before his youngest child Viz. Mary R. WOLFF arives at the age of twenty one years or marries, then it is my will that the two negroes above named Viz. George and Creswile remain in trust untill she Mary R. WOLFF arrives at the age of twenty one years or marries, and then to be sold and equally divided between John S., Milton Y., Charles S., James R., and Mary R. WOLFF. And it is my express will and intention that the said negroes George and Creswile shall be in no event liable for the present or future debts

55

of my son George F. WOLFF, but shall remain securely vested for his use and that of his five children in the said Lewis SAXON and John F. W. SAXON who an hereby authorized to him out exchanged or sell sd. negroes as they may think most beneficial to the said George F. WOLFF and his five children above named. 3rd, I give to my daughter Isabella SAXON my negro woman Venies about seventy years of age and all the furniture of every description (Illegeable) now in her pofsefsion and the notes and accounts that may be due me at my death. And it is further my will that she pay all the debts that I may owe at the time of my death. Lastly, I appoint John F. W. SAXON my executor to carry into effect this my last will and testament. Signed, sealed, and acknowledged in presence of us this 26 day of February, 1842.

Christopher Burns   Mary Wolff (SEAL)
H. Saxon
R. C. Saxon
Recorded in Book A, Page 46, Bundle 101, Package 10. Proven date Jan. 4, 1845. W. D. Watts, Ordy. Recorded date not available

WILL OF GEORGE MADDEN

South Carolina Laurens District. In the name of God, Amen. I George MADDEN of said district, being of sound and disposing mind and memory, but weak in body, and calling to mind the uncertainty of life and being desirous to dispose of all such worldly estate as it hath pleased God to blefs me with, do make and ordain this my last will in the manner following, that is to say. I desire that so much of my personal property be sold immediately after my decease and the monies arising therefrom all my just debts and funeral expences be paid. I give to my wife Nancy MADDEN all the ballance of my property both personal and real estate during her life as widowhood. And if my wife should marry immediately after her marriage all my property, both personal and real shall be sold and my wife to receive a childs part of both personal and real estate and if my wife should not marry, immediately after her death my estate shall be sold both real and personal estate on one and two years credit and my executor hereafter named to make a good and sufficient title to said real estate, and all my estate both real and personal estate to be equally divided amongst my children except Elizabeth WILBON and Lacklin L. MADDEN and for them to have none until the ballance of my children get as much as they have had. And then for Elizabeth WILBON to have ten dollars for her full share to and her heirs forever. And the ballance of my estate to be equally divided amongst Nancy N. MADDEN, Laclin L. MADDEN, Fanny MADDEN, Sarah MADDEN, Rebecca MADDEN, Polly MADDEN, Amy MADDEN, and Lewey MADDEN to them and their heirs forever. And lastly, I do constitute and appoint my said wife executrix and my son Lacklin L. MADDEN executor of this my last will and testament. In testimony whereof I have hereunto set my hand and affixed my seal this the third day of October in the year of our Lord, one thousand eight hundred and forty two. Signed, sealed, published, and declared

as and for the last will and testament of the above named George
MADDEN in the presents of us.

Wm. Graves   Geo. Madden (LS)
Thomas X Dison
     his mark
Illegeable
Recorded in Will Book A, Page 46. Original will not in files of
Probage Judge. W. D. Watts O. L. D. Proven August 28, 1844.
Recorded date not available.

WILL OF ALFRED PERRETT

In the name of God, Amen. I Alfred PERRETT, being of sound and
disposing mind and memory, but weak in body and calling to mind
the uncertainty of life, and being desirous to dispose of all
such wordly estate as it hath pleased God to blefs me with, do
make and ordain this my last will in manner following, that is
to say. I desire that after my death that my body be decently
buried and my funeral expences paid, then my just debts to be
paid. Then I bequeath and desire my beloved wife Mary PERRETT
to have my land on which I live embracing the house etc. during
her life time of widowhood. And I also bequeath to my wife Mary
one waggon and harnefs, one horse, one black mare, 1 colt, one
sorrel mare, and two mules, stock of hogs, and cattle, household
and kitchen furniture and plantation tools necefsary to the farm.
I desire that my son Bryant PERRETT and my daughter Nancy Caroline PERRETT to be and to have as much as the rest of my children
which I have given property to, for them to be made equal and
then I bequeath and have given before to my daughter Sarah A.
A??MORE six hundred and fifteen dollars in property agreeablt to
a memorandum made. And I have and do give unto my daughter
Abafail C. ELLISON five hundred dollars in property agreeable to
said memorandum. And I do and have given unto my daughter Lucinda F. MCDONALD five hundred and sixty five dollars in property
agreeable to said memorandum. And I do and have given unto my
son Thombury A. PERRETT six hundred and ten dollars in cash, and
1 horse, and after making all of them equal, that is my son
Bryant and Nancy, the remainder of my property I wish my wife
Mary to have during her life, and at her death to be equally divided among my children. I wish my son Thombury A. PERRETT and
my wife Mary PERRETT to act as executor and executrix in order
to carry out the intention of this my last will and testament
made by me. In testimony whereof I have hereunto set my hand
and affixed my seal this the 28th day of April, 1845. Signed,
sealed, published, and declared as and for the last will and
testament of the above named Alfred PERRETT in the presence of us.

Abram Machen   Alfred Perrett (SEAL)
C. B. Riley
Thosl. J. Sullivan
Recorded in Will Book A, Page 47. Original will not in files of
Probate. W. D. Watts Ordy. Laurens District, Laurens County.

Continued on page 58

Continued from page 57
Proven date July 3, 1845.

WILL OF SOLOMON FULLER

South Carolina Laurens District. In the name of God, Amen. I Solomon FULLER Senior, of the aforesaid State and District, being of sound and disposing mind and memory but weak in body, and calling to mind the uncertainty of life and being desirous to dispose of all such worldly estate as it has pleased God to blefs me with, do make and ordain this my last will in manner following viz. That it is my will and desire that my executors hereinafter named after my death have me decently buried in a christian like manner and as soon thereafter as it may be convenient to sell so much of my personal estate which can be best spared as may be necefsary the proceeds of which shall be put to the proceeds of my present crop, should there be a suplus over and above as support for the family. And out of the monies arising therefrom all my just debts and funeral expences be paid. 2nd. I give unto my two sons in law and their children (one) the sum of one dollar each to them and heirs forever. 3rd. It is my will and desire that my two sons Harrison M. FULLER and Solomon T. FULLER shall each have a horse worth sixty dollars and my daughter Mary a horse worth sixty dollars and a saddle worth twelve dollars to put them on an equal footing with those of my children that has already received those things, when they arrive of age or marry or sooner if convenient. It is further my will and desire that whenever any of my children shall marry that they have each a cow and calf, one feather bed and furniture, and such other things as my wife may conveniently spare the same being taken into consideration in the general division of my estate hereinafter named. I give unto my beloved wife Phebe FULLER all my state both real and personal of whatever it may be not herein before disposed of to be during her natural life or widowhood and after her death to be equally divided among all my children hereinafter named share and share alike. After making them equal should some of them have received mor than others before that time to them and their heirs forever Viz., Ellison I. FULLER John R. FULLER, Harrison M. FULLER, Mary FULLER, and Solomon T. FULLER, which dicision is to be effected by a sole of all my property real and personal except my negro girl Milley which my daughter Mary FULLER is at liberty to take at valuation as so much of (Illegeable) property and divided accordingly. But in case my wife should marry, then it is my will and desire that the property both real and personal should be divided immediately between my children Viz., Elison I. FULLER, john R. FULLER, Hanison M. FULLER, Mary FULLER, and Solomon T. FULLER, share and share alikt, to them and their heirs forever. Except the share of my wife in which she in only to hold a life interest and at her death to be equally divided among the five last mentioned children. Lastly, I do constitute and appoint my brother Alsey FULLER and my two sons John R. FULLER and Hanison M. FULLER executors of this my last will and testament, hereby revoking all other and former will or wills by me made. In witnefs whereof I have hereunto set my hand and affixed my seal this 27th day of August, one thousand eight hundred and thirty four in presence of.

Henry W. Paslay   Solomon Fuller (SEAL)
Wm. Fuller
George Robert
Recorded in Will Book A, Page 48. Proven Sept. 2, 1844. Recorded date not available. Original will not in files of Probate Judge. W. D. Watts, Ordy. Laurens District, Laurens County.

WILL OF SAML. MCWILLIAMS

The State of South Carolina Laurens District. In the name of God, Amen. I Samuel MCWILLIAMS of the district aforesaid, being of sound and disposing mind and memory, but weak in body, and calling to mind the uncertainty of live and being desirous to dispose of all such wordly estate as it hath pleased God to blefs me with, do make and ordain this my last will in manner following that is to say. I desire that all my estate, both real and personal to belong to my wife Martha MCWILLIAMS enduring her life as well real as personal and after her decease I give to my daughters Martha MCWILLIAMS and Mary MCWILLIAMS one hundred and fifty dollars each and also give the above mentioned girls the beds and all the household and kitchen furniture and the saddles which they now use (shall be) they shall have and hold all the above articles mentioned forever. I give my son Alex MCWILLIAMS all my real estate lying west of Cane Creek to have and to hold forever. All the rest of my estate both real and personal of what nature or quality whatsoever it may be sold and equally divided amongst my several children. And I give the same to them their heirs executors, administrators and afsigns forever. And lastly, I do constitute and appoint my son Alex MCWILLIAMS executor of this my last will and testament by me heretofore made. In testimony whereof I have hereunto set my hand and affixed my seal this 7th of Feby., 1845. Signed, sealed in presence of us as the last will and testament of Samuel MCWILLIAMS.

Joseph Ball   Saml. McWilliams (L. S.)
Wm. McGowan
May McWilliams
Pleasant Newbry
Recorded in Will Book A, Page 48. Original files not in Probate. Proven date Mar. 10, 1845. W. D. Watts, Ordy. Laurens District. Laurens County.

WILL OF NANCY C. WATTS

South Carolina Laurens District. In the name of God, Amen. I Nancy C. WATTS of the State and District aforesaid, being weak in bodily health, but of sound and disposing mind and memory, and being forcibly reminded that it is appointed unto all persons once to die, do make, constitute, and appoint the following as and for my last will and testament. First, It is my will and

desire that my executor to be hereafter named do take pofsefsion
as early as posible after my decease of all the property that I
may be pofsefsed of at my decease consisting of notes, negroes,
household furniture, and so forth and divide and pay it out in
the following manner. First pay my funeral expences and just
debts. Secondly, I give to my executor in trust my two negro
girls Fanny and Dorcas for the sole benefit and comfort of my
two youngest daughters Sarah P. and Margarete E. WATTS (to wit)
Fanny to my daughter Saray P. WATTS and Dorcas to my daughter
Margarett E. WATTS both to be valued at my death by good judges
of property, the valuation of which each of them, at that time,
is to account for to my estate. Should either of my daughters
Sarah P. or Margarete E. WATTS die without ifsue or leaving a
child or children at the death and the child or children should
die without ifsue, then in the case or either of those cases the
negroes and their ifsue are to return back to my estate, and be
equally divided between my other surviving children, or the
child or children of such of my children as may be dead. The
child or children taking amongst the such part as their parent
if living would be entitled to. Thirdly, It is my will and desire that my executor do sell if necefsary my household furniture and negro girl Martha, but if pofsible and would prefer
some one of my children taking the negro girl Martha at a price
agreed on by them and my other little plunder divided among them
without a sale. Fourthly, It is my will and desire that all of
my children living at my death have an equal protion of my estate
share and share alike making Sarah P. and Margarete E. WATTS
account of course for the valuation put upon the two negro girls
willed in trust for them. (Illegeable) Fifthly, I do appoint
my executor to be hereafter named trustee for my two daughters
Sarah P. and Margarett E. WATTS. And it is my wish for all the
monies that may be coming to them (as well as the two negro girls
Fanny and Dorcas) from my estate to be kept by him for their im-
mediate use and benefit as long as they may live. Sixthly, I do
constitute and appoint as my sole executor of this my last will
and testament my son James W. WATTS, hereby revoking and annulling all wills by me heretofore made. And I do confirm this my
last will and testament and no other. Signed, sealed, published
and declared by the said Nancy C. WATTS, as and for her last
will and testament before us whose names are hereunto subscribed
in her presence and in the presence of each other, in the year
of our Lord, one thousand eight hundred and forty five, and 8th
day of March, 1845. Witnefs:

H. M. Phinny   Nancy C. Watts (L.S.)
J. E. Grey
John D. Williams
Recorded in Will Book A, Page 48. Proven March 10, 1845.
Recorded date not available. W. D. Watts, Ordy. Original will
not in files of Probates Judges. Laurens District, Laurens County.

WILL OF MILTON PITTS

In the name of God, Amen. Know all men that I Milton PITTS of
the District of Laurens and State of South Carolina, being of
sound mind but afflicted in body, and calling to mind that it is
appointed unto all men once to die, do think proper to dispose
of all the earthly goods with which it hath pleased the Lord to
blefs me in manner following. 1st. I commend my soul to God,
who give it and my body to the earth from whence it was taken.
2nd. My will is that all my just debts be paid as soon as necefsary or convenient. 3rd. My will is that whatever property or
estate whether personal or real which remains after my debts and
funeral expences are discharged be, and it is hereby constituted
the property and estate and pofsefsion of my wife Mary PITTS for
her use and benefit to be subject to her entire control forever.
4th, I hereby constitute and appoint my father in law said Mary
PITTS father, William LOVELL, my sole executor of this my last
will and testament at that he be empowered to act in reference
to my estate in whatever way may seem to him to be the interest
of dear and affectionate wife sd. Mary PITTS. In witnefs whereof I have set my hand and seal this 13th day of November, 1844.
Signed sealed and in presence of.

Wt. E. Lindsey   Milton Pitts (L. S.)
Noah Johnson
Chaplin Lindsey
Recorded in Will Book A, Page 50. Proven May 25, 1845. Record-
ed date not available. W. D. Watts, Ordy. Original will not in
files of Probates Judges. Laurens District, Laurens County.

WILL OF KETURAH WALKER

In the name of God, Amen. I Keturah WALKER of the State of South
Carolina, Laurens District, being of sound and disposing mind and
memory, and knowing that it is appointed unto all once to die,
and not knowing haw soon I shall be called and being desirous to
dispose of all such worldly estate as it hath pleased God to
blefs me with, do ordain, make, and institute this my last will
and testament revokin all others hither to made. First, I bequeath my soul to God, who gave it to me, and my body to the
dust from where it sprang to be buried in a decent christian like
manner. After paying all my just debts and funeral expences, I
give devise and dispose of my property in the following manner,
that is to say. Immediately after my death I desire that the
whole of my property both real and personal be sold and to be
equally divided among all my children, that is to say, Allen
WALKER, Bones WALKER Hogan WALKER, Azairiah WALKER, Elizabeth
SHAW, Debly Ann WILCOTT, Emely SHAW, Emaline MADDEN, and the
children of Patsey MILAM Decd. Viz. William, John, Debly Ann,
Jane, and Elizabeth, they are to have the same share as their
mother would have if living, the shares of the two youngest Jane
and Elizabeth to remain in my executors (hereinafter named) until
they become of age or married. It is exprefsly understood that

my executor is fully authorized to make good and lawful titles to my land. And lastly, I do constitute and appoiny my beloved son Hogon WALKER executor to this my last will and testament by me hitherto made. In testimony whereof I have hereunto set my hand and affixed my seal this 9th day of March, 1843. Signed, sealed, published, and declared as and for the last will and testament of above named Kiturah WALKER, in presence of us.

	her
John H. Coleman	Keturah X Walker (L.S.)
Wm. Nelson	mark
Azariah Walker	

Recorded in Will Book A, Page 50. Proven May 5, 1845. Recorded date not available. Original will not in files of Probates Judge. W. D. Watts, Ordy. Laurens District, Laurens County.

WILL OF AGNES PARK

South Carolina Laurens District. In the name of God, Amen. I Agnes PARKS of the district and state aforesaid, reflecting upon the uncertainty of life, and being of sound and disposing mind and memory, do make and ordain this my last will and testament viz. Item 1st. It is my will and desire that all my just debts be paid in the first place. Item 2d. I then give and bequeath unto my daughter Molly STEWART five hundred dollars to her and her heirs forever. Item 3d. I give and bequeath to the children of my deceased daughter Isabella FOWLER the sum of eight hundred dollars to be equally divided amon them and their heirs forever. Item 4th. I give and bequeath to my daughter Elizabeth BLAKELY the sum of eight hundred dollars to her and her heirs forever. Item 5th. I give and bequeath to my grand daughter Nancy SIMPSON oldest daughter of my son Andrew PARK the sum of three hundred dollars to her and her heirs forever. Item 6th. I give and bequeath to my son Andrew PARK the sum of two hundred dollars to him and his heirs forever. Item 7th. I give and bequeath unto my grand daughter Nancy (the daughter of Sally HUTCHINSON) who intermarried with on PEARSON the sum of two hundred dollars to her and her heirs forever. Item 8th. I give and bequeath unto Celema BREWARER (now living with me) the sum of two hundred dollars to her and her heirs forever. Item 9th. I further will and desire that the residue and remainder of my estate (if there should be any at my death, after satisfying the aforesaid legacies) should be equally divided among all the legatees in this my will heretofore named and none others. Item 10th. I do hereby nominate, constitute and appoint my friend and relation Dr. John W. SIMPSON sole executor of this my last will and testament hereby revoking all other wills or codicils I have heretofore made. In testimony whereof I have hereunto set my hand and seal this the eighth day of January, in the year of our Lord, one thousand eight hundred and forty two. Signed, sealed, and acknowledged as her will in the presence of.

	her
J. D. Wright	Agnes X Park (SEAL)
B. L. James	mark

Continued on page 63

Continued from page 62
C. L. Illegeable
Recorded in Will Book A. Page 51. Original will not in files of
Probate. Proven date Mar. 25, 1844. W. D. Watts Ordy. Laurens
District. Recorded date not available.

WILL OF MANOAH ROBERSON

In the name of God, Amen. I Manoah ROBERSON of the District of
Laurens and State of South Carolina (farmer), being of sound mind
and disposing memory, but calling to mind the uncertainty of life
and being desirous to dispose of all such worldly estate as it
hath pleased God to blefs me with, do make and ordain this my
last will in manner following that is to say. I give and bequeath to my loving wife Sucretia ROBERSON during her natural
life or widowhood the following property viz. the plantation
whereon I now live together with every thing thereon and all the
personal estate during her natural life or widowhood. After her
death or widowhood the remainder of the estate to go to her two
daughters that is to share and share alike. If my dearly beloved
wife Lucretia ROBERTSON remains on the plantation well, if she
moves off the plantation is to be sold and the money put at interest by my executor untill my two daughters comes of age of
twenty one years of age. If she remains on the plantation all
is to belong to her as before mentioned. And lastly, I constitute
and appoint William OWINGS executor of this my last will and
testament by me hereby revoking all other wills and testament by
me mede. In testimony whereof I have hereunto set my hand and
affixed my seal this the eighteenth day of November, one thousand eight hundred and forty four. Signed, sealed, published and
delivered as and for the last will and testament of the above
named Manoah ROBERTSON in the presence of us.

	his
John Garrett	Monah X Robertson (L.S.)
Emily Hilton	mark
her	
Mary X Owings	
mark	

Recorded in Will Book A, Page 51. Proven Dec. 9, 1844. Recorded date not available. W. D. Watts, Ordy. Laurens District.
Laurens County. Original will not in files of Probate Judge.

WILL OF JOHN JOHNSON

South Carolina, Laurens District. In the name of God, Amen. I
John JOHNSON of State and District aforesaid, being of sound and
disposing mind and memory, but weak in body, and calling to mind
the uncertainty of life, and being desirous to dispose of all
such worldly estate as it hath pleased God to blefs me with, do
make and ordain this my last will in manner following, that is
to say. I desire that my executor hereinafter named immediately
after my decease sell (at his own discretion) so much of my personal estate as will pay all my just debts and funeral expences.
After the payments of all my just debts and funeral expences, it

is my will and desire that my daughters, Viz; Mary Elizabeth,
Katharine, Martha, and Jennetta JOHNSON each have a good feather
bed and furniture. After the payment of all my just debts and
funeral expences, I give and bequeath to my wife Nancy JOHNSON
the whole of the ballance of my estate viz; all my land and negroes and all other property of what kind so ever and for and
during the term of her natural life. After the decease of my
wife Nancy JOHNSON, it is my will and desire that those of my
daughters as above named, that shall remain single have the whole
of my estate, both real and personal which I have given and bequeathed to my said wife Nancy JOHNSON to have and to hold to
keep together for their own benefits and use free from rent or
hire while any two of them shall remain single. Again, it is my
will and desire that those of my daughters who shall live together and hold my estate as above disposed of. If they shall by
mutual consent agree to break up housekeeping that my executor
sell the whole of my estate both real and personal viz. My land
upon one and two years credit and my personal property upon a
credit of twelve months. Again, it is my will and desire that
all of the monies arising out of the sale of my property both
real as well as personal be equally divided among my surviving
children Viz.; Ezekiel, Aaron, Lofton, Frederick, and Isaac
JOHNSON and my five daughters above (Illegeable) my said son
Isaac JOHNSON executor of this my last will and testament by me
heretofore made. In testimony whereof I have hereunto set my
hand and affixed my seal this third day of Feby., in the year of
our Lord, one thousand eight hundred and forty four. Signed,
sealed, published, and declared as and for the last will and
testament of the above named John JOHNSON in the presence of us.
Witnefses:

                                          his
James Blackbun   John X Johnson(L.S.)
George H. Brown   mark
Susannah King
Recorded in Will Book A, Page 52. Original will not in files of
Probate Judge. Proven Nov. 15, 1844. Recorded date not avil-
able. W. D. Watts, O. L. D.

                    WILL OF RACHAEL ODELL

State of South Carolina Laurens District. In the name of God,
or the eternal will Amen. I Rachael ODELL being in a low state
of health, but of sound and disposing mind do make and ordain
this my last will and testament in the following manner or form.
In the first place, it is my will and desire that after my decease (and my remains are decently interred after the christian
form and manner) all my just debts should be discharged as soon
as convenient. Secondly, I bequeath to my daughter Margaret,
the wife of Edward SCRIBNER, the sum of one dollar, also to my
daughter Mary, the wife of Thos. SCRIBNER one dollar. Thirdly,
To my daughter Elizabeth ODELL, I give one bed and furniture,
likewise to my daughter Rachael A. C. ODELL, I give one bed and
furniture. And the ballance of my personal estate to be sold and

proceeds thereof to be equally divided between my five younger children viz.; Thomas ODELL, Elizebeth ODELL, Samuel ODELL, Levi C. W. ODELL, and Rachael A. C. ODELL. Fourthly, It is my desire that my interest in the estate of Baruch ODELL decd. should be equally divided between my five afore mentioned children viz.; Thomas ODELL, Elizabeth ODELL, Samuel ODELL, Levi C. W. ODELL, and Rachael A. C. ODELL. Fifthly, I bequest my interest in a tract of land lying in the State of Illinois, Shelby County, containing forty acres, more or lefs to my five younger children to wit; Thomas ODELL, Elizabeth ODELL, Samuel ODELL, Levi C. W. ODELL, and Rachael ODELL. Finally, I do nominate and appoint my friend John ODELL as executor to carry this my last will and testament in to affect, believing, hoping and trusting that he will act in all cases with a single eye to strict justice the mutual interest, satisfaction and comfort of my legatees. Signed, sealed and delivered this the sixteenth of February, in the year of our Lord, one thousand eight hundred and forty four, and in the sixty eighth year of the American Independence.

	her
Josephus C. Babb	Rachael X Odell (L.S.)
Richard M. Owens	mark
John Lusk	

Recorded in Will Book A, Page 52, Bdle. 94, Pkg. 11. Proven date Mar. 12, 1844. Recorded date not available. W. D. Watts, Ordy. Laurens District.

WILL OF PRESLEY OWINGS

Being much afflicted in body, but of sound mind and memory, and knowing that is appointed for all men to die once believing the time of my desolation in near approaching, I do bequeath my estate which it hath been please God to give as follows. First, I recommend my soul into the hands of almighty God, who gave it me hoping he will receive it. Secondly, I recommend my body to the dust from whence it came neatly to be entered at the expense of my executors. Thirdly, I give and bequeath all my estate both real and personal unto my wife Marget OWINGS during her natural life that she may live comfortable on the same during the term of her existence while in this world. Fourthly, My desire is that my son Lanson OWINGS live on my land and make what he sees cause so that he takes good care of my said wife and keep her from suffering for anything that she particular needs to live on. And fifthly, at her death my will is that all of my estate both real and personal shall be exposed to public sale and equally divided between my lawful heirs. And lastly, I nominate and appoint my two sons Abner OWINGS and Lanson OWINGS my sole executors to carry this my last will and testament into effect and in power them to collect all my just debts and if there should be any demand against me, I authorise my said executors to sell of my estate enough to pay the same and to defray the expense of proving this my will. And I do acknowledge this to be my last will and testament, in witnefs I have hereunto set my hand and seal this tenth day of March, 1836.
Continued on page 66

65

Continued from page 65
Test: Robotson Moore   Presley Owings (LS)
      Stephen Garrett
              his
      Jonathan X Jones
              mark
Recorded in Will Book A, Page 53, Bdl. 95, Pkge. 12. Proven
March 3, 1845. Recorded date not available. W. D. Watts O. L. D.

WILL OF DAVID MARTIN

South Carolina Laurens District. In the name of God, Amen. I
David MARTIN of the district and state aforesaid, being of sound
and disposing mind, memory, and discretion, but calling to mind
the uncertainty of life, do make and ordain this my last will
and testament in manner following. First, I direct my executor
hereinafter appointed as soon after my death as convenient, to
pay my funeral expences and all my just debts out of any money,
I may leave on hand and the debts due me. Second, I desire that
my executor, shortly after my death call in three respectable
freeholders to value all my lands, negroes, and other personal
property; one third of which I devise and bequeath to my beloved
wife Nancy MARTIN during her widowhood; one other third to my
son Adison P. MARTIN and the remaining third to the said Adison
P. MARTIN in trust for the sole and separateuse of my daughter
Levenia Frances MARTIN during her life, except her third of my
live stock, household and kitchen furniture and crop on hand,
which I give her absolutely and without being subject to the
trust aforesaid. And at her death I devise and bequeath the
same except as before excepted, to such child or children and
grand child or grand children, as she may leave. The grand child
or grand children to take the share their parent would take under
this will if living, but should she die without leaving such
child or children, grand child or grand children, in that event
I devise and bequeath her legacy aforesaid, subject to the exception aforesaid, to the said Adison P. MARTIN or to such child
or children as he may leave, should he die before his said sister. Should my said daughter however leave a husband and die
without a child or children or grand child or grand children as
aforesaid, then I devise and bequeath two thousand dollars of
the legacy in which she has a life estate, to such husband and
the balance thereof to the said Adison P. MARTIN or his child or
children as aforesaid. This clause of my will is intended to
embrace my whole estate after payment of funeral expences and
debts. And my desire is that the aforesaid division (Illegeable)
off from the northern end of my land, commencing on the extreme
north east corner of said land at Mavricks line, thence west
towards my residence, keeping morth of the ninety six road and
continuing untill one third, in value, of my whole land is a
measured for my said daughter to be held together with the balance of her legacy in trust as above provided by the said Adison
P. MARTIN with all the power necefsary to the protection and pre-
sevation of the same for the uses and purposes aforesaid, and
with a view to that end. I hereby declare to the title to the

66

same to be vested in the said trustee and in him to continue.
After having laid off my daughter's share of the said land, then
the balance is to be divided equally between my said wife and
the said Adison P., my wife's interest to be limited to her widowhood and to include the homestead. And it is my desire that
the slaves and other personalty be put in three equal lots according to valuation and distributed as before directed. My
daughter's share to be held in trust as aforesaid except what I
have given her absolutely. It is also my wish **that** my son and
his mother should continue to reside at the homestead place and
keep their respective shares of my estate in common during the
widowhood of my said wife or untill Adison marries. But should
my said wife marry again, then I devise and bequeath the portion
in which she has an interest during widowhood to my said son and
daughter, my daughter's share thereof to be held in trust as the
rest of her said legacy by the said Adison P. and subject to the
same limitations. And in lieu of said legacy to my wife, I bequeath to her two negro fellows and a negro woman to be selected
by her out of my stock of negroes, at her marriage, but she is
not in making the selection to choose any of the mechanics. Also
the dividends that may thereafter be due and receiveable on
twenty five shares of my rail road stock and the same number in
the rail road bank during her life. And at her death the said
negroes and stock to be equally divided between my (Illegeable)
the share of the latter to be held in (Illegeable) limitations.
And I would here state that the legacies to my son and daughter
are to be held subject to the contingincy of their mother's marrying again, so that she may have the oppertunity of selecting
the negroes given her in that event as aforesaid. Third. I
devise and bequeath all the residue, if any, of my estate to my
said son and daughter upon the trusts and limitations above set
forth. And should my wife not marry again, at her death, I devise and bequeath the legacy given her during widowhood as follows, to wit, one half thereof to my son and the other to him in
trust as aforesaid for his said sister upon the same trusts and
limitations as the rest of her legacy. Fourth. On further reflection I give and bequeath to my said wife absolutely her
third part of my live stock, household, and kitchen furniture,
and the crop that may be on hand at my death. Fifth. I constitute and appoint Adison P. MARTIN executor of this my last will
and testament. In witnefs whereof I have hereunto set my hand
and seal this 30th day of June, in the year of our Lord, one
thousand eight hundred and forty six. Signed, sealed, and declared as the last will of David MARTIN in the presence of us.

A. L. Wilson   David Martin (SEAL)
Wm. Rook, Jr.
W. T. Tinsley
W. H. Dillard
Recorded in Will Book A, Page 54. Recorded date not available.
Original will not in files of Probate. Proven date Aug. 21st,
1846. Wm. D. Watts, Ordy. Laurens District.

WILL OF SILAS HILL

South Carolina Laurens District. In the name of God, Amen. I Silas HILL of the district and state aforesaid, being of sound and disposing mind and memory, but weak in bodily strength and bearing in mind the uncertainty of human life, for the purpose of disposing of any my worldly pofsefsions, do hereby declare and ordain this my last will and testament, that is to say. Item 1st. I will and desire that my funeral expences and all my just debts first be paid. Item 2nd. I will and bequeath my whole estate both real and personal to my beloved wife Rebecca HILL during her natural life or widowhood. Item 3rd. I will and desire that my wife, afsisted by my three brothers Thomas HILL, James HILL and John HILL, shall give to my sons and daughters a liberal education such as they may desire, or as may be thought most advisable. Item 4th. Should any of my children arrive at age or marry during the widowhood of my wife, I will and desire that she pay over to such child or children so arriving at age, or marring the sum of three thousand dollars each, or its value in property such property to be appraised and valued by my executors hereinafter to be mentioned, and my three brothers, or any two of them. Item 5th. In the event that my wife should marry, then on her marriage, I will and desire my whole estate, both real and personal, to be sold, and one third part of the whole amount not including my portion or portions which may be given off. I will and bequeath to my beloved wife Rebecca HILL absolutely and forever, and the balance I desire to be equally divided among my children, such child or children as may have received any portion or portions, accounting for the same so as to make all equal. Item 6th. Should my wife die without marrying, then I desire all my children to have an equal portion of my whole estate after it is sold each child or children accounting for what they have received so as to make all equal. The children of any deceased son or daughter taking among them what their father or mother would have taken if living and should any of my sons or daughters, die before a final division of my estate as above provided for, not leaving a child or children, I desire his or her share to be equally divided amongst the rest of my children and the grand children if any, as above prescribed. Item 7th. It is my will and desire that my three brothers, Thomas HILL, James, and John HILL will aid and afsist my wife Rebecca HILL (who is hereby appointed my sole executrix) in the management and control of my estate so long as she may live single, and superintend the raising and education of my children. And I hereby empower my said executrix with the advice and approbation of said brothers or any two of them to purchase any property for the benefit of the state which to them amy seem advisable for the benefit of the estate. My said executrix hereby having full power and authority to execute and deliver good and sufficient titles for the same. In testimony whereof I have hereunto set my hand and affixed my seal hereby acknowledging this to be my last will and testament this the twenty ninth day of June, in the year of our Lord, one thousand eight hundred and forth five. Signed, sealed, and acknowledged in the presence of

John G. Klink   Silas Hill (SEAL)
Saml. R. Todd
John D. Wright

Recorded in Will Book A, Page 55. Proven Dec. 18, 1845. Recorded date not available. W. D. Watts Ordy. Laurens District. Original will not in files of Probate Judge Office. Laurens District, Laurens County.

WILL OF MARY MARTIN

State of South Carolina. I Mary MARTIN of Laurens District in said State, do make and appoint this my last will and testament Viz. 1st. I will and direct that my executor hereinafter named do pay my funeral expenses and all my just debts as soon after my death as may be convenient. 2nd. I will and direct that my executor have the family burying ground at my fathers old place walled in with rock that he have the enclosure made sufficeintly large to contain the remains of all the family. 3rd. I will and bequeath to my friend Robert VANCE five hundred dollars to be held by him in trust for the sole and seperate use of my step daughter Margarett Crolina MARTIN free from the control of any husband which she may have. The said sum of money to be loaned and the interest paid to the said Margarett Caroline MARTIN annyally during her life. And at her death the said five hundred dollars to be equally divided amongst her children, the child or children of a deceased child representint its parent. And in the event of the said Margarett Caroline MARTIN dies leaving no child or children or lenial descendant that then and in that case my will and desire is that the said Robert VANCE pay over the said five hundred dollars to my friend Dr. Anthony F. GOLDING to him and his heirs forever. 4th. I will and bequeath that the remainder of my estate, both real and personal of every kind and description shall be divided into three equal shares, one share of which I will and bequeath to my sister Cynthia WHITWORTH to her and her heirs forever, one other share I will and bequeath to Wm. D. WATTS, Esqr. in trust for the use and benefit of my sister Artemased AUSTIN and her husband Samuel AUSTIN, during their joint lives, and during the life of survivor and my will and desire is that the said Wm. D. WATTS vest the said share in such property real and personal as may be most to the interest of my sister and her husband, and permit them to use and enjoy it, or loan out the same and pay to them the interest annually during their joint lives, and the life of the survivor. And at the death of the survivor that the said share with the increase if any, be equally divided amongst the children of the said Artemased, the child or children of a deceased child to take the share which the parent would be entitled to if living, but if at the death of the survivor of the said Artemased and Samuel, there shall be no child or children or lenial descendant of the said Artemased living, then and in that case, I will and direct that the said William D. WATTS, Esqr. trustee under this will deliver up and pay over the said share to my sister Cynthia WHITWORTH and her heirs other and remaining share. I will and bequeath to Dr. Wm. PHILLIPS in trust for the use and benefit of my sister Elizabeth G. AUSTIN and her husband Robert AUSTIN, during their joint lives and the life of the survivor, and my will and desire is that the said Dr. Wm. PHILIPS vert the said share in such property real and personal as may be most to the interest of my sister and her husband, and permit them to use and enjoy it, or loan out the same and pay to them the interest annyally during their joint lives, and the life of the survivor. And at the death of the survivor, that the said share with the increase if any, be equally divided amongst the children of the said Elizabeth G. AUSTIN. The child or children of a deceased child to take the share which their parent would be entitled to if living but if at the death of the survivor of the said Elizabeth G. and Robert, then shall be no child or children or lenial descendant of the said Elizabeth G. living. Then and in that case, I will and direct that the said Dr. Wm. PHILIPS trustee under this will deliver up and pay over the said share and increase if any, to my sister Cynthia WHITWORTH and her heirs. Lastly, I do hereby nominate, constitute, and appoint my friend Dr. Anthony F. GOLDING sole executor of this my last will and testament hereby revoking all former and previous wills by me at any time made. In witnefs whereof I have set my hand and seal this twenty sixth day of August, eighteen hundred and forty six. Signed, sealed, and acknowledged in presence of.

T. G. Williams   Mary Martin (SEAL)
Eliza Goodman
Rhoda E. C. Williams
Recorded in Will Book A, Page 56. Proven Oct. 26, 1846. Recorded date not available. W. D. Watts, Ordy. Original will not in files of Probate Judge.

WILL OF JONATHAN MOTES

South Carolina Laurens District. In the name of God, Amen. I Jonathan MOATS of Lauren District in the State aforesaid, being of sound and disposing mind, memory, and understanding, do make and ordain this to be my last will and testament. 1. I will and desire that all my just debts and funeral expenses be paid. 2. I will and bequeath unto my wife Susan one negro woman named Rachael during her natural life or widowhood and after the death or marriage of my wife, I will and desire that the said negro woman Rachael belong to my daughter Dicy Ann REYNOLDS wife of Benjamin REYNOLDS to her and her heirs forever. I will and desire also that my wife Susan be comfortably and decietly maintained so long as she live or may remain single by my son in law Benjamin REYNOLDS and my daughter Dicy Ann, his wife. And in consideration of this, I gave to them more of my property than to any other children. If my wife Susan should marry again, then my will is that my son in law Benjamin REYNOLDS and Dicy Ann his wife, be discharged from all further liability to her.

3. I will to my daughter Dicy Ann REYNOLDS the tract of land whereon I now reside and one negro boy named Joe, and one negro woman named Lucy and her boy child named Jack to her and her heirs forever. 4. I will to my daughter Betsey MOATES, wife of Chesley MOATES, one hundred dollars to be paid by my executor hereafter to be appointed to her and her heirs forever. 5. I will to my daughter Mineva PINSON, wife of John PINSON, one hundred dollars eighty dollars of which I have to pay for being security for the said John PINSON my son in law, husband of my daughter Minerva. And twenty dollars to be paid by my executor to her and her heirs forever. 6. I will all the balance of my property of every kind and discription what ever to my daughter Dicy Ann REYNOLDS to her and her heirs forever. 7. I Do hereby appoint my son in law Benjamin REYNOLDS executor of this my last will and testament. And I do hereby revoke all former wills by my made and declare this to be my last will andtestament. In witness whereof I have here unto set my hand and seal this 30th day of December, 1845. In presents of:

G. Thomas
H. Finley Senr.
Reuben A. Griffin

his
Jonathan X Moats (LS)
mark

Recorded in will book A, Page 57, Bdl.104, Pkge. 7. Proven and recorded date not available.

WILL OF GEORGE COOK

South Carolina Laurens District. In the name of God, Amen. I George COOK of the state aforesaid, being of sound and disposing mind and memory, but weak in body, and calling to mind the uncertaininty of life, and being desirous to dispose of all such wordly estate as hath pleased God to blefs me with, do make and ordain this my last will in manner following, that is to say. I desire that the tract of land whereon I now live be sold immediately after my decease and out of the moneys arising therefrom all my just debts and funeral expences be paid after payment of my just debts and funeral expences. I give in trust to my executors herein after named for the sole benefit of my daughter Elizabeth KNIGHT and her bodily heirs, one negro boy Toby which I value at three hundred and twenty five dollars, which boy at the death of my daughter above named shall be sold and the money arising from the sale of said boy equally divided among her bodily heirs. All the rest of my estate both real and personal I give and bequeath to my beloved wife Polly COOK during her natural life time, and I give to each of my children (to wit namely) James, Joshua, Nancy, Allen B., John, William E., Mary, Martha, Abraham, and George three hundred and twenty five dollars to be paid to each at the death of my wife. But if convenient for my wife to pay it to them as they become of age, it is my wish for her to do so. Andy my will is that at the death of my wife and the above named legacies are paid over all my property real and personal be sold and equally divided among my children. And I do hereby appoint my son Joshua COOK as a trust friend to receive

my daughter Elizabeth KNIGHTS legacy at the death of my wife
which legacy shall be used to the sole benefit of my daughter
Elizabeth during her lifetime and then go to her bodily heirs.
And lastly, I do appoint my said wife executrix and my sons James
COOK and Joshua COOK executors of this my last will and testament
by me heretofore made. In testimony whereof I have hereunto set
my hand and affixed my seal this the twenty third day of July,
one thousand eight hundred and forty five, and in the seventieth
year of the Independance of the United State of America. Signed,
sealed, published, and declared as and for the last will and
testament of the above named George COOK in presence of us.

J. J. Atwood   George Cook (L. S.)
R. Thomas
William Rose
Recorded in Will Book A, Page 58. Original will not in files of
Probate. Proven date Aug. 15, 1845. Recorded date not avail-
able. W. D. Watts, Ordy. Laurens District.

WILL OF TEMPERANCE GOLDING

South Carolina Laurens District. In the name of God, Amen. I
Temperance GOLDING, of the State and district aforesaid, being
of sound and disposing mind and memory, but weak in body and
calling to mind the uncertainty of life, and desirous to dispose
of all such worldly estate as it hath pleased God to blefs me
with, do make and ordain this my last will and testament, in
manner following, that is to say viz. I desire that immediately
after my decease or as soon after as convenient, that all my
just debts and funeral expences be paid. After the payment of
my just debts and funeral expences, I desire that my two negroes
viz, Giles and Becca, be kept together by my executor hereinafter
to be named and the proceeds of the aforesaid negroes to be applied to the use and future maintainance of my husband James
GOLDING and my three sons viz.; Foster GOLDING, John GOLDING,
and Franklin GOLDIN, so long as my husband James GOLDING shall
live, and after his death, then I will and desire that the above
named negroes with the increase of the girl Becca, be divided
equally between my three sons as above named. I desire further
that all the residue and balance of my estate of whatever quality
or kind soever, it may be, be equally divided between my aforesaid mentioned to be employed at the discretion of my executor,
until my youngest son Franklin GOLDING arrives at the age of
twenty one years. And lastly, I do constitute and appoint my
trusty friend Dr. William PHILIPS executor of this my last will
and testament by me heretofore made, this the 24th day of July,
1845. As witnefs my hand and seal. Signed, sealed, published,
and declared as and for the last will and testament of the above
named Temperance GOLDING, in the presence of us.

                                              her
Test: William Philips   Temperance X Golding
       Clementina B. Philips   mark
Mary E.Mary E. Gill
Continued on page 73

Continued from page 72
Anthony T. Golding
Recorded in Will Book A, Page 60, Bdl. 108, Pkg. 11. W. D.
Watts, O. L. D. Proven and recorded date not available.

WILL OF SAMUEL GOODMAN SR.

South Carolina Laurens District. In the name of God, Amen. I
Samuel GOODMAN Senr. of the District and State aforesaid, being
of perfect mind and memory, but calling to mind the uncertainty
of death, being desirous of making a distribution of such worldly estate as it has pleased heaven to blefs me with in this life
do make and ordain this my last will and testament in the manner
following. Viz.; I loan to my beloved wife during her life,
the following property (Viz) the plantation or tract of land formerly belonging to Gillam GOODMAN containing 57 acres more or
lefs. Also ten acres to be taken from the tract of land I now
live on begining at the corner near the branch between Lewis
BALLS and my own land and run paralel with the old lines untill
it joins Mrs. AUSTINS land, also one negro woman named Aniky and
her son Lewis, her daughter Eliza, also one horse, two cows and
calves, all of her own choice, five large hogs, give hogs of
one year old, one good cow, and pigs, one good feather bed and
furniture, one bedstead and cord, one large trunk, one small
trunk, one good table, six seting chairs, plantation tools of
every third and gear sufficient for her farm and as much kitchen
furniture as she thinks will be sufficient for her use together
with a sufficiency of meat, coffee, sugar, flour, corn, fodder,
and oats, to last her from my death untill she has time to make
a crop. Now if the house on the plantation above given to my
beloved wife is not repaird. at my death my executor is to have
it repaird. immediately for my wife in a comfortable manner with
all other necefsary out buildings suitable for her convenience
and pay for it out of my estate. Now my will is that all the
before mentioned property with the future isue and increase of
the famales that may remain at my wife's death shall return to
my estate and be sold by me executor and the moeny be equally
divided between all my children as may be living at the time the
dividend takes place. And the children of such as may be dead
the child or children of such as may be dead taking amongst themselves such of my estate as their parent if living would have
been entitled to. Secondly, I give and bequeath unto my son
James GOODMAN the part of the tract of land whereon I now life
supposed to contain above two hundred acres. After taking off
the parcel of land lying between said tract and my son Saml.
GOODMAN, begining for a dividing line at a large post oak a line
tree near the corner of Mrs. AUSTINS cotton field near the Mill
road from thence a little below the corner of Drury Sims. Old
field leaving the wet weather over to the right hand and land
enough to the right hand of said drain for a good mill road. My
son James is to be at liberty to take the land above bequeathd.
to him at five dollars pr. acre or let return to my estate and
be sold by my exec. and draw his part in money. Also my son
Saml. GOODMAN is to be at liberty to take the above parcel of

land adjoining that is to be cut off by the dividing line as above describd. at five dollars pr. acre, or let it return to my estate and be sold by my executor. Now the above mentioned ten acres of land cut off for my wife's convenience at her death is to return to the old tract from whence it was taken. Also I give and bequeath unto my beloved wife at my death all the property I have and am to get with her to do as she pleases with forever. Fourthly, Having previously advancd. to son Saml. GOODMAN in maoney and property amounts equal to one hundred and fifty dollars, haveing in like manner advancd. my son Gillan GOODMAN an amount equal to one hundred and fifty dollars and having like manner advancd. my son David GOODMAN an amount equal to one hundred dollars and having in like manner advand. my daughter Rhoda, wife of James NICKLES, one hundred and twenty dollars. And having in like manner advancd. my daughter Maria, wife of James COOK, and amt. equal to one hundred and fifty dollars. And having in like manner advancd. my daughter Jamima, wife of William COOK, an amt. equal to one hundred and seventy five dollars. Fifthly, I give and bequeath unto my son James GOODMAN one bed, bedstead, and furniture, one cow and calf, one sow and pigs, one ewe and lamb, my shot gun, allowing him the filly, saddle and bridle he now claims all which I value at one hundred and fifty dollars. I have chargd. my son Gillam with the sum of two hundred and ninety five dollars for land given him. Also I charge my son Saml. GOODMAN with the sum of four hundred and forty five dollars, for land given him. Also, I charge my son David GOODMAN with two hundred and fifty dollars for land given him, which charges is to be deducted out of then portions of my estate. It is also my wish and desire that all my just debts be paid as soon as posible this being done my will and desire is that the whole of the balance of my estate both real and personal be sold by my executor and be equally divided between such of children as may be living. And the children of such as may be dead the child or children of any, decd. child taking among themselves such part as their parent if living would be entitled to. Sixthly, My will and desire is that if any of my children to whom bequeath have been herein before made and shall hear after receive should die leaving no child nor children or leaving child or children and the child or children should dye, that then and in that case the same and every part of property thereof shall return to and be equally divided between such of my children as may then be living. And the chidlren of such as may be dead in the manner already directed. Seventhly, My wish and desire is that each of my chidlren shall enjoy as nearly as practicable an equal protion of my estate. Lastly, I nominate, constitute, and appoint my friend John D. WILLIAMS to be my executor hereby giving him all the power virtue and authority necefsary to the full and complete execution of this my last will and testament. In testimony whereof I have hereunto set my hand and affixed my seal this the 9th day of October, Anno Domno, 1829. Signd., seald., publishd., and declared by the said Samuel GOODMAN senr. as and for his last will and testament in the presence of.

Continued on page 75

Continued from page 74
M. W. Chrestman   Samuel Goodman (SEAL)
X Jas. G. Williams
X E. D. Williams
Recorded in Will Book A, Page 61, Bdl. 29, Pkge. 2. Proven date
Jan. 3, 1831. Recorded date not available. David Anderson, Ordy.
Laurens District.

WILL OF FRANCIS STEWART

South Carolina Laurens District. In the name of God, Amen. I
Francis STEWART, being of sound and disposing mind and memory,
but weak in body and calling to mind the uncertainty of life and
desirous to arrange my worldly affairs, do make and ordain this
my last will and testament in the manner following to wit. 1st.
I give to my daughter Mary STEWART one small tract of Duncans
creek containing thirty seven acres more or lefs bounded by the
lands of Hofh MCKELVY, Robert H. LITTLE, Francis STEWART, and
others otherwise known as Shepherds tract. 2nd. I desire that
the tract of land on which I now reside containing one hundred
and fifty acres more or lefs, be divided into three equal shares
by the acre, and I give to my son Wm. STEWART one third of said
land allowing him first choice. 3rd. I give to my son Robert
STEWART one third of said land allowing him second choice. 4th.
And I give to my son John Allen STEWART the remaining third of
said tract of land. I give the lands above specified to my
children herein named and to their heirs and afsigns forever.
5th. And I desire that the remainder of my estate consisting of
horses, cows, hogs, household and kitchen furniture, notes and
money, be equally divided among my four children herein named af
after paying my just debts and funeral expences according to valuation. 6th. It is my will and desire that Sarah LIPP the
mother of the above named children have a support from them during her natural life out of the property which I have bequeathed
to them provided she shall live among them as they may mututally
agree. But they shall not be bound to pay for her boarding if
she should choose to live with any other person. 7th. And lastly, I do constitute and appoint my friends William BLAKELY, son
of William, and James L. YOUNG executor of this my last will and
testament, hereby revoking all other and former wills and testament by cut heretofore made. In testimony whereof I have hereunto set my hand and affixed my seal this the sixth day of May,
one thousand eight hundred and forty five (1845). Signed, sealed, published, and declared as and for the last will and testament of within named Francis STEWART in presence of us.

Alexander McKelvy   Francis Stewart (L.S.)
John Dalrymple
Hugh McKelvy
Recorded in Will Book A, Page 63. Proven and recorded dates not
available. W. D. Watts, Ordy. Original not in files of Probate
Judge. Laurens District, Laurens County.

75

WILL OF WILLIAM CARTER

South Carolina Laurens District. In the name of God, Amen. I William CARTER being of sound and discretionary mind, but being in feeble health or knowing that it is appointed unto all men once to die, do make constitute and declare this my last will and testament revoking all other wills heretofore made by me. First, I will and bequeath unto my beloved wife Martha CARTER the tract of land whereon I now reside known as the Cross Hill Tract, together with the adjoining tract at this time occupied as a temporry residence by Mr. Allen VANCE. I further give and bequeath unto my wife the following negroes, to wit. Jack and Liza his wife, Betsy and her three children Caroline, Essex, and John, Diannah and her child, Margaret, and also my negro man Ike. I give also to my wife all such household and kitchen furniture as she may think proper to select. I give further to my wife, my sorrel and bay mares, eight heads of cattle, fifteen head of stock hogs, my Barouch and harness, waggon and harness, and all such other plantation tools together with a sufficiency of provisions as will be a comfutency, for her support and for the support of my dear children for one year. It is my will and desire that my executors hereafter named do assist and council with my wife in selecting these comforts for her, and my childrens benefit. It is my will and desire that my unfurnished house together with all the lumber and utencils bot for its competion, shall be furnished so far as may rendered comfortable to my wife and children. Second, I desire and will that my tract of land known as my upper place adjoining lands of William LIGON and others, be sold at publick sole on a credit of one, and two years, by my executors hereafter named, and I hereby authorise sd. executors to make true and lawful titles to the said land. Third, I desire and will that all my other personal estate not before disposed of shall be by my exeuctors shold on a credit of twelve months. Fourth, I desire and will that my executors pay all my just debts and after payment of such dibts and all accounts notes, and monies arising from my estate shall be equally divided among all my surviving children as they become of age, or shall marry. Fifthly, My will and desire is that all the property both real and personal before bequeathed to my beloved wife Martha CARTER, shall be for her support and for the support of my death children. But should my beloved wife marry, I desire all said property both real and personal and that may be in her possession at said marriage to be immediately under the entire control of my executors and to be by them disposed of or managed in whatever maner they may seem best for her benefit and for the benefit of my children. Sixthly and lastly, I do hereby constitute and appoint as my whole and sole exeuctors of this my last will and testament my brother in law Danile LIGON and my brother Henry N. CARTER. Witness my hand and seal this 20th day of November, 1845. Signed, sealed, delivered and published in presence of.

J. H. Coleman   Wm. Carter (SEAL)
Continued on page 77

Continued from page 76
William Lindsay
Jn. P. Watts
Recorded in Will Book A, Page 65, Bdle. 100, Pkge. 1. Proven
Nov. 27, 1845. Recorded date not available. W. D. Watts, Ordy.
Laurens District, Laurens County.

WILL OF EDWARD MARTIN

South Carolina Laurens District. In the name of God, Amen. I
Edward MARTIN of the district and state aforesaid, being of
sound mind, memory, and discretion, but weak in body and calling
to mind the uncertainty of life, do make and ordain this my last
will and testament in manner and form following, Viz. First: I
will and desire that my executors hereinafter appointed pay my
funeral expences and just debts out of any ready money I may
leave on hand or by a sale of such of my personal estate as they
think best to sell. Secondly: I give, bequeath and devise the
residue of my estate both real and personal to my brother David
MARTIN and my friends John ARMSTRONG and James DAVIS and the survivors and survivor of them, in trust neverthelefs, to permit
my beloved wife Mary MARTIN and my two children Robert Jefferson
MARTIN and Margaret Caroline MARTIN to have, pofsefs, use, and
enjoy the same during the widowhood of my said wife, the children
to be supported and educated out of the proceeds of the farm.
But should my said wife marry or either of my said children come
of age or marry before the marriage of said wife, in any one of
those events I authorise the said trustees and the survivors and
survivor of them to divide the said estate by appraisement or
sale into three equal parts. One of which I give and devise to
the said David MARTIN, John ARMSTRONG, and James DAVIS and the
survivors and survivor of them in trust for the sole and separate
of my said wife during her life without being liable in any form,
either the property or income for the debts of any future husband. And I hereby vest her with the power to dispose of the
same by will, but such power is not to effect the legal title of
the trustees during her life estate. Thirdly: I give and devise
one other of the part aforesaid to the said David MARTIN, John
ARMSTRONG, and James DAVIS in trust, to permit my son Robert
Jefferson MARTIN to have the pofsefsion use and enjoy, out of
the same during his life, and at his death I give and devise the
same to such child or children as he may have surviving him. But
should he die in the life time of his said sister Margant Caroline, without such child or children, in that event I give and
devise said share to the trustees aforesaid, and the survivors
and survivor of them in trust for the sole and separate use of
his said sister during her life, and at her death to such child
or children as she may leave surviving her. Fourthly: I give a
and devise the remaining part of said estate to the trustees
aforesaid and the survivors and survivor of them in trust to
permit my said daughter Margart Caroline MARTIN to have the pofsefsion, use and enjoyment of the same for her sole and separate
use during her life. And at her death I give and devise the same
to such child or children as she may leave surviving her, but

should she die in the lifetime of her said brother without such child or children, in that event I give and bequeath the same to the trustees aforesaid and the survivors and survivor of them in trust for the use and benefit of the said Robert Jefferson MARTIN during his life and at the death to such child or children as he may leave surviving him. Fifthly: Should my executors herein after affociated deem it most for the benefit of my said legatees to make a division of my estate according to the provison of my will above set forth, I hereby authorise them to do so, whenever they think it adìvseable, the legatees to show the estate as before stated. And the said trustees in the event of the estate's being converted into mony an authorise to vest the funds in other property for the use of the said legatees upon the same trusts and limitations as before provided. I hold both my said children die without leaving a child or children in that event I give and devise their legacies aforesaid to my next of kin.   Lastly, I hereby constitute and appoint David MARTIN, John ARMSTRONG and James DAVIS executors of this my last will and testament, hereby revoking all former wills by me heretofore made. In testimony whereof I have hereunto set my hand and affixed my seal this 18th day of January, in the year of our Lord, one thousand eight hundred and forty five. Signed, sealed, and declared as and for the last will of the above named Edward MARTIN in the presence of us.

Henry W. Paslay   Edward Martin (SEAL)
Turner R. Milam
W. A. Waldrop
Recorded in Will Book A, Page 66, Bdl. 99, Pkg. 12.   Proven and recorded date not available. W. D. Watts, O. L. D.

WILL OF GEORGE DILLARD

South Carolina Laurens District. Owing to the uncertainty of life and the certainty of death, and my weak and dehilitated state of health, I am admonished. While I believe that I am in a disposable state of mind to arrange and settly my worldly businefs. I give and bequeath the whole of my lands to my wife Martha DILLARD during her natural life allowing her the privilege at any time she may think proper to sell the whole, or any part of it if she chose. If my wife Martha DILLARD should sell either the whole or any part of my lands it is my will and pleasure that she retains one third of the price of said lands, and that the other two thirds of said price be equally divided between my children, viz; Susan JOHNSTON, Elizabeth, A. J. DILLARD, Elvira DILLARS, J. B. DILLARD, I. A. DILLARD, and Sebran DILLARD. It is further my will and pleasure that all my personal property be sold on a credit if twelve months, and after all my debts and funeral expences be paid out of the proceeds of said property, then it is my will and pleasure that my two daughters Elizabeth and Elvira DILLARD be paid fifty dollars each, and that they be allowed to keep the beds they now claim, as the other children have already been advanced to that amount. It is also my will and pleasure that Samuel PACKER my grandson be paid out of the proceeds of my personal estate one hundred and fifty dollars and no more. It is my will and desire that my wife Martha DILLARD keep as her own not subject to division the amount recieved from the estate of Susan DILLARD deceased, which is supposed to be about four hundred dollars. Then the balance to be divided as follows viz.; one third to my wife Martha DILLARD and the other two third equally between my children (Viz) Susan JOHNSTON, Elizabeth DILLARD, A. J. DILLARD, Elvira DILLARD, J. B. DILLARD, and Sebran DILLARD. The above is my last will and testament, and I hereby annul all others Decr. 16th, 1846. Signed, sealed, and acknowledged in the presence of.

Thos Wein
Jas Hill
L. T. Rodes
N. Harris

his
George X Dillard (LS)
mark

Recorded in Will Book A, Page 69. Original will not in files of Probate Judge. W. D. Watts, O. L. D. Proven and recorded date not available.

WILL OF GEORGE MCCRARY

South Carolina Laurens District. In the name of God, Amen. I George MCCRARY, being of sound mind, memory, and understanding, do make and declare this my last will and testament in manner and form following. First. I resign my soul into the hands of almighty God, and my body, I remit to the earth to be decently buried at the discretion of my friends, and my worldly estate I give and devise as follows. First, I give and bequeath to my two grand children Robert OWENS and Sarah OWENS, children of my deceased daughter Sarah OWENS, one hundred dollars to be equally divided between them. Secondly, I give and bequeath to my grand children, children of my deceased daughter Sophy SMITH two hundred dollars to be equally divided among them. Thirdly, I give and bequeath to my daughter Elizabeth MCCRARY, the plantation a tract of land whereon she now resides. Embracing all the land on the side of the branch where she lives, the branch to be the line, also I give and bequeath to my daughter Elizabeth MCCRARY my negro fellow William. Fourthly, I give and bequeath to my daughter Lucinda FURGUSON my negro women Jade and Nina, together with their future ifsue. Fifthly, I give and bequeath to my daughter Frances SHELDEN my negro boy Jim and girl Caroline, together with their future ifsue. Sixthly, I give and bequeath to my son Edwin MCCRARY the plantation or tract of land whereon I now reside embracing all the land up to John LUKES" land and the branch line of the tract of land before bequeathed to my daughter Elizabeth MCCRARY. Also I give and bequeath to my son Edward MCCRARY my two negro fellows, Lands and George, and all my household furniture, except one bed, bedsead, and furniture. Seventhly, I give and bequeath to my son Chastine MCCRARY all the rest and residue of my land, bounded by land before bequeathed to my son Edwin MCCRARY, John Luke estate of John LITTLE, and land before bequeathed to my daughter Elizabeth MCCRARY. Also I give and bequeath to my son Chastine MCCRARY my two negro boys Patrick and Martin, and one bedstead, bed, and furniture, not before disposed of. Eighthly, All the rest and residue of my estate not before disposed of, of what kind and nature soever I will and desire shall be equally divided between my heirs according to law after payment of my just debts and funeral expences. And lastly, I do hereby constitute and appoint my son Edwin MC-CRARY, whole and sole executor of this my last will and testament and I do hereby utterly disallow, revoke and disannul all and every other former wills and testaments by me in any wise made. In witnefs whereof I hereunto set my hand and seal this ---- day of -----in the year of our Lord, 1845. Signed, sealed, published and declared by the testator as and for his last will and testament in our presence, who at his request in his presence and in the presence of each other have subscribed our names as witnefses

Test: Edmond Adair
Robert I. Adair
James H. Adair

his
George X McCrary
mark

Recorded in Will Book A, Page 71. Recorded and proven date not available. Original will not in files of Probate Judge. W. D. Watts, Ordy. Laurens District.

WILL OF JOHN DENDY

South Carolina Laurens District. I John DENDY of the State and district aforesaid, being old and in feeble health, but of disposing mind, do make this my last will and testament. I will that as early after my decease as it can be done legally that all my estate real and personal be sold by my executors hereinafter named upon the usual credits and after paying all my just debts and funeral expenses I dispose of the balance of my estate as follows to my children equally viz. I give one share to my daughter Elizabeth TINSLEY upon her accounting for three hundred dollars heretofore advanced to her. One share to my son Youngsets DENDY, upon his accounting for six hundred dollars heretofore advanced to him. One share to my daughter Nancy the wife of Branch LIGON, upon her accounting for three hundred dollars heretofore advanced to her. One share to W. D. WATTS intrust for the use my daughter Posey, the wife of Lanford POWER to be managed by the said trustee in the way he may think best for her comfort during her life. And at her death I give the same or the remainder thereof equally between her children the child or children of a decd. child taking among them the share the parent would be intitled to if living upon her accounting for the same of three hundred dollars her to fore advanced to her having her to fore advanced to my daughter Sally the wife of David CRADDOAH the sum of three hundred dollars and after wards deeded to Thomas N. DENDY in trust for my said daughter a negro woman Lucy and her children, Jim, Peggy, and Elliott, and her future increase, she is to secur no more of my estate. One other share I give to my son Daniel C. DENDY in trust for. the use of my son Thomas N.

DENDY during her life and at his death I give the same equally
to his children the child or children of a decd. child taking
among them the share their parent would have been intitled to if
living upon the trustee accounting for the negro woman Mary and
her child Martha and future increase at valuation as so much of
the share of his certig in trust which negroes and increase I
have heretofore deeded to the said Danile C. DENDY for the purpose above set forth which said trusts and limitation, I hereby
republish. I further direct that the share willed in trust to
Thomas N. DENDY be liable for my liabilities as his security.
One other share I give to Daniel C. DENDY in his own right to
him and his heirs forever together with one bed, bedstead, and
furniture extra of his distributive share. And I hereby appoint
the said Daniel C. DENDY executor of this my last will and testament. In testimony whereof I have hereunto set my hand and seal
this the 24th day of September, 1847. Test.

Charles Williams   John Dendy (SEAL)
Lem G. Williams
James A. B. Hood
Recorded in Will Book A, Page 73. Proven and recorded dates not
available. Bdle, 109, Pkge. 2. W. D. Watts, Ordy. Laurens
District, Laurens County.

WILL OF JOHN MILLER

South Carolina Laurens District. I John MILLER of the district
and state aforesaid, being of sound and disposing mind and memory, but knowing the uncertainty of life, do make and ordain
this my last will and testament in manner and form following.
First. I will and desire that all my just debts and funeral expences be paid out of my estate by my executor hereinafter named.
Second. Whereas I executed an agreement with my wife Margaret
MILLER on the 29th day of February, 1836, wherein it was agreed
that I should relinquish all claim to one third of my estate,
both real and personal to her to be disposed of by her at will
and she on her part agreed to relinquish all claim to the remaining two thirds of my estate. And whereas shortly thereafter I
put the said Margaret in pofsession of one third of my estate
including the land I now reside on with her. And whereas the
said Margaret has executed a deed or deeds of conveyance of the
said land to two of my son, Charles and Washington MILLER, but
without my consent. Now if the said agreement and the said
deeds should be void in law and equity, I devise and bequeath
the said one third of my estate relinquished to my wife aforesaid together with the other two thirds of my estate, both real
and personal to all of my children, to wit: Matthew MILLER,
Nancy GARRETT, Rachael ADINGTON, Mark MILLER, Mary HARRIS, Charles MILLER, and Washington MILLER, share and share alike. But
should the said agreement and the said deed or deeds prove ef-
fectual, then I devise and bequeath the remaining two thirds of
my estate to my children Matthew MILLER, Nancy GARRETT, Rachael
ADINGTON, Mark MILLER, and Mary HARRIS. Third. I desire and

bequeath all the residue of my estate of whatever description to my children Matthew, Nancy, Rachael, Mark, and Mary, share and share alike. But on reflection should my said wife survive me, then I devise and bequeath the one third of my estate, which she is now in pofsesion of to her during her life, and at her death to pafs under the previous clauses of this will as therein, directed. Lastly, I constitute and appoint my trusty friend William HENDRICKS executor of this my last will and testament. In testimony whereof I have hereunto set my hand and seal this 8th day of July, Anno Domini, Eighteen hundred and forty six. In presence of us.

C. P. Sullivan   John Miller (L. S.)
Wm. Hance
R. E. Todd
Recorded in Will Book A, Page 75. Original will not in files of Probate Judge. Proven and recorded date not available. W. D. Watts, O. L. D.

WILL OF AGNES WILLIAMSON

South Carolina Laurens District. In the name of God, Amen. I Agnes WILLIAMSON of the State and District aforesaid, being in a low state of health, but of sound and disposing mind and memory do make this my last will and testament. First. I desire that all my just debts and funeral expences be paid out of my estate. I then give to my son James MCCOLLUMS one negro woman called Sarah and her increase after the date of this will and two hundred dollars in money out of the undo of my estate to him and his heirs forever. And to my son Dr. William WILLIAMSON, I give one hundred and seventy dollars to him and his heirs forever. To my daughter Jane WILLIMSON, I give a negro girl named Ede Caroline and her increase and a walnut burea to her and her heirs forever. 2nd. I give and bequeath to Albert MILLER and Franklin MILLER in trust for the sole use and benefit of my daughter Agnes MILLER wife of Hamon MILLER, and her children during their lives a negro girl called Sally Cumi, and her increase. The said negro and her increase to remain in the unterrupted possession of said daughter during her life, and to be nether subject to time sale or in any other way for the debts or contracts of Hamon MILLER. And at the death of my daughter the trustees are to dispose of her and her increase in the way they think best for the interest of all the children of my aforesaid daughter. I also give to the said trustees for the purposes before mention a note which I hold on the said Hamon MILLER for one hundred dollars and interest there on with James MCCOLLUM security, but I direct that the security to be released from any liability on said note and interest. 3rd. All the rest and residue of my estate real and personal which I may die possessed, I will that my executor shall sell on a credit of twelve months, and after paying the debts and cash legacies before mentioned first. Should there be any money remaining that a neat plain site of stons be placed at the head and foot of the gravs of James WILLIAMSON my late husband

82

and my own. And should there still be funds left, I give the same equally between (Illegeable) WILLIAMSON, Jane WILLIAMSON and the trustees of Agnes MILLER for her use as aforesaid. In testimony whereof I have hereunto set my hand and affixed my seal this 9th day of January, one thousand eight hundred and forty five. Signed, sealed, published, and declared as and for the last will and testament of the above named Agnes WILLIAMSON, in the presence of us.

John Nickels
Willis Benham
Jas. Davis

her
Agnes X Williamson (L. S.)
mark

Recorded in Will Book A, Page 76, Bdl. 106, Pkge. 13. Proven date not available. Recorded date not available. W. D. Watts, Ordy. Laurens District.

WILL OF MILDRED A. HENDERSON

South Carolina Laurens District. In the name of God, Amen. I Mildred A. HENDERSON, being weak of body, but of sound mind memory and understanding, thanks be to almighty God, for the same, and knowing that it is appointed for all men once to die, and after death the judgement, do make and constitute this my last will and testament in manner and form following. I commend my soul to almighty God, who gave it, and my body to be decently entered at the discretion of my friends and my worldly estate I will and dispose of as follows. 1st. I will and direct that seven hundred dollars be paid to my brother Abner G. GARY in full of all demands and services rendered including also a note which David MARTIN holds against my brother Abner G. GARY and myself jointly, it being a joint note for upwards of three hundred dollars which not must be paid out of the seven hundred dollars before mentioned. And Abner T. GARY has to remain on my plantation until the sale of my estate as overseer. Secondly. I will and desire that my daughter Francis E. HENDERSON shall receive as much of my estate as will make her an amount equal to a seperate share of which my step children William T. HENDERSON, Robert Y. HENDERSON, and Sarah C. HENDERSON, may receive from their grandfather John BOYCE decd. estate. Thirdly. All the rest and residue of my estate real and personal of what nature so ever not before disposed of, I will and desire to be equally divided between my daughter Francis E. HENDERSON and my three step children William T. HENDERSON, Robert Y. HENDERSON, and Sarah C. HENDERSON. Fourthly. I will and desire that my sister Pennesy Francis MARTIN shall take my child Francis E. HENDERSON and raise her and I request that my brother in law of Fairfield, John A. MARTIN be guardian for my daughter Francis E. HENDERSON by his giveing good security according to the requisition of the court of Ordinary. In witnefs whereof I have hereunto set my hand and seal this 25th day of June, in the year of our Lord, one thousand eight hundred and forty five. Signed, sealed, published, and declared by the testatrix in the presence of us to be her last will and testament who in her presence and in the presence of each other have subscribed our names as witnefses.

William Young   Mildred A. Henderson (L.S.)
Thomas Wier
John G. Kern
Recorded in Will Book A, Page 78, Bdle. 96, Pkge. 23. Recorded
and proven date not available. W. D. Watts, Ordy. Laurens Dis-
trict, Laurens County.

WILL OF JOHN OSBOURNE

I John OSBORN of Laurens District in the State of South Carolina
being of sound and disposing mind and memory, and being desirous
to dispose of all such worldly estate as it has pleased God to
blefs me with, do make and ordain this my last will in manner
following that is to say. I give to my son Robertson OSBORN a
negro girl named Clarrissa, to him and to his heirs forever. I
give to my beloved wife Delphia OSBORN should she survive at my
death all the balance of my estate, both real and personal, except so much as may be neccessary to pay debts, for and during
her natural life to remain in her pofsession for her maintainance and support. Of the property herein before given to my
beloved wife during her natural life. I give to my son Robertson
OSBORNE in trust for the children of my son James OSBORN, a negro
man named Kit. And it is further my will that the said Robertson
OSBORN shall receive out of the proceeds of the sale of my property not herein specifically mentioned, the sum of one hundred
and seventy five dollars previous to the distribution of the same
in trust likewise for the children of my son James OSBORN. I
give to my son Clabourn OSBORN a negro woman named Kate. To my
daughter Nancy BARNS a negro woman named Ritter and a boy named
Peter. To my Robertson OSBORN a boy named Lewis and a boy named
Turner. And to my son Robertson OSBORN in trust for Jane OSBORN
the wife of my son John OSBORN, and the children which he now
has or may hereafter have, a negro man named Aleck and a girl
named Emily together with whatever sum of money arises from the
sale of my property, not specifically willed being one fifth part
of the same. And it is further my will that the proceeds of the
said trust estate shall not be subject to the payment of the
debts of my son John OSBORN. And it is further my will that
should any of the negroes herein willed to either of my children
and which are to remain in the pofsession of my wife during her
natural life, do before coming into their pofsession that the
value of the said negro or negroes be made up to said child out
of the residue of my estate previous to its final distribution.
It is further my will that immediately after the death of my
wife, should she survive me or so soon, as the crop which may
then be on hand, shall be gathered and disposed of my executor
hereinafter named, shall cause all the balance of my estate,
both real and personal, of what nature or quality soever it may
be not herein before specificaly disposed of, to be sold. And
after paying my just debts and all necessary expences upon my
estate. The residue be equally dividedamongst my several children

84

herein before named. The share which may be going to my son
James OSBORN to pafs into the hands of my son Robertson OSBORN
in trust for the children of my son James. And it is further my
desire that my son Robertson shall permit my son James to enjoy
the profits of the property given to him in trust for my son
James children during his life time. And lastly, I do constitute
and appoint my friend Thos. F. JONES my executor of this my last
will and testament by me heretofore made. In testimony whereof
I have hereunto set my hand and seal this eighth day of March,
one thousand eight hundred and forty five. Signed, sealed, published, and declared as and for the last will and testament of
the above named John OSBOURN. In presence of us.

```
                                         his
Collyar Barksdale               John X Osbourne (L.S.)
Beverly Barksdale                   mark
Alfred Barksdale
```
Recorded in Will Book A, Page 80. Original will not in files of
Probate Judge. Recorded and proven date not available. W. D.
Watts, Ordy. Laurens District.

WILL OF WM. BLAKELY SENR.

South Carolina Laurens District. In the name of God, Amen. I
Wm. BLAKELY, Senr. of the district and state aforesaid, being old
and infirm, but of sound and disposing mind and understanding,
and calling to mind the uncertainty of life, and being desirous
to dispose of all such worldly estate, as God hath been pleased
to blefs me with, do make and ordain this my last will and testament, as follows to wit. It is my will that as early as practi-
able after my death, that all the estate real and personal, that
I may die pofsessed of, be sold by executors hereinafter named,
on such credit as is usual in such cases. And in the first place
all my jsut debts and funeral expences paid out of the proceeds
of said sale. Then the balance of the proceeds of the sale and
all monies notes, and accounts that may be owing me at my death.
That owing by me children as well as others I dispose of as follows. In equal portions to my children which are here named,
Jonathan, John, William, James, David, Thomas, and SAmuel, and
my daughters Catharine and Isabella and in the event that either
of my sons or daughters should be dead for their child or children, to take among them the share or shares their parent or
parents would have taken if living. But the share of my son
Jonathan, I give to my son William BLAKELY, in trust for the use
and benefit of my said son Jonathan and his family, to be applied for said purpose at the discretion of the said trustee, with
the exception of fifty dollars which I direct the trustee to pay
to Allen BARDSDALE on a judgement he holds against my said son
Jonathan, out of the share of said Jonathan. The said trustee
to have the power to put the said trust fund into the hands of
the said Jonathan. At any time he may deem it prudent to do so
in the life time of said Jonathan, and if he should still retain
the trust fund, untill the death of the said Jonathan BLAKELY.
Then I direct the trustee to pay one third of what remains to

the widow of the said Jonathan, that is if it is the wife he now has. And the other two thirds in equal parts to his children as they come of age or marry, but should his present wife die, and he marry another, then the whole is to go to his children as above directed. The share of my son John is also a trust estate having already decided to him by a deed of trust three negroes, which deed of trust I hereby refer to the amount of the value of said negroes, which said deed will show. I direct to so much of his distributive share of my estate and if that amount should not be his full distributive share, I direct that the balance shall go into the hands of the same trustee subject to the same trusts and limitations as the negroes mentioned in said deed of trust. And should the value of said negroes be more than this equal share, I direct the trustee named in said deed of trust to pay back to my estate so much as is over paid, as the intention of this will is to make all my children equal (so far as the amount is concerned) and to vest the shares of Jonathan and John BLAKELY in the hands of trustees. Lastly. I nominate, constitute and appoint my son Wm. BLAKELY executor of this my last will and testament, hereby revoking all other and former wills by me heretofore made. In testimony whereof I have hereunto set my hand and seal this the 13th day of December, 1845. Signed, sealed, published, and declared in the presence of us.

                                            his
James L. Young   Wm. X Blakely Senr. (L. S.)
F. N. Folker   mark
Henry M. Bryon
Recorded in Will Book A, Page 82, Bdle. 92, Pkge. 1. Recorded and proven date not available. W. D. Watts, Ordy. Laurens District.

                        WILL OF BENJAMIN BROWN

In the name of God, Amen. I Benjamin BROWN of the State of South Carolina, Laurens District, being of sound and disposing mind and memory, but calling to mind the mortality of my body. And knowing that it is appointed unto all men once to die, do make and ordain this my last will and testament in the following manner, that is to say. First, as teaching such worldly estate as it hath pleased God to blefs me with in this life. After paying my just debts and funeral expences I give and dispose of my property in the following manner, that is to say. I lend to my daughter Ann BROWN and my wife Polly BROWN all my estate, both real and personal, so long as my wife Polly BROWN and my daughter Ann BROWN shall remain on my premises, together for their support and use. It is my will that if Polly BROWN thinks proper to sell any of my negroes, she shall have the right so to do and the proceeds of such negro or negroes, to be accounted for in the final settlement after the death of Anne BROWN or Polly BROWN. It is also my will that my grandson Thomas Jefferson TYGART, shall have a moderate English education Sau (read, write and cypher,) tolerably to be paid for out of my estate as wanted at the death of my daughter Anne BROWN or my wife Polly BROWN.

It is my will that all my property both real and personal shall be equally divided between my lawful heirs. And lastly, I do constitute and appoint my wife Polly BROWN executrix and in case of her death, my friend J. M. YOUNG executor of this my last will and testament by me made. In testimony whereof I have hereunto set my hand and affixed my seal this 19th day of February, one thousand eight hundred and forty seven. Signed, sealed, published, and declared in presence of us.

J. M. Young
Rofs. Benham
A. G. Young

his
Benjamin X Brown
mark

Recorded in Will Book A, Page 84. Recorded and proven date not available. Original will not in files of probate. W. D. Watts, Ordy. Laurens District.

WILL OF JOHN M. CAMPBELL

South Carolina Laurens District. In the name of God, Amen. I John M. CAMPBELL laboring under great bodily disease but in the exercise of all the faculties of mind and reason with which God has blefsed me, I therefore do make and publish this my last will and testament. In the first place I wish my body to be decently interred and all my just debts to be paid. In the second place it is my request all the balance of my estate including one horse, saddle, and bridle, and all monies due me to be given to my sister Mary AIKINS two children viz.; John AIKIN and Elizabeth AIKIN. I do hereby make and ordain James AIKIN executor of this my last will and testament. In witnefs whereof I have hereunto set my hand and seal this 26th April, 1848. Signed, sealed, and declared in presence of us, who have subscribed in the presence of each other.

John R. Spearmand
William Hitt
Henry N. Carter

John M. Campbell (L.S)

Recorded in Will Book A, Page 85, Bdle. 101, Pkge. 5. Proven and recorded dates not available. W. D. Watts, Ordy. Laurens District, Laurens County.

WILL OF JANE MONROE

State of South Carolina Laurens District. In the name of God, Amen. I Jane MONROE, of the State and District aforesaid, being weak in body, but of a sound and disposing mind and memory, calling to mind the uncertainty of life, and being desirous to dispose of such worldly effects as it has pleased God to blefs me with do make, and ordain this my last will and testament in manner and form following Viz: It is my desire that after all my just debts and funeral expenses are paid that such disposition as I now direct be made of such property as are left. 1. It is my desire that my thirds of the tract of land whereon I now live containing (originally) two hundred and two acres, more or lefs the third of which I bequeath and give to my three children now living, that is to say, Margaret MONROE, Danl A. MONROE, and John H. MONROE to be equally divided between them by sale or otherwise as they may agree, the aforesaid gift-subject to a deduction of fourteen acres, which has been my me conveyed, by sale to William EAST and my rights given him for the same. It is my desire that each of my aforesaid children have and I do give to each of them one bed, bedstead, and furniture, but it is further my wish that my daughter Margaret MONROE have her choice of the aforesaid beds and furniture, and each of said sons, to have their beds, etc. of equal value and all the rest and residue of my said estate including household and kitchen furniture, stock of every description and kind. And I do hereby give and bequeath to my three children aforesaid, to them and their heirs forever, to be by them divided by sale or otherwise as may chose. It is my desire, and I do give to my daughter Margaret MONROE my loom, with all the apparatus to the same belonging to her and her heirs forever. And I do also, give and bequeath to my daughter Margaret, my clock to her and her heirs forever. And lastly I do nominate, constitute, and appoint my respected brother Larking S. MONROE, and my son Daniel A. MONROE, my executors to this my last will and testament, revoking all other wills by me at any time by me heretofore made. In witnefs I have hereunto set my hand and affixed my seal 22nd day of May, one thousand eight hundred and forty seven. Signed in presence of us.

Elihu Watson
Wm. East
James Joye

her
Jane X Monroe (S. L.)
mark

Recorded in Will Book A, Page 86, Bdle. 103, Pkg. 12. W. D. Watts, O. L. D. Proven and recorded date not available.

WILL OF ABNER PYLES

State of S. Co. Laurens District. In the name of Supreme, Amen. I Abner PYLES of the above State and District, being of sound mind and disposing memory, do make ordain and declare the sequel to be my last will and testament. In the first place, I do declare that as there was provision made some years ago (at my request) by Richard and Maryan SHALKELFORD, grandfather and grandmother, of my oldest daughter Metilda TEGUE desd. by conveying to her the said Metilda and her ifsue, a negro woman by name Gin and all her children, except a boy called Jerry, who was at the same time bequeathed to my son Newton PYLES, the above bequest together with what I afterward gave to my sd. daughter, I am bound to believe is an equitable share of my poor emoluments. I do further from causes leading thereto, give unto my grand daughters Elizabeth and Eliza TEGUE, one hundred dollars each, to be paid over to them as soon as those sums can be raised out of my property. Secondly, I give and bequeath to my beloved son Milton PYLES eight hundred dollars in addition to what he has already received which may be found entered in my large fo.E. Thirdly, As my beloved son Adison PYLES is at this time in affulent circumstances and I have so little at this time for diftribution I am well afsured his generous heart will be satiffied with what he had recd. before he left here, which will be found entered in the above named fo C. together with articles left in my care for sale. Also the sum of eighteen dollars and fifty cents which I recd. from H. YOUNG esq. the amount of which sum and the value of said articles I wish my exect. to pay over to the sd. Adison PYLES or his order. Fourthly, I do also give unto my beloved son Newton PYLES what may be found charged to him the said Newton in the sd. fo. E. together with what will be devised to him in another clause in the sequent. Fifthly, To my beloved son Madison PYLES, I give and bequeath two hundred dollars in addition to what may be found entered in the sd. fo. E. Sixthly, To my only surviving daughter Susannah H. TRIBBLE and her child or children, I give and bequeath a negro woman by name Anne, and her children, Viz.; Lucinday, Rosette, Warren, and Nelly together with the other goods and chattles which she the sd. Susannah carried with her when she left me. Seventhly. To my youngest child T. Jefferson PYLES, I give and bequeath a negro man called Rich, also a lad named Jim, and a young woman by named Lucy. The tract of land whereon I now reside containing three hundred acres more or lefs must be sold upon terms my exect. may deem best together with all the residue of my little property except my library containing a variety of useful books, tracts and manuscript all of which books I wish to be equally divided between my sons Newton PYLES and Jefferson, reserving a few that amy be suitable to their sister Susannah H. TIRBBLE. Eighthly. It is also my will that after all debts and C. are paid off that the surplus should be equally divided between my son Newton and Jefferson PYLES, each, or either of whom I do hereby nominate and appoint as my lawfull Exect. for this my last will and testament, and I trust they will always keep in view the character of the truly good and honest man, the noblest work of God or nature which you please. Signed, sealed, and acknowledged to be the last will and testament of me Abner PYLES this 12th day of April Common era, 1844, of the American Republic sixty eight and in the presence of.

W. T. Campbell   Abner Pyles (L. S.)
Wm. Blakely
W. A. Waldrop
Recorded in Will Book A, Page 87, Bdle. 107, Pkge. 19. Proven and recorded dates not available. W. D. Watts, Ordy. Laurens District, Laurens County.

WILL OF HUGH MAHAFFEY

State of South Carolina Laurens District. In the name of God, Amen. I Hugh MAHAFFEY of the State and District aforesaid, being of sound and disposing mind and memory, but weak in body, do make and ordain this my last will and testament, in manner following. In the first place after my decease; Immediately I direct all my just debts and funeral expences to be paid. 2ndly. I give and bequeath to my daughters Cynthia MAHAFFEY and Clarinda MAHAFFEY, the tract of land which I now live on to them equally them and the heirs of their bodies forever. And to each of them one bed and furniture and to Cynthia one loom and apperataz pertaining to it with a quilling wheel. And to Clarinda one wheel and cards and a cupbourd and one cow and calf to each of them. One brown mare now in fole to Cynthia, and one sorrel filly to Clarinda. 3rdly. After my death it is my desire that the balance of my effects not otherwise disposed of be sold and equally divided amoungst all my children. 4thly. I give the same to them and the heirs of their bodies forever. 5thly. And lastly, I do constitute and appoint my friends William MAHAFFEY and Hosea MAHAFFEY executors of this my last will and testament by me here tofore made. 6th. I appoint the above named executors as trusts to the legacies I have left to my two daughters Cynthia MAHAFFEY and Clarinda MAHAFFEY. In testimony whereof I have hereunto set my hand and seal this thirty first day of December, eighteen hundred and forty six. Signed, sealed, and published as the last will and testament of the above named Hugh MAHAFFEY, in the presence of us.

                                              his
Lewis Mahaffey   Hugh X Mahaffey (L. S.)
Sanford B. Mahaffey   mark
Cynthia N. Mahaffey
Recorded in Will Book A, Pg. 89, Bdl. 104, Pkge. 3. Recorded and proven date not available. W. D. Watts, Ordy. Laurens District.

                    WILL OF CHARLES EAGERTON

South Carolina Laurens District. In the name of God, Amen. I Charles EAGERTON of the state and district aforesaid, being of sound and disposing mind and memory, but weak in body and calling to mind the uncertainty of life, and being deserous to dispose of all such worldly estate as it hath pleased God, to blefs me with, do make and ordain this my last will and testament in manner following, that is to say. I will and desire that as soon after my decease as may be consistent with the interest of my estate, all my just debts and funeral expenses be paid. After the payment of my just debts and funeral expenses, I will and bequeath to my beloved wife Frances EAGERTON the following property Viz. All of my real estate. I also bequeath to my beloved wife the following negro slaves Viz. namely; Dinah, Fill Lee, the blacksmith and Lee, commonly called little Lee, Addison, and Jane, Edney together with ifsue and increase of the aforesaid slaves. I also will and desire that my beloved wife shall have all of my stock of horses, cattle, sheep, and hogs, together with all and every article of my property not hereinafter to be mentioned, to have and to hold during the natural life of my said wife Frances, with the exception of the household and kitchen furniture, which I give her the right of disposing of at her death as she may think proper. All of the aforesaid property willed as aforesaid to my beloved wife Frances EAGERTON, I wish her to have and to hold during her natural life with the exception of the household and kitchen furniture as aforesaid. I will and bequeath to my adopted son and nephew, John Edward JONES, the following negro slaves viz. namely; Harriet and George, children of the aforesaid negro woman Dinah, together with increase of the aforesaid negroes reserving however the right of pofsefsion of the aforesaid negores Harriet and George in my beloved wife as long as she may like. Should my nephew John Edward JONES die leaving no ifsue then and in that case, I desire that the negroes left as avoce to the said John Edward shall revert to my beloved wife Frances. I will and bequeath to John Joseph, Frances and Matiton GATES, children of Robert GATES deceased, all of my demands for and on account of the said Robert, and his children as aforesaid (my demands being considerable and which will appear on an examanition of my papers) the demands as above stated, I have to the aforesaid children for the regard interlained for the said Robert GATES while living as well as for the affiction which I have toward his children. After the demise of my wife Frances EAGERTON, and not before I will and desire that all my property, both real and personal as left to my wife Frances during her natural life, be sold by my executor hereinafter to be named, and the proceeds then be equally divided share and share alike, between my sisters Clarifsa SCOTT and Elizabeth OLIVER, and to the heirs of their body. The aforesaid Clasifsa and Elizabeth, now living in the State of North Carolina as I believe. Being pofsefsed of eight share of rail road stock in the Charleston Cincinate and Louisville Company, the scrip of which is now in the hands of W. D. Watts, Esqr. Ordinary of the district. I will and bequeath the aforesaid eight shares at my decease and not before to my friend Anthony Y. GOLDING of the State and district aforesaid, as a compensation to him for the trouble which he may have in aiding and afsisting my beloved wife Frances EAGERTON in the management of her businefs, and the future distribution of the aforesaid legacies. And further I wish it distinctly understood that the property which I have bequeathed to my beloved wife Frances, in fee simple in this instrument, is not so vested in her as to allow her the right to dispose of it to Benjamen HOLT or his wife Amelia or her children, or to Nathan CHAPMAN and his wife Sophia or children, should they have ifseue. And lastly, I do constitute and appoint my friend Anthony Y. GOLDING of the state and district above mentioned executor of this my last will and testament, revoking all former wills and testament by me heretofore made. In testemony whereof I have hereunto set my hand and affixed my seal this twenty sixth day of June in the year of our Lord, one thousand eight hundred and forty six, and in the seventieth year of American Independence. Signed, sealed, published, and declared as and for the last will and testament of the aforesaid Charles EAGERTON and in the presence of us. The erasures and interlining done before signing. Elizabeth OLIVER my sister as mentioned in the foregoing instrument is dead, as I believe I therefore bequeath to her children the legacy to which she would be entitled was she living. All the above done before signing.

Continued on page 92

Continued from page 91
Patrick Todd   Charles Eagerton (SEAL)
Sarah Wright
William Todd
Recorded in Will Book A, Page 91, Bdle. 144, Pkge. 17. Proven
and recorded dates not available. W. D. Watts, Ordy. Laurens
District.

WILL OF GEORGE JOHNSON

State of South Carolina Laurens District. I George JOHNSON of
the state and district aforesaid, being weak in body, but of
sound and disposing mind and memory, calling to mind the uncertainty of life, and being desirous to dispose of such worldly
effects as it has pleased God to blefs me with, do make and ordain this my last will and testament in manner and form following Viz. It my desire that all my just debts be paid out of the
sales of my crop, but should prove insufficient I then desire
that my executor hereinafter named sell such other property as he
may think best and apply the money arising from such sale to the
payment of such of my said debts as may remain unpaid, out of
the sale of the crop as aforesaid, and after the said debts including my funeral expenses are paid. I then desire and give to
my beloved wife Martha and to the four small children viz. George
Washington, Willard Simpson, Sarah Ann, John Wesley, the tract
of land whereon I now live containing one hundred and seven and
a half acres together all my household and kitchen furniture,
plantation tools, my stock of cattle, hogs, sheep, and two horses
Jim, and Bell, also one bay colt Fanny. I also desire that my
wife and the aforesaid four children before mentioned have, and
I do give to them my negro Mars Washington to them and their
heirs forever. But should my wife marry, I then desire that all
such bequeathed to them as may then be found, be sold and my
wife receive one third of money arising from the sale thereof,
and the remaining two thirds to be equally divided amongst my
aforesaid children to them and their heirs forever. I give and
bequeath to my other three eldest children viz; William, Abraham,
and Margaret A. MILLER, wife of John MILLER senr. a tract of land
containing forty one and a half acres, adjoining land of Anderson
JOHNSON and others, to equally divided amongst by sale or otherwise as they may agree to them and their heirs forever. I also,
give and bequeath to my aforesaid daughter Margaret A. MILLER my
bay mare Mary, to her and her heirs forever. And lastly, I do
nominate, constitute, and appoint my respected brother Anderson
JOHNSON, my executor to this my last will and testament, revoking all other wills by me at any time heretofore made. In testimony whereof I have hereunto set my hand and affixed my seal this
21st day of February, 1847. Test:

Elihu Watson   George Johnson (L. S.)
Jesse Enterkin
Larkin S. Monroe
Recorded in Will Book A, Page 93, Bdl. 1?7, Pkg. 18. Recorded and
proven date not available. W. D. Watts, Ordy. Laurens District.

WILL OF DAVID CURETON

South Carolina Laurens District. In the name of God, Amen. I David CURETON of the State and District afforesaid, being of sound and disposing mind and memory, but weak in body, and calling to mind the uncertainty of life and being desirous to dispose of all such worldly estate as it hath pleased God to blefs me with, do make and ordain this my last will and testament in the maner and follows (Viz). 1st. I desire that immediately after my decease that my just debts be paid together with my funeral expences be respectfully paid. 2nd. I desire that Marcus DANDY have the prefference of the boy Jame at the price of seven hundred dollars and if the said Marcus DANDY shall refuse to take the said boy at the above mention price the boy Jame may have the right of choseing his own marster and that the said seven hundred dollars is to be paid to Elihue PAYNE at his own dicrsion. 3rd. Thirdley and lastly. I give and bequeath to my nephew Elihue PAYNE all my estate both real and personally to have and to hold during of his natral life, and at his death to be equally divide between his four children namely; James C. PAYNE, Richard PAYNE, Levington PAYNE, and Mary A. PAYNE to have and to hold all and singler the said estate. I do constitute and appoint the said Elihue PAYNE and George WELLS executors of this my last will and testament by me heretofore made. In testimoney whereof hereunto I set my hand and affix my seal this twenty ninth day of December, in the year of our Lord, one thousand Eighteen hundred and forty six.

William H. Adams   David Cureton (LS)
James A. Foshee
David F. Foshee
Recorded in Will Book A, Page 95, Bdl. 101, Pkg. 6. W. D. Watts O. L. D. Proven and recorded date not available.

WILL OF CALVIN ABBERCROMBIE

South Carolina Laurens District. In the name of God, Amen. I Calvin ABBERCROMBIE, being weak but of sound, disposing mind, memory, and understanding do make and ordain this my last will and testament. First, I direct all my just debts to be paid and my body to be decently buried. Second. I give and bequeath unto my wife Mary the tract of land whereon I now live containing about two hundred and twenty two acres during her life, and at her death to my son Lindly ABBERCROMBIE to him and his heirs or assigns forever. And it is my will that the said Lindly shall occupy and cultivate his present farm and such other part of the premises as his mother may not need. Stay upon the premises and take good care of his mother during her life. Third. I give and bequeath to my son Lindly ABBERCROMBIE the tract of about eighty acres of land whereon the widow Elizabeth ABBERCROMBIE of my son John decd. now lives in trust to and for the following use and purpose to wit, for the use and benefit of said wodow during her life and widowhood and at her death or marriage to be equally divided among the heirs of my said son John, but not to be liable for the debts or contracts of the said widow Elizabeth. Fourth. I give and bequeath to my wife Mary a negro girl by the name of Sarah about ten or eleven years old to have and to hold the said negro girl Sarah her heirs and assigns forever. Fifth. I give and bequeath unto my wife Mary the whole of the balance of my personal estate of every description whatsoever consisting principally of two negroes one by the name of Wessly and the other Bathena, horses, cows, hogs, household furniture, plantation toos, etc. for her use, benefit and subsistance during her life and at her death what may be and remain of the said property give in this clause to my wife. I wish and direct to be sold by my executors hereinafter appointed and the proceeds of the sale to be equally divided among the following children, to wit, Harriet, the wife of Jno W. NASH, Mary the wife of Hiram SIMS, Rebecca the wife of Kellet BABB, Calvin ABBERCROMBIE, Junr., Elizabeth the wife of Holway CAMPBELL, James ABBERCROMBE, Christy the wife of Wm. RIDGWAY, Ruth the wife of Alfred SIMS, Johnathan ABERCROMBIE and Lindly ABERCROMBIE, except Johnathan, and I will and desire him to have one hundred dollars more than the rest. Sixth. I appoint my sons Lindly ABBERCROMBIE and Johnathan ABBERCROMBIE executors of this my last will and testament. Witness my hand and seal this the 21st September, 1837. Published and acknowledged in presence of.

Asa Garrett   Calvin Abbercrombie (LS)
Isham Bolt
William F. Downs
Recorded in Will Book A, Page 96. Original will not in files of Probate Judge. W. D. Watts, O. L. D. Proven and recorded dates not available.

WILL OF CINTHIA WHITWORTH

South Carolina Laurens District. In the name of God, Amen. I Cinthia WHITWORTH of the State and District aforesaid, being of sound and disposing mind and memory, but weak in body and calling to mind the uncertainty of life and being desirous to dispose of all such worldly estate as it hath pleased God to bless me with, do make and ordain this my last will and testament in manner following, that is to say. I will and desire that as soon after my decease, as convenient all my just debts and funeral expenses be paid by my executors hereinafter to be named. After the payment of my just debts and funeral expenses, I will and bequeath to my beloved daughter Frances Elizabeth WHITWORTH, and to the heirs of her body all of my real estate that I now own or may die possessed of. I also will and bequeath to my beloved daughter Frances and to the heirs of her body all of my negro slaves by name Viz: Judy, Big Tom, Cherry, Mecca, Cleopatria, Easther, Mike, and Tom commonly known by the name of Thom Pitts together with the future issue and increase of said negro slaves. I also bequeath to my beloved daughter Frances all of my ready mony as well also as all my bonds, notes, or accounts, together with all my stock of horses and mules, sheep and hogs, with all my household and kitchen furniture together with all and every description of property which I may die possessed of, be it of what kind or quality soever, to have and to hold all of the above named property during her natural life, and to the heirs of her body. I wish it distinctly understood that I do not desire that there shall be any sale of my property, as there can be no necessity for such sale. I do hereby nominate and appoint my trusty friend and relation Daniel RUDD, of Newberry District, my trustee and the sole trustee over the property devised as above to my daughter Frances Elizabeth WHITWORTH to manage as best as he can for the sole use and benefit of my said daughter Frances with the following prociso to it. Should my daughter Frances die leaving bodily heir or heirs, then and in that case I will and desire that her child or children inherit all of the estate that she may die possessed of, to be if more than one child, equally divided among them, except the sume of one thousand dollars which I will and bequeath to the husband of my said daughter Frances, should she have one living at time of demise. And lastly, I do constitute and appoint my trusty friends and relations Daniel RUDD the trustee of my daughter Frances as above mentioned and Henry BURTON both of the State aforesaid, and District of Newberry, executors of this my last will and testament by me heretofore made. As witness my hand and seal, in the year of our Lord, one thousand eight hundred and forty six, and the fourteenth day of May. Signed, sealed, published, and declared as and for the last will and testament of the aforesaid Cinthia WHITWORTH and in the presence of us.

Anthony ?. Golding   Cinthia Whitworth (LS)
John H. Goodman
A. G. Cook
Recorded in Will Book A, Page 98. Original will not in files of Probate Judge. Proven and recorded date not available. W. D. Watts, O. L. D.

WILL OF WILLIAM SPEARS

In the name of God, Amen. I William SPEARS of the District of Laurens, being weak in body, but of sound and disposing mind and memory and calling to mind the uncertainty of life, do make the following dispositition of what worldly property it hath pleased God to blefs me Viz. As soon as convenient after my decease my executor herein after named will sell so much of the property as can best be spared by my family as will satisfy all my just debts and funeral expenses. My land and the other property which may remain after the above named expences an satisfied I wish to remain as they are for the use of my family during the natural life of my beloved wife, Elizabeth SPEARS. And should my son Andrew SPEARS think proper to live with his mother and sister, on the terms he has been doing, I wish him to do so. And at the death of my wife Elizabeth, I wish all my estate both real and personal to be sold and equal distribution thereof to be made amongst all my children agreeable to law. And I do hereby constitute and appoint my son William SPEARS executor of this my last will and testament. In testimony whereof I have hereunto set my hand and seal this tenth day of January, one thousand eight hundred and forty five. Witnefses.

John Stewart   Wm. Speers Senr. (L. S.)
J. P. Hutcherson
M. B. Sheldon
Recorded in Will Book A, Page 100, Bdle. 105, Pkge. 13. Proven and recorded dates not available. W. D. Watts, Ordy. Laurens District, Laurens County.

WILL OF NANCY NEELEY

In the name of God, Amen. I Nancy NEALY of Laurens District, being of sound mind and memory, but weak in body, and disirous to dispose of all such worldly estate as it hath please God to blefs me with, do make and ordain this my last will in the following manner. 1st. I give to my beloved sister Elizabeth NEALY all my personal property during her natural life, after her death, I wish for what is left to be sold by my executor here in after named, and equally divided between my two brothers George NEALY and James NEALY, I give the same to them there heirs, executors, administrators, and assigns forever. 2nd. I give unto my beloved sister and brother Elizabeth NEALY and Samuel NEALY all my real estate or tract of land during there natural lives and after there deaths I want it to be equally divided between my two brothers George NEALY and James NEALY, and I give the same to them there heirs, executors, administrators, and assigns forever. 3rd. And lastly, I do constitute and appoint my brother George NEALY executor of this my last will and testament by me there to fore made. In testimony I have here unto set my hand and seal this 30th day of Sept., 1846. Signed, sealed, published, and delivered as the last will and testament of the above named Nancy NEELY in presents of us.

B. T. Watts   Nancy Neeley (SEAL)
I. M. Hill
W. T. Nealy
Recorded in book A, Page 101, Bundle 112, Package 11. Proven date Dec. 5, 1850. Recorded date not available. W. D. Watts, Ordy.

WILL OF JOSHUA FRANKS

In the name of God Amen. Know all men by these preasants that I Joshua FRANKS of the State of South Carolina Laurens District, being of feeble state of body, but of sound mind, do write this my last will and testament. I do therefour bequeath to my son Robert P. FRANKS six hundred dollars. I do likewise, bequeath to my son NIles FRANKS the sum of six hundred dollars. I do also bequeath to my son Joshua S. FRANKS six hundred dollars. I do also bequeath to my son William L. FRANKS six hundred dollars. I do likewise, bequeath to my son Abner C. FRANKS six hundred dollars this sum annext to the name of my several above named sons is to place them equal with my daughter Mary HELLAMS my daughter Nancy BOLT and my son George FRANKS who have here to fore received at my hand each of them property to the amount of six hundred dollars. The remainder of my property after my just debts are paid. I do bequeath to my beloved wife Prudance FRANKS during her natural life, then out of the same, I do bequeath to Samuel SAXON, Joshua SAXON, William N. SAXON, John W. SAXON, Mary SAXON, and Thomas L. SAXON, six of my grand children one hundred dollars to each of them after this is done the balance is to be sold and equally divided amongst my several named children in this division the six above named gran children only has the clame of one child. Further more I do now appoint my son Jofhua S. FRANKS and William L. FRANKS, my executors to excute this my last will and testament. In witnefs whereof I do set my hand and seal this the 17th day of November, one thousand eight hundred and forty seven, and the seventy second year of American Independance. Signed in presence of.

Wm. Clardy   Jofhua Franks (L. S.)
Lewis Saxon
Arechibd Henderson
Proven date 30th day of Jany, 1848. Recorded date not available. Recorded in Will Book A, Page 102, Bundle 102, Pkg. 2. W. D. Watts, Ordy. Laurens District.

WILL OF WM. MADDEN

In the name of God, Amen. I Wm. MADDEN of the State of South Carolina, Laurens District, being of sound and disposing mind and memory, and knowing that it is appointed unto all men to die, and not knowing how soon, I shall be called, and being desirous to dispose of all such worldly estate as it hath pleased the Lord to bless me with, do make and ordain this my last will and testament (revoking all others hithertoo made). 1st. I give my soul to God, who gave it to me, and my body to the dust from whence it sprang to be buried in a decent christian like manner. 2nd. After paying all my just debts and funeral expences, I give demise and dispose of my property in the following manner, that is to say. I give my beloved wife Sarah MADDEN during her natural lifetime or widowhood, my negro man Solomon, my negro woman Rose, two bed steads and furniture, so much of my stock, household and kitchen furniture, as my executors hereinafter named may think she needs. Also the use of a part of the tract of land whereon I now live during his her lifetime or widowhood, which ever takes place. First the land is to be returned to my son Moses MADDEN as is hereinafter willed to him, the negro man Solomon, negro woman Rose with stock, household and kitchen furniture to be immediately sold and equally divied among all my children, Malsa MADDEN, Eliza GRADEN, Polleyar MADDEN, Sofshia MADDEN, Hulaz MADDEN and Moses MADDEN. I give to my Malso MADDEN one hundred and sixty acres of lands to be cut off of the east and of my lands joining to the said Malso MADDEN, whereon he now lives. I give to my daughter Sophia MADDEN my negro boy named Calvin and horse valued to sixty five dollars, one cor and calf, beds, steads, and all the bed clothes known as surd. I give to my daughter Hulda, my negro girl named Lucy, one horse valued at sixty five dollars, one cor, and calf, beds steads, and all the bed clothing known as hess. I give to my son Moses MADDEN my negro woman Milvy, one road waggon, and harnefs one bay mare, and bay mule, one cow and calf, and a part of the tract of land whereon I now live, supposed to be two hundred acres more or less, after taking of what I have willed to my son Malsa MADDEN. I wish and desire the balance of my property not willed as above to be immediately sold after my death, to pay my debts, Viz, the tract of land containing one hundred and twenty four acres joining lands of Elihu MADDEN, Hampton FINLY, and Mrs. S. BOYD, one boy named Joe and all my crop of cotton on hand. And lastly, I do hereby constitute and appoint my sons Malso MADDEN and Moses MADDEN executors to this my last will and testament by me here tofore made. In testamony whereof I have hereunto set my hand and affixed my seal this 13th day of Oct., 1849. Signed, sealed, and published and declared as and for the last will and testament of the above named Wm. MADDEN in the presence of us.

J. Sa. Coleman   Wm. Madden (LS)
Hampton Finly
B. F. Madden
Recorded in Will Book A, Page 103. Original will not in files of Probate Judge. W. D. Watts, O. L. D. Proven and recorded dates not available.

WILL OF PATTILLO FARROW

South Carolina Laurens District. I Pattillo FARROW of the District of Laurens in the State aforesaid, do make, publish and declare this as my last will and testament. AS to such worldly estate as it has pleased God to blefs me with, I hereby bequeath as follows Viz. It is my will and pleasure that such amount as I may have received since August, 1848, and such as may hereafter be received on a judgment which I have on the late Doc. Samuel FARROW be so applied by my executors that my sister Mrs. Nancy FARROW is to have the use of it during her life, and at her death to be equally divided among her children thus living. I also, give and bequeath unto my sister the further sum of fifty dollars to be paid her annually during her life. I give and bequeath unto my beloved wife Jane S. FARROW and my children Viz, James FARROW, Anny P. SIMPSON, wife of John Wister SIMPSON, Susan W. FARROW, Thomas FARROW, Henry P. FARROW, Rosanna FARROW, and Luli Ann FARROW the whole of my estate both real and personal to be valued and appraised and return made thereof to the ordinary, together with all outstanding demands due me, to be and remain in the pofifion of my wife for the purpose of maintaining, raising and educating of my children, which I desire to be done at the discretion of my executors such of my children being of age and desireing to receive a portion of my estate, may do so, my executors causing the same to be valued by three disintrested persons, not to exceed a childs part and causing a return to be made to the ordinary there of as an advancement. On the death or marriage of my wife I desire the whole of my estate to be sold and divided between my wife and children as follows Viz. Two ninths of the whole value I give and bequeath unto my beloved wife to be disposed of by her by will or otherwise, and the balance I give and bequeath unto my children above named to be equally divided between them. The sum of money which I advanced in common among my friends for the use of John L. JAMES, I desire to remain unmolisted so long as my executors under the circumstancy of the case may deem it proper. I desire it to be understood on a settlement of my estate that I have made on advancement to my daughter Anna P. and my son in law James the sum of twelve hundred dollars. Should it become necessary in the management of any of my negroes from bad character or habits to sell, swap, or exchange any of them, I hereby authorise and direct my executors to do. And if a sale to reinvest the money in and then if desirable or otherwise to employ the funds for the benefit of my estate. I hereby nominate, constitute, and appoint my sons, James FARROW, Thomas FARROW, and my son in law John Wister SIMPSON executors of this my last will and testament. In witnefs whereof I have here unto set my hand and seal this sixteenth day of October, 1849. Signed, sealed, published, and declared as and for the last will and testament of Pattillo FARROW who subscribed the same in the presence of each other and the testaton.

Sam R. Todd   Pattillo Farrow (L. S.)
John Ga?lington
William Anderson
Recorded in Will Book A, Page 104, Bundle 101, Pkg. 21. Recorded date not available. Proven date 19th day of November, 1849. W. D. Watts, Ordy. Laurens District.

WILL OF JOHN SIMPSON

South Carolina Laurens District. In the name of God, Amen. I Jno SIMPSON of Laurens District and State above mentioned, being of sound and disposing mind and memory, but weak in body, and calling to mind the uncertainty of life, and being desirous to dispose of all such worldly estate as it hath pleased God to bless me with, do make and ordain this my last will in manner following that is to say. First, I desire my body to be decently buried at the discretion of my executors hereafter to be named. Second, I desire that my estate both real and personal be sold, and out of the monies arising therefrom, pay all my just debts, and funeral expences. After payment of my debts and funeral expences, I give to my wife Harriet, the balance of my estate during her natural life, and widowhood. 3rd. After her decease or at the expiration of her widowhood, I give the same to my children, share and share alike, with the exception that those who have received advancement must account for them in the division of said estate. I give the above stated property to them and their heirs forever. Lastly, I hereby nominate and appoint Henry R. SHELL, executor of this my last will and testament. I acknowledge this and no other to be my last will and testament. In witnefs whereof I have set my hand and seal this the seventeenth day of August in the year of our Lord, one thousand eight hundred and forty six. Signed, sealed, and published by the testator to be his last will and testament. In presence of us who have subscribed our names as witnefses in presence of the testator and in presence of each other.

James Hipp   Jno Simpson (SEAL)
Isaac Lovelefs
Joseph Hipp
Recorded in Book A, Page 106. Recorded date not available. Proven date not available. Original will not in files of Probate Judge.

WILL OF LARKIN S. MONROE

South Carolina Laurens District. In the name of God, Amen. I Larkin S. MONROE of the State and District afore said being weak in body, but of sound disposing mind and memory, calling to mind the uncertainty life, and being desirous to dispose of such worldly effects as it has pleased God to blefs me with, do make and ordain this my last will and testament in manner and form following Viz. It is my will and desire that soon after my death as my executors here in after may deem advisable, sell the tract of land containing thirty eight acres more or lefs, purchased by me as a part of the tract, belonging to the estate of Jane MONROE decd. My waggons, and bay mare and colt and out of the money arising from sales pay all my just debts and funeral expenses and if this should prove insufficient to pay the debts and C. aforesaid, I then desire my executors aforesaid to sell so much of my other personal property as they may think best and pay and satisfy the remainder of my said debts or in lien of the personal property which is as desired to be sold to satisfy the remaining part of debts as left at the action of said executors They are authorized to sell so much of the tract of land whereon I now live as will pay and satisfy said debts as aforesaid and after all my just debts and funeral expenses are fully paid and satisfied. It is then my desire and I do give and bequeath to my loving wife Rebecca MONROE during the term of her natural life or widowhood for the purpose of raising my four children and C. the tract of land whereon I now live (except so much as my said executors my sell for the prupose above mentioned) together with all my stock of cattle, hogs, with the household and kitchen furniture, plantation tools and C. And it is my wish that in case of marriage of my wife aforesaid the tract of land aforesaid be sold and that my said wife receive one third of the money arising from said sale, and the other two third go to and be equally divided amongst my children then living. And lastly, I do hereby nominate, constitute and appoint my respected friends Anderson JOHNSTON and Elihy WATSON my executors to this my last will and testament, revoking all other wills by me at any time hereto fore made. In testimony whereof I have hereunto set my hand and affixed my seal this 25th May, 1879 or 1849. Witnefs:

Wm. East   Larkin S. Monroe (SEAL)
R. W. Vance
James M. Oxner
Recorded in Book A, Page 107, Bundle 104, Package 6. Proven date June 30, 1849. Recorded date not available. W. D. Watts, Ordy.

WILL OF JOSEPH AVARY

South Carolina Laurens District. I Joseph AVARY of the State and District aforesaid, being somewhat unsond of body, but of sound and disposing mind, do make this my last will and testament. Article 1st. After my death I desire my body to be decently and plainly buried and my funeral expenses to be first paid out of my estate and after that all the just debts I may be owing at my death. Article 2d. I give and bequeath to my son Joseph AVARY and my daughter Cynthia AVARY the same amount of my estate as I have give to each of my other children when they left me and commenced the world for themselves. Article 3th. I give and bequeath to my beloved wife Rhoda AVARY, the whole ballance of my estate both real and personal for her to use and enjoy during her natural life, and after her death, I desire the ballance, or what ever may then be on hand of my estate to be sold and to be equally divided amongst all my sons and daughters or their lawful heirs, with the exception of my son Joel AVARY, he is to have no share, as I have allready given him more than I am able to give the ballance. Article 4th. I do hereby constitute and appoint my wife Rhoda AVARY and my son Joseph AVARY my executors to execute this my last will and testament. Witnefs my hand and seal this 27th Sept., 1848.

E. B. Gamorell   Joseph Avary (L. S.)
A. McKnight
Joseph Sullivan
Recorded in Will Book A, Page 108, Bdle. 99, Pkge. 7. Recorded and proven date not available. W. D. Watts, Ordy. Laurens Dist.

WILL OF JOSEPH SULLIVAN

South Carolina Laurens District. In the name of God, Amen. I Joseph SULLIVAN being sound of body and of disposing mind, do make and constitute this my last will and testament. First, I devise my body decently, not ostentationsly buried. Secondly, I desire my funeral expenses and all my just debts paid. Thirdly, The following property I do hereby, deed and convey and vest all the right and title in, to my brother Thomas I. SULLIVAN, in

trust to hold the same, permitting my wife to reside on a cultivate the land, toll of the mills and labour of the slaves, to
maintain and support her (viz.) I deed and convey to him the
ballance of my lands after cutting of two settlements hereinafter
named, which I suppose will contain something between nine hundred and one thousand accordingly, the mills etc., also ten negro
slaves, George and his wife Dicy, Morris, Patty, Edmond, Anderson
Hector, Will, Lucy, and old Bacchus, also all of my household
and kitchen furniture, one close carriage and buggy, one waggon,
all my plantation and black smith tools, Gray, six horses or
mules, and a sufficiency of cattle, hoggs, and sheep to comfort
with the plantation and hands. Also a sufficiency of provision
for the family until a crop is made, (also five hundred dollars
in cash, which I desire she may have the command of to render
her comfortable), and at the death of my wife Temperance SULLIVAN
I do hereby desire and bequeath the above lands and negroes to
my three sons Milton A., Wm. Dunklin, and Charles Pleasant SULL-
IVAN or the survivor or survivor of them as the case may be, and
the other property above devised if any remains to be equally
divided amonst all of my children. Fourthly. I give and bequeath to my son John H. SULLIVAN, the amount of one hundred dollars to pay his debt to me in my store. I also deed to George
W. SULLIVAN a negroe boy named Bird, in trust for the use of my
son John H. to be held in the same manner as the other property
set of for him in a deed of trust. Fifth. To my daughter Kiziah
J. MCCULLOUGH I bequeath one hundred and fifty dollars. And I
also deed to Dr. James M. SULLIVAN a negro boy named Isaac in
trust, for the use of my daughter Keziah I. to be held by him in
the same manner as the other negroes I deeded him in trust for
her use etc. Sixthly. I bequeath to my daughter Mary Ann EPPS
five hundred dollars, which my executor will lay out in property
for her use and retain and hold the title to the same as the
other property I give her. Seventhly. I do hereby convey and
deed to George W. SULLIVAN to be held by him in trust until my
son Milton A. arrives of age, then the title to vest in him, the
following property, one tract of land to be out of the upper end
of my lands which I suppose will contain three hundred and fifty
acres, a corner to be made at the forks of the road going to
Andrew MCKNIGHTS and to run from thence along the road leaving to
Charles POSEYS old place until it reaches the fence, thence to
run a straight line from thence to the mouth of a branch at the
river a little below where Mrs. POSEY drowned herself, to include
all above said line adjoining and binding on Andrew MCKNIGHT,
John BOLT, Willis CHEEK, Josiph AVARY, Pleasant SHAW, and John
MEARS lands. Also the following negroe Lewis and his wife Lifsy
their children Agnise and Robert, also Sandy and Caroline, also
four hundred dollars in cash, for the use and benefit of my
daughter Malinda C. SULLIVAN, the said land and negroes to be
held in trust in the same manner, that my daughter Mary Ann EPPS
is by deed. The money left in this bequest I desire the trustee
to stock the farm with and put the negores on it to work, etc.
Eighthly. I bequeath the following property to my daughter
Temperance SULLIVAN (the title to vest in George W. SULLIVAN

(until my son Milton A. arrives of age then to vest in him under
the same limitations and restrictions as the property I deeded
to my daughter Mary Ann EPPS) one tract of land, suppose to contain five hundred acres, including the Hickory Tavern, begining
on a stake 3 x in Sims old field near a pond, running thence N.
40 W 20 to an Ash 3 x tence N 52 E 28.00 to a red oak 3 x thence
S 37 E 9.00 to a stake 3 x binding on Robert MANLY's land thence
to 41 E 21.00 to a stake 3x thence S 44 E 74.00 to a small Per-
simmon 3 x binging on Edmond BOLTS land, thence S 55 W 37.00 to
a stake 3 x thence S 60 E 26. to a stake 3 x tence West 22.50 to
a stake 3 x thence cornering with Isfsu R. GRAY, thence W 63 W
47.50 to a stake 3 x binding on Mrs. AVARYS land and from thence
to the beginning. Also six negroes, Adam, Francis and her child
Matilda, George, Pool, Sceally, and Nancy, and six hundred dollars the above property to be held in trust for her use etc. as
a reference to the deed above will more fully shown. Ninth. The
whole ballance of my estate not bequeathed in the above bequest's
I do hereby give and bequeath to my three sons Milton A., William
D., and Charles P. SULLIVAN, consisting in part of nineteen negroes Viz.: John, Inda, Jane, Linda, David, Ned Jun., Francis,
Ned Sr., Sam, Suse Arnold, Susan Jemas, little John, Martha,
Aaron, Tom, Humphrey, Rachel, Stephen, and his wife Matilda.
Merchandise that may be on hand at my death, cash, notes of
hand and book accounts due me (after paying debts and other legacies) add debts due me as a member of the firm of G. W. SULLI-
VAN and Co., all the stock and provisions on hand, and all produce of any kind or sort on hand (excepting what is for my wife)
all choses in action and whatever else if any thing remains of
my estate, I bequeath to my said three sons Milton A., Wm. D.,
and Charles P. SULLIVAN. Further more I desire my executor to
sell the last named six slaves above (Viz) Aaron, Tom, Humphrey,
Rachel, and Stephen and Matilda, on as long a credit as he may
deem prudent, with intrust from date. Tenth. I wish and desire
my sons and two youngest daughters to have a good education and
imprefs the same on my executors and hope that my wife will manage so as to educate them as far as can be done at home, without
infringing on their portions for board clothing and schooling.
My three sons I desire to have a collegiate education if their
abilities should be deemed sufficient by my executor and my other
brothers. Lastly. I constitute and appoint my brother Thomas I.
SULLIVAN to execute this my will and testament my executor.
Signed, sealed, and acknowledged in the presence of this 27th
day of May, 1846.

E. B. Gambrell   Joseph Sullivan (LS)
W. H. Mauly
Thomas Mauly
Recorded in Will Book A, Page 109, Bdle. 182, Pkge. 12. Original
will not in files of Probate Judge. W. D. Watts, O. L. D.
Recorded dates not available. Proven Nov. 12, 1849.

WILL OF JNO. FOWLER

In the name of God, Amen. I Jno. FOWLER of the District of Laurens and State of South Carolina, being of sound mind do make and ordain this my last will in the manner following (to wit). After all my just debts are paid, I will the whole of my estate both real and personal to my wife Elizabeth FOWLER during her lifetime or widowhood for her use, and the use of my unmarried children as though I were living. And at her death to be disposed of as follows. I desire that my land be laid of and valued by three disinterested persons, to my six sons, (to wit) William Wade, Wiley Y., Jno. F., Wesly Jr., and William in trust for the use and benefit of Jesse and my negroes. I will to be put in lots and valued in the same way as the land, and after my daughters (with the exception of Elizabeth LOWRY the wife of James LOWRY,) are made equal with my sons. I then will that the balance of my estate except the negroes, should be sold, and all my children be made to share equal except the aforesaid Elizabeth LOWRY, wife of Jas. LOWRY. The share Jesse to be paid over to my son William, who is to have charge of his whole estate in trust for the sue of my son Jesse, and the trustee is so to use his trust estate that Jesse is not to spend it or any part except the annul income. In making distribution of my estate amongst my children, I desire that all that I have ever given or may hereafter give to any one of them, should be accounted for as my meaning is for them all to sheare equal except the aforesaid Elizabeth LOWRY, wife of James LOWRY, for whom if any provisions is made by this will. It will be in an after clause or by a codicil. I nominate and appoint my son William FOWLER, and friend Jno. H. HENDERSON to execute this my last will given under my hand and seal this day. In the event of my marrying, I give her one third part of my whole estate during her life, and then for it to return to my estate and be distributed agreeable to my will, Augst, 16th, 1851.

Wm. B. Gary   Jno. Fowler
Henry H. Watkins
Wm. Bargefs
Recorded in Will Book A, Page 112. Recorded and proven date not available. W. D. Watts, Ordy, Laurens District. Original will not in file of Probate Judge.

WILL OF WILLIS D. CHEEK

State of South Carolina Laurens District. Know all men by these presence, that I Willis D. CHEEK of the state and district aforesaid, being of sound disposing mind and memory, do make and publish this my last will and testament. First, I desire that my executrix and executor, do sell at public auction my tract of land known as the Berry Pool tract supposed to contain one hundred and forty acres, also anything else of my personal property which my wife may not want to keep for the use of the farm. And for them to pay all of my just debts out of the proceeds. And I

further desire should my wife need funds for the use of the small
children, such as schooling and c. that she, and my executor be
authorised to sell any of the personal property left her to defray the expences. Second. I give and desire to my beloved
wife Prifsilla CHEEK, all the rest and residue of my real estate
where I now live. Also all my personal proberty, my negroes,
horses, cattle, hogs, household and kitchen furniture, farming
utentials, with every species of property not mentioned above,
to have and to hold so long as she lives. After her death, then
all of the above property that has not been disposed of, to be
sold and equally divided amongst all of my children, or if any
be dead and have heirs, for these heirs to get their part. Third
I ordain and appoint my beloved wife Prissilla CHEEK as executrix
and my son Jno. CHEEK executor of this my last will and testament.
In testimony whereof I have hereunto set my hand and seal and
published and declared this to be my last will and testament, in
the presence of the witness as named below. This the 5th day of
October in the year of our Lord, one thousand eight hundred and
forty nine. Signed, sealed, published, and declared by the said
W. D. CHEEK as and for his last will and testament. In the presence of each other and at his request have hereunto subscribed
our names as witnesses.

James Nesbitt   W. D. Cheek (L. S.)
W. W. Hitch
Wm. A. Todd
Recorded in Will Book A, Page 113, Box 111, Pkg. 13. Recorded
and proven date not available. W. D. Watts, Ordy. Laurens Dist.

WILL OF ANDREW HAMILTON

October 30th, 1848. South Carolina Laurens District. I now
make my last will and testament as follows. I bequeathe my negroes to my nephew James DOWNEY Viz. William Archey Lilah, and
Robert Absolom, the said negroes to be the property of Mr. Samuel
DOWNEY until James DOWNEY becomes of age or marrys and then they
to be his and his bodily heirs forever. I bequeathe to my niece
Eliza DOWNEY one negro woman named Mary and child Maria Elizabeth
to be the property of Samuel DOWNEY until Eliza DOWNEY becomes
of age or otherwise marries. Then they to be hers and her bodily
heirs forever. And if either should die without a bodily heir
the property to return back to the family. I want my personal
property and my negro boy Thomas to satisfy my debts and the remainder to be divided equally between Samuel HAMILTON, Alexander
HAMILTON, Martha DERRAH, Mary DOWNEY, and Elizabeth SCOLES. And
this to be my last will and testament signed and sealed in the
presence of (L. S.) This my last will and testament signed and
sealed in the presence of

Test: Robert McDaniel   Andrew Hamilton (SEAL) L.S.
      Nancy Pitts
      W. R. Molloy
October 30, 1848.
Continued on page 106

Continued from page 105
Recorded in Book A, Page 114, Bundle 124, Package 1. Proven
date Oct. 8, 1849. Recorded date not available. W. D. Watts,
Ordy.
I do appoint Samuel DOWNEY to be the executor of my estate here
before. Witnefses

WILL OF ELLIS CHEEK

In the name of God, Amen. I Ellis CHEEK of the State of South
Carolina and District of Laurens, being in a low state of health
but of sound mind and memory, do make and constitute this my
last will and testament in manner following (VIZ). After all my
just debts and funeral expences are paid, I desire that all my
estate both real and personal shall be sold by my executors here
in after named on a credit not lefs than one year, nor more than
two years. And the money arising there from with the debts due
or owing to me from my children or others either by notes or
accounts thereunto added to be equally divided among my children
herein after named VIZ. William CHEEK, Richard CHEEK, Salley
SENTELL, Mary RHODES, Jane RHODES, Cafsey FARROW, Willis D. CHEEK
Linney RIDDLE. And lastly, I do hereby nominate constitute and
appoint my son Willis D. CHEEK and my friend William ROFS my
executors to this my last will and testament. Signed, sealed,
and declared in presence of us this 12th of January, 1838.

                                                        his
James B. Higgins   Ellis X Cheek (L. S.)
Samuel Mills
Benjamin B. Higgins
Recorded in Will Book A, Page 115, Bundle 82, Pkg. 6. Recorded
date not available. Proven date 17th day of September, one thou-
sand and eight hundred and thirty eight. W. D. Watts, Ordy.
Laurens District.

WILL OF NEWMAN GARY

I Newman GARY of the District of Laurens and State of South Carolina, being of sound and disposing mind and memory, but calling
to mind the uncertainty of life, and being desirous of disposing
of such worldly estate as it hath pleased God to blefs me with,
do make and ordain this my last will and testament in manner and
form following that is to say. First. It is my will and desire
that after my death all my just debts and funeral expenses be
paid out of such moneys as I may leave on hand and the debts
owing to me. Second. I will and bequeath to my beloved wife
Elizabeth GARY, my whole estate real and personal during her natural life. Third. After the death of my wife, it is my will
and pleasure that suitable tomb stones be erected over the graves
of myself and my wife by my executors hereinafter named to be
paid for out of my estate. And that all the remainder of my
estate of every description real and personal be valued and
appraised in three lots or portions, the negroes to be appraised
in families, so as not to separate them if pofsible. These lots
or shares to be as nearly equal in value as may be practicable,

and the appraisement to be made by three respectable and disinterested free holders to be selected by my executor. Fourth. After the division and appraisement of my estate above directed be made, I give and bequeath to my friend Daniel MANGUM one portion or third part thereof, which is to include my land and buildings, to be held by him in trust for the sole and separate use and benefit of my daughter Mary R. MCDOWELL, the wife of Thomas MCDOWELL, during her natural life, the said property in no event, or the income thereof to be subject to the debts, contracts, control, or management of her husband. And after her death, I give and bequeath the said third part or portion of my estate to the children of my said daughter Mary R. MCDOWELL in equal shares the children of any deceased child to take amongst them the share to which their parent would be entitled if living. Fifth. I give and bequeath one other third part of my estate, appraised and divided as aforesaid, to my grand daughter Louisa Elizabeth GARY, the daughter of my deceased son Jefse R. GARY, And should she die under age without children and unmarried, then it is my will that the same be divided between my daughter Mary R. MCDOWELL and the children of my deceased daughter Pamela C. PYLES. My said daughter Mary R. MCDOWELL to take one half there of to be held by the trustee above named subject to the same trusts and limitations set forth in the fourth clause of my will. And the remaining half to be equally divided amongst the children of my said daughter Pamela C. PYLES, the child or children of any deceased child to take the share to which their parent would be entitled if living. Sixth. I give and bequeath the remaining one third part or portion of my estate to the children of my deceased daughter Pamela C. PYLES in equal shares. And if either of said children should die under age unmarried and without children his or her share to go to the survivor or survivors. And should the whole of the said children die under age without children and unmarried, then I give and bequeath one half of their portion of my estate mentioned in this clause to the trustee of my daughter Mary R. MCDOWELL to be held by him subject to and upon the same trusts and limitations contained in the fourth clause, and the remaining half I give to my grand daughter Louisa E. GARY daughter of Jefse R. GARY. Lastly, I nominate and appoint Addison T. MARTIN executor of this my last will and testament hereby revoking all other wills by me heretofore made. In testimony whereof I have hereunto set my hand and seal this 25th day of November, 1848. Signed, sealed, published, and declared in presence of.

Daniel Mangum   Newman Gary (SEAL)
Bela R. Mangum
Asa B. Davis
Recorded in Will Book A, Page 119, Bdl. 110, Pkge. 13. Recorded and proven date not available. W. D. Watts, Ordy. Laurens District.

WILL OF ELIZABETH POOL

In the name of God, Amen. I Elizabeth POOL of Laurens District and State of South Carolina, being of sound and a disposing mind and memory, and calling to mind the uncertainty of life and being desireous to dispose of all such worldly estate as it hath pleased God to blefs me with, do make and ordain this my last will in the manner following (VIZ). lst. I desire that after my decease all my estate both real and personal be sold and divided between my children as. 2nd. I give to my gran daughter Mary E. MOSELY one tenth of my estate to be held by my son Berry P. POOL untill she attains the age of twenty one. 3rd. After the above leacy I desire that the balance of my estate be equally divided between my children (to wit) Berry P. POOL, William POOL, Rebecca PATTERSON, Nancy CAMPTON, and Mary COOLMAN. 4th. I desire that if my grand daughter Mary E. MOSELEY should not live to attaine to the age of twenty one the interest she may be entitled to under this my will be disposed of according to the third clause of my will. 5th. I give and bequeath the interest my daughter Mary COOLEMAN may be entilled to under this my will to my son Berry P. POOL to advance to her as he may think she stands in need. And lastly, I do constitute and appoint my son Berry P. POOL executor of this my last will and testament by me heretofore made. In testimony whereof I have hereunto set my hand and affixed my seal this 24 day of September, 1850. Signed sealed and acknowledged in the presence of us.

	her
W. S. Smith	Elizabeth X Pool
Saml Mills	mark
A. S. Hutchinson	

Recorded in Will Book A, Page 121, Bundle 110, Pkg. 15. Recorded date not available. Proven date 23rd of October, 1850. W. D. Watts, Ordy. Laurens District.

WILL OF WHITEHEAD WILKS

The state of South Carolina. I Whitehead WILKS do make and constitute this my last will and testament in manner following. Item lth. I will and devise to my wife Eliza WILKS the tract of land whereon I now live (provided Silas BAILEY does not take it under a contract between he and I) during her natural life, and if Silas BAILEY takes the land under said contract then I bequeath her the six hundred dollars which said Bailey is to pay for said land, one bed stead, bed, and furniture, a horse, and biggy on the plantation, a negro girl named Jane, the above named money and property I give to my said wife during her natural life. And after death to be equally divided into three parts, one of which I give to my daughter Eliza HENDERSON. One third to the children of my deceased son Cornilius WILKS. And one third to my son Joseph WILKS to be setled in trust as hereinafter stated. Item 2. I will and bequeath to my son Thomas G. WILKS all the interest and claim which I have from my father's estate which is all that I intend giving him. Item 3. I will and direct that all the ballance of my estate be sold by my executors and the proceeds of the same with whatever may be owing to me after the payment of my debts be divided into three shares. One of which I give and bequeath to my grand children (the children of my deceased son Cornelius WILKS). One third I give and bequeath to J. H. IRBY and Dr. Jno. H. DAVIS together with that part named after the death of my wife, in trust for the sole use and benefit of my son Joseph WILKS during his life and after her death to such child or children that may be living of his. One third I give and bequeath to my daughters Eliza HENDERSON with a request that my son in law Saml. HENDERSON, may vest the same in property and have it settled in trust for the use and benefit of his wife during life and then to her children. I do hereby constitute and appoint J. H. IRBY and Dr. Jno. H. DAVIS my executors to this my last will and testament. Nov. 8th, 1847. Signed, sealed, and acknowledged in the presence of.

Sml. Fleming   Whitehead Wilks (L.S.)
R. E. Todd
Wm. T. Blakely
Recorded in Will Book A, Page 123, Bdle. 114, Pkge. 10. W. D. Watts, O. L. D. Proven and recorded dates not available.

WILL OF DR. JOHN NICKELS

In the name of God, Amen. I John NICKELS of the District of Laurens and State of South Carolina, being of sound and disposing mind and memory, do make constitute and ordain this my last will and testament in manner and form following, that is to say. First. It is my will and desire that all my just debts be paid as soon after my death as may be practicable. Second. It is my will and desire that as soon after my death as the money can be collected, either from debts due me or the proceeds of the farm, there shall be made up and paid to each of my daughters Catherine N. HOLMES, Mary S. ANDERSON, and Isabella Jane WRIGHT the sum of two thousand dollars provided however, that any money they or either of them or their husbands may have previously received from me or debts paid for them by me shall be considered and recoved in as making a part or whole of said sume of two thousand dollars as the case may be. Third. I give and bequeath to my daughter Isabella Jane WRIGHT household and kitchen furniture, stock and C. to an amount equal that given to either of my other daughters at the discretion of my wife to be delivered to her where called for. Fourth. I give and bequeath all the rest and residue of my estate real and personal, to my beloved wife Jane NICKLES during her natural life. And at her death I give and bequeath to Dr. John W. SIMPSON the following negroes, to wit; a woman named Rachel with her children Evelene Jackson, Preston, Perry and Cornelia; also a man named Fielding and his wife Pemna with then children, Simon, Jefferson, Isaac, Jane, Creecy and Fielding. Hester a woman and her daughter Ellen with her children Baizilla, Andrew, and Othella Margaret. Also a negro man Jim and his two brothers Joseph and Isaac, a man named Clarborn, a man named Jim Wynn and a woman named Polley, in trust for the use and benefit of my daughter Catherine N. HOLMES during her natural life. And at her death the said negroes to be disposed of as follows, to wit, one half of the increase to belong to her husband, and all the above named negroes and the remainder of their increase to be equally divided amoungst her children. The child or children of a deceased child to take the share to which their deceased parent if living would be entitled. But should she die without leaving a husband or child or children survering her, or the child or children of a deceased child, then it is my will and desire that all the aforesaid negroes with their whole increase be equally divided between my other two daughters Mary E. and Isabella Jane if living. And if either be dead leaving no child or children, thm surviving then the whole to go to the last survivor. But if either be dead leaving a child or children living then such child or children to take the share to which their mother if living would be entitled. And if my said daughter Catherine N. HOLMES should die leaving no child or children living nor child or children of a deceased child, but should leave a husband, then it is my will and desire that such husband should have and take one half of the increase of the aforesaid negroes. And all the ballance of the increase with the negroes named in this clause shall be disposed of as is here in provided in the event of my said daughter dying without leaving a husband, child, or children, or the child or children of a deceased child. And it is further my will wiat my said daughter Catherine N. HOLMES shall have the pofsefsion and use of the aforesaid negroes and their increase (after the termination of the life estate of my wife) during her natural life. But the said negroes and increase in no event to be subject to the debts or contracts of her present or any future husband after the death of my wife. Fifth. I give and bequeath to Dr. Jno. W. SIMPSON the following negroes to wit, a man named Edmond and his wife Peggy with her children Tom, Aggy, and Anthony. Moriah and her child Emely, also a woman named big Lucy and her daughter Mira with her children Simeon, Sally Ann and Lenides, the woman named little Lucy with her children, Nancy, David, and Iarrat. William a man and his wife Mitia with her children Lorenza, Sally, and Stepney, a man named Simon and his wife Moriah with two of their sons Jackson and Blueford together with their future increase in trust for the use and benefit of my daughter Mary E. ANDERSON during her natural life. And at her death to be disposed of as follows, to wit, one half of the increase of the same to belong to her husband. And all the above named negroes with the remainder of their increase to be equally divided amongst her children the child or children of a deceased child to take the share to which their parent should have been entitled to if living. But should my said daughter die without leaving a husband or child or children surviving her or the child or children of a deceased child. Then it is my will and desire that all the aforesaid negroes with their whole increase be equally divided between my two other daughters Catherine N. HOLMES and Isabella Jane WRIGHT if living. And if either be dead without a child or children sur-

viving her then the whole to go to the survivor. But if either
be dead leaving a child or children living then such child or
children to take the share of said negroes and their increase to
which their mother if living would be entitled. And if my said
daughter Mary should die leaving no child or children nor the
child or children of a deceased child surviving her, but should
leave a husband, then it is my will and desire that her said
husband should take and have one half of the increase of said
negroes and all the ballance should be disposed of as in provided. In the case of my said daughter (dying without leaving a
husband, child, or children, or grand child or grand children
surviving her). And further it is my will that my said daughter
Mary E. ANDERSON may have the pofsefsion and use of the said
negores and their increase during her life, the same in no event
to be liable for any debt or contract of her present or any
future husband. Sixth. I give and bequeath to Dr. John W. SIMP-
SON after the death of my wife the following negroes, to wit,
Noah a man, and his wife Betsy with her children William, Henry,
Dannel, Martha, Adeline, Lucinda, Lewis, Adella and Lama. Also
a woman named Kitty Ann, with her children Parthenn Frances,
Milly Sophia, and Matilda. A woman named Sylvia with her children Jim a man, Calvin, Harriette and her child Louisa Frances an
and Caroline with her child Fanny Jane, in trust for the use and
benefit of my daughter Isabella Jane WRIGHT during her natural
life. And at her death the said negroes to be disposed of as
follows, to wit, one half of the increase to belong to her husband and all the above named negroes with the remainder of their
increase to be equally divided amoungst her children. The child
or children of a deceased child to take the share to which their
parent if living should be entitled. But should my said daughter
die without leaving a husband or child or children surviving her
or the child or children of a deceased child. Then it is my
will and desire that all the aforesaid negores with their whole
increase be equally divided between my two other daughters Catherine N. HOMES and Mary E. ANDERSON if living and if either be
dead leaving no child or children surviving then the whole to go
to the survivor. But if either be dead leaving a child or children surviving, then such child or children to take the part to
which their mother would have been entitled if living. And if
my said daughter Isabella Jane should die leaving no child or
children or the child or children of a deceased child surviving
her, but should leave a husband, then it is my will and desire
that such husband should take and have one half of the increase
of the aforesaid negroes. And all the ballance should be disposed of as is provided in the case of my said daughter dying
without leaving a husband, child or children or grand child or
grand children surviving her. And it is further my will that my
said daughter Isabella Jane shall have the use and pofsefsion of
the aforesaid negroes and their increase during her life, but
the same in no event to be subject to the debts or any contracts
of her present or any future husband. Seventh. It is my will
and desire that should any difference in value be apparent in
the several lots of negroes now bequeathed to Dr. John W. SIMPSON

for the use and benefit of my said daughters Catherine N. HOLMES Mary E. ANDERSON, and Isabella Jane WRIGHT at the time the same shall come into their pofsefsion. The several lots be valued and the difference made up to those having the lefs valuable portions out of the residue of my estate before the final division of the same. Eight. After the death of my wife Jane NICKELS, I will and direct that my real estate in Laurens Dist. be divided and laid off into three equal parts or tracts as near as may be and to be valued one of which tracts I give and bequeath to each of my said daughters Catherine N. HOLEMS, Mary E. ANDERSON, and Isabella Jane WRIGHT during their respective lives and at their death their respective parts of said land be equally divided between each their children. But should either of my said daughters die without leaving a child or children surviving them or gran child or grand children, then the tract or parcel of land herein bequeathed to such of them as may so die to be disposed of in the same manner and to be subject to the same limitations as are provided in the fourth, fifth, and sixth clauses of this will, relative to the negroes therein bequeathed and mentioned. Provided however that the husband or husbands of my said daughters are to take no part of the said real estate on the death of either of my said daughters. And I do further direct that if the part or tract of land laid off to either of my said daughters should exceed in value that of the others or either of them. The difference in value is to be made up out of the residue of my estate before a final division thereof so that each may be equal. Ninth. It is my will and desire that all the rest and residue of my estate after the death of my wife be sold by my executor and the proceeds thereof be equally divided amoungst my three daughters Catherine N. HOLMES, Mary E. ANDERSON, and Isabella Jane WRIGHT, except my rail road and bank stock which is to be divided amoungst them equally without sale. Lastly. I do hereby nominate, constitute and appoint Dr. John W. SIMPSON my executor of this my last will and testament. In testimony here in I have hereunto set my hand and seal this twenty fifth day of February in the year of our Lord, one thousand eight hundred forty eight. The word child in the fourth clause and negroes the same. The word after the death of my wife in the fifth clause and the same words after the death of my wife in the sixth clause were underlined before signing. Signed, sealed, and delivered, declared, and published as my last will and testament in presence of.

Willis Benham   John Nickels (SEAL)
J. H. Lockhart
Wm. F. Martin
Recorded in Book A, Page 123, Bundle 111, Package 20. Proven da date October 23, 1850. Recorded date not available. W. D. Watts Ordy.

WILL OF FRANCIS SIMS

South Carolina Spartanburgh District. In the name of God, Amen.

I Frances SIMS of the State and District aforesaid, being weak
in body, but of perfect mind, and memory, thanks be to God.
Calling to mind the mortality of my body, and knowing that it is
appointed for all men once to die, I make and ordain this my last
will and testament that is to say. Principally and first of all
I give and recommend my soul into the hands of almighty God,
that gave it, and my body I recommend to the earth to be buried
in a decent christian manner. Nothing doubting but at the general resurrection I shall receive the same again by the mighty
power of God. And touching such worldly estate wherewith it has
pleased God to blefs me with in this life, I give and dispose of
the same in the following manner and form. Item 1s. I give and
bequeath unto my beloved daughter Hainey FOWLER, Precilla CHEEK,
and Polly WALKER all my wearing clothes, extra. Item 2nd. My
will is that my estate both real and personal be sold and the
money equally divided between my children and their heirs Starling SIMS, William SIMS, and the children of my daughter Elizabeth, Eliza I. GIDDING, William C. GIDDINGS, John L. GIDDING,
to have one share among them equally. Hainey FOWLER, Priscilla
CHEEK, and Polly WALKER, and their heirs to equal shares with my
sons Starling and William. Item 3rd. My will is that the one
sixth part of my estate above willed to my grand children remain
in the hands of my executors until they are of lawful age to
receive it. I likewise make and ordain my son William SIMS and
my son in law Willis D. CHEEK my executors of this my last will
and testament. I do hereby ratify and confirm this and no other
to be my last will and testament. In testimony whereof I have
hereunto signed, sealed, and acknowledged the same in presence
of all the subscribing witnefs this June 4th, in the year of our
Lord, one thousand eight hundred and forty five. And in the sixty seventh of American Independence.

her
Frances X Sims (SEAL)
mark

William Jones
R. S. Woodruff
Daniel Lanford
The word Walker interlined and their heirs before signed. I give
my daughters and grand daughter Elizabeth I. GIEONS.
Recorded in Will Book A, Page 128, Bdl. 111, Pkge. 10. W. D.
Watts, O. L. D. Proven and recorded dates not available.

WILL OF WILLIAM ROOK

In the name of God, Amen. I William ROOK of South Carolina and
Laurens District, being of sound and disposing mind and memory,
but weak in body, and calling to mind the uncertainty of life,
and being desirous to dispose of all such worldly estate as it
hath pleased God to blefs me with, do make and ordain this my
last will and testament, in manner following, that is to say. I
give and bequeath to my beloved wife Mrs. Elizabeth ROOK one
third part of my land including the buildings, and also as many
of my negroes as she may choose and select for her own use and
benefit. My will and desire further is, that my said wife have
as much of my stock plantation tools, household and kitchen

113

furniture, and provision sufficient to serve her twelve months as she may think proper to choose. Again it is my will and desire that my said wife do permit my son Saml. ROOK to have the use of the one half of my house bequeathed to her. Again my will and desire is that my said son Saml. have the house bequeathed to my said wife after her decease laid out to him in the distribution of my real estate. Again, I do hereby will and devise that my estate both real and personal be divided amongst my children according to the provisions of the act of distributions of this State, with the exception of the share which my daughter Catharine LYLES, wife of Benjm. LYLES should have. I further will and divise the share of my said daughter Catharine LYLES to my sons Thos. I. ROOK and William ROOK in trust for the sole and seperate use and benefit of my said daughter Catharine LYLES during her life. And at her death to be equally divided amongst her children that may then be living. In witnefs whereof I have here set my hand this day of Feby., in the year of our Lord, one thousand eight hundred and forty eight. Signed, sealed, and acknowledged in the presence of us.

P. C. Caldwell   William Rook Senr. (SEAL)
John Suber
Charles C. Wells
Recorded in Book A, Page 129, Bundle 124, Package 14.   Proven date Nov. 5, 1850. Recorded date not available. W. D. Watts, Ordy.

WILL OF WILLIAM LIGON

In the name of God, Amen. I William LIGON of Laurens District South Carolina, being of sound and disposing mind and memory, and calling to mind the uncertainty of life and being desirous to dispose of all such worldly estate as it hath pleased God to blefs me with, do make and ordain this my last will and testament hereby revoking and making void all former wills by me at any time heretofore made in manner following that is to say. Itim 1st. I bequeath my soul to God who gave it me and my body to the dust from whence it sprang to be interred in a christian like manner. After paying all my just debts and funeral expences, I demise and dispose of my property in the following manner that is to say. Item 2nd. It is my will and desire that my administrators as soon as practicable after my decease do sell at public sale all my estate both real and personal on a credit of twelve months. (Excepting such property as I may hereafter bequeath or loan to my wife Elizabeth LIGON). And equally divide the monies arising therefrom between all my children, to wit, Thomas LIGON, Susan MILAN, Patsey CARTER, William LIGON, Daniel LIGON, Joseph T. LIGON, Robert B. LIGON, John W. LIGON, and George A. LIGON, the children of my son James LIGON, decd. to take the share amongst them that would have fallen to their parent, and the children of my daughter Elizabeth HENDERSON decd. to have the share that would have fallen to her amonst them, all my children to share alike. After first having made my youngest children (viz) Joseph T. LIGON, Robert B. LIGON, John W. LIGON, and George A. LIGON, equal with my other children to whom I have made, and may hereafter make advancements for which they are to account in said division without interest reference is to be had to my family book for all the advancements made and for which I have them charged in said family book. Item 3rd. I will and bequeathed to my beloved wife Elizabeth LIGON one thousand dollars to be paid to her in money, one bed and furniture of her own selection her saddle, and one years provision of every thing necefsary for herself and family and stock to be hers and her heirs forever. Item 4th. I loan to my said wife all the tract of land whereon I now live and my negro man Reuben and his wife Rose, negro boy Joe and girl Nancy, negro boy Sam. girl Sary and girl Vilet with their future increase from this time two beds and furniture of her own chosing all the crockery, and glafs ware and all the silver spoons, and my two large looking glafses, cupboard and sideboard, two horses, two bridles, and one saddle of her own chosing, two cows and calves, one sow and pigs, of her own selection, my Barouch and harnefs, and all the fowls on the premises to have and to hold to her own use during her natural life or widowhood. This provision being for my said wifes dower at law, and exprefsly in line thereof and upon the death or marriage of my said wife. It is exprefsly my meaning and intention that the above mentioned land and negroes with the increase of the negroes beds, and furniture, crockery and glafs ware, silver spoons, looking glafses, cupboard, and sideboard, horses, saddle, bridle, cows, and calves, Barouch and harnefs and all loaned property return into the hands of my administrators to be sold by them the land on a credit of one and two years and the negroes and other loaned property on a credit of twelve months and the monies arising therefrom to be equally divided amongst all my children, the heirs of such as are or may be dead to take the share of their respective parent as hereinbefore directed and my wife is not to be accountable for the wear or misfortune of the property loaned to her. Item 5th. I give and bequeath unto my trusty and faithfull fervant Reuben five dollars to be paid to him by my administrators annually during his life. Item 6th. As I appoint no executors I desire my son Daniel LIGON, Henry ONEALL and John MILAM to administer upon my estate with the will annext by me made. In testimony whereof I have hereunto set my hand and affixed my seal this the twentieth day of June, one thousand eight hundred and forty seven. Signed, sealed, published, and declared, as and for the last will and testament of the above named William LIGON in presents of us.

Jas. E. Lockhart   Wm. Ligcn (SEAL)
Aaron Wells
Thomas Nelson
Silas Walker
Recorded in Will Book A, Page 130, Bdle. 118, Pkge. 7. Recorded and proven dates not available. W. D. Watts, Ordy. Laurens District.

Continued on page 116

Continued from page 115
CODICIL
Whereas I William LIGON of Laurens District have made and duly
executed my last will and testament in writing bearing date the
twentyth of June, 1847, and therein loaned to my wife during her
life or widowhood a negro girl Sarah and her future increase.
Now I do hereby revoke the said loan of the said girl Sarah and
in lieu thereof do loan to my said wife my negro girl Katy to be
hers during her life or widowhood. And at her death or marriage
the said girl Katy to go back into the hands of my administrators
and be disposed of as directed in my said will with the to her
property loanded and my girl Sarah to be sold as my other property at my decease and disposed of as directed in my said will.
Signed, sealed, published, and declared by the said William LIGON
as for a codicil to his last will and testament and to be taken
a part thereof. In presents of this 12th day of June, 1850.

Lafaytte Martin   Wm. Ligon (SEAL)
Thos. Walker
W. N. Carter

WILL OF ANTHONY GRIFFIN

In the name of God, Amen. I Anthony GRIFFIN of Laurens District
in the State of South Carolina, being weak in body health, but
of sound and disposing mind, and calling to mind the uncertainty
of life, and being desirous of making a disposition of such
worldly estate as it has pleased Heaven to blefs me with in this
life, do make and ordain this my last will and testament in the
manner following, that is to say. First. I give and bequeath
unto my daughter Frances Amanda GRIFFIN, to her and to her bodily
heirs forever, my negroe girl Jude (or any other negroe girl of
mine she may choose to select instead of Jude), one good feather
bed, bed shead, and furniture, one good horse, one good cow and
calf, one sow and pigs, my beauraugh and my gold watch. Secondly. After the above bequeaths given to my daughter Frances Amanda GRIFFIN my will and desire is that the whole of my estate
both real and personal be sold by my executors hereinafter named
as early practicable after my death. And after paying all my
just debts and funeral expences, to be divided amongst my children as I will hereafter direct. Thirdly. Having advanced in
money and property to and for my son Doct. William H. GRIFFIN,
and amount much more than I am able to give to my other children
after paying my just debts, a charge amount of which I have his
makes for, all of them I wish my executors to give up to him
except five hundred dollars ($500) of them, that amount I wish
collected of him and applied to the payment of my debts an divided amongst my children as I will hereafter direct. Fourthly. I
have some notes on my son Richard F. GIRFFIN, which notes I direct my executors to give up to him without etaching any thing
from him for them, as I have not advanced to him as much as I
have to some of my other children. Fifthly. My will and desire
is that my executors do pay (out of the residue of my estate) to
my daughters Jane L. FULLER and Martha F. HIGGINS ($10) ten

dollars each in cash and in lieu of all their interest in my estate. Sixthly. My will and desire is that after the above bequeaths and after paying all my just debts, my executors do divide all the balance of my estate equally between my son Richard F. GRIFFIN and my three daughters Mary W. WATTS, Sarah A. PHINNEY, and Frances Amanda GRIFFIN, share and share alike between them four. Seventhly and lastly. I constitute and appoint my relitive Ino. D. WILLIAMS and my friend W. D. WATTS my sole executors hereby giving them full power. Virtue and authority to carry out this my last will and testament and revoking all others heretofore made. In testimony whereof I have hereunto set my hand and affixed my seal this the 4 day of November, Armo Damin, 1849. The interlining on the third line from the bottom of this page was done before signing. Signed, sealed, published, and declared by the said Anthony GRIFFIN as and for his last will and testament in the presence of us.

John D. Brown   A. Griffin (L.S.)
Willis Brown
James Babb
Recorded in Will Book A, Page 133. Recorded and proven date not available.

WILL OF JEMIMA DAY

In the name of God, Amen. I Jemimah DAY of the District of Laurens and State of South Carolina, being of sound and disposing mind and memory, but weak of body, and remembering the uncertainty of life, being desirous of disposing of such worldly estate as it hath pleased God to blefs me with, do make, constitute, and ordain this my last will and testament in manner and form following, that is to say. First, It is my will and desire that all my just debts and funeral expenses be paid. Second. I will and bequeath my whole estate real and personal of every description to Charles SIMMONS and Pamela SIMMONS his wife, during their join lives and after the death of either, to the survivor during life. And after the death of both of them, I will and bequeath my said estate real and personal of every description consisting of land, negroes, stock, furniture, and so forth to the two children of the said Charles and Pamela SIMMONS to wit, Pamela Adeline SIMMONS and Charles Young Lafayette SIMMONS to then and their heirs forever. In testimony whereof I have hereunto set my hand and seal this 23 day of August, 1850. Signed, sealed, and published in presence of.

Wm. Graves Sen.   Jemima Day (SEAL)
Wm. W. Graves
Wm. E. Caldwell
Recorded in Will Book A, Page 134, Bdle. 110, Pkge. 9. Recorded and proven dates not available. W. D. Watts, Ordy. Laurens District.

WILL OF ISABELLA BOYD

State of South Carolina Laurens District. I Isabella BOYD of
the State and District aforesaid being weak in body, but of sound
and disposing mind and memory, and calling to mind the uncertainty of life and being desirous to dispose of such worldly effects
as it has pleased God to blefs me with, do make and ordain this
my last will and testament in manner and form following VIZ. It
is my desire that as soon as practicable after my death that all
my just dues be collected and all my just debts and funeral expenses be paid out of the same, and the balance whatever it may
be of said money. I give and bequeath to my grandson Abraham
Miller JOHNSON, to him and his heirs forever, but should the
said Abraham Miller JOHNSON die before he arives to the age of
twenty one years, or marry's it is my desire that the aforesaid
legacy go to and be equally divided between my two sons herein
after named. I give and bequeath to my two sons William H. BOYD
and Samuel A. BOYD all the residue and remainder of my estate
real and personal Viz. The tract or parcel of land lying on the
east side of the Quaker branch originally containing sixty nine
and ¼ acres and joining the tract whereon I now live, and by a
late survey the two said original tracts are inclosed in one
platt together with the said tract of land whereon I now live.
And which I have heretofore disposed of by deed of gift to my
aforesaid two sons William H. BOYD and Samuel A. BOYD, which
deed of gift I do not revoke, but give the same to them and
their heirs forever, together with my stock of horses, cattle,
hogs, cows, fodder, wheat, oats, one waggon and gear, plantation
tools, household and kitchen furniture, with every other article
or species of property which I may die pofsed of. I give and
bequeath to my before mentioned two sons to be equally divided
between them and their heirs forever. But should either of the
aforesaid sons die leaving no ifsue, it is my desire in that case
that the portion or property of every description left to the
son so deceased pass into the pofsefsion and be the property of
the surviving son. And lastly, I do constitute and appoint my
aforesaid two sons William H. BOYD and Samuel A. BOYD executors
to this my last will and testament, hereby revoking all other
wills by me at any time heretofore made. In testimony whereof I
have hereunto set my hand and affixed my seal this 25th day July
1842. Signed and C. in presence of us.

her
Isabella X Boyd (L. S.)
mark

Wm. W. Floran
A. Chilles Dendy
Elihu Watson
Recorded in Will Book A, Page 135, Bundle 111, Pkg. 8. Recorded
date not available. Proven date 16th of Dec. 1850. W. D. Watts
Ordy. Laurens District.

WILL OF M. D. PINSON

South Carolina Laurens District. In the name of God, Amen. I
M. D. PINSON of State and District aforesaid, being of sound and

disposing mind and memory, but weak in body, and calling to mind
the uncertainty of life, and being desirous to dispose of all
such worldley estate as it hath pleased God to blefs me with, do
make and ordain this my last will in manner following, that is
to say. First, I desire my body to be buried by my family and
friends in a decent maner, according to the usual custom of the
coutry. Secondley, I desire my whole estate after my death to
be sold on such a credit as my executor may think best with the
following exception. So long as my wife Elizabeth and all my
children can remain together comfortably and sattisfactoriley, I
sett a part the following property for there support, to wit.
Such portion of my plantation together with the homestead as may
be nessarey for that purpose, with the following slaves, Harry,
Sam, Peter, Tom, Milly Lucy, Hanah, and Seleaney, 1 carriage,
three mules and one horse, waggon and harnefs, and plantation
tools, stock sufficent of cattle and hogs, and a sufficiency of
provision for my family for next year, together with all my
household furniture. If my wife and children can not remain together in a pleasant and comfortable situation or where they desire to separate, I wish the aforesaid property to be sold and
divided with a like all the rest of my estate. I wish out of
the sale of my property all my just debts and funeral expences
paid. I give to my wife Elizabeth one childs part all my estate
both real and personal, my eight children to wit, Washington,
Mary, Louisa, Elizabeth, Joseph, Virginia, Martha, and Alpheus.
I desire to all share equal in the division of my property in
equal shares with my wife Elizabeth both of real and personal
estate. And I desire in the event of any of my children dieing
without issue or marryinc in that event that such child or childs
share may be equally divided with all the other children then
living. Lastley, I do constatue and appoint Geo. W. SULLIVAN
executor of this my last will and testament, by me heretofore
made, commenceing one page one and ending on page three. In
testimoney whereof I have hereunto set my hand and affixed my
seal this the 15th day of Octr. 1850. Signed, seal, and published and declared as and for the last will and testament of the
above named M. D. PINSON in the presence of us.

Wm. A. Stone   M. D. Pinson (L. S.)
Jno. Finley Jnr.
    his
M. D. X Pinson
    mark
Ruth C. Madden
Recorded in Will Book A, Page 136, Bdle. 111, Pkge. 9. Proven
and recorded dates not available. W. D. Watts, O. L. D.

WILL OF PETER HAIRSTON

South Carolina Laurens District. In the name of God, Amen. I
Peter HAIRSTON of Laurens District and State aforesaid, being
weak of body, but of sound mind, memory, and understanding praise
be to God for it. And considering the uncertainty of life and

to the end that I may be better prepared to leave the world when
it shall please God to call me hence, do make and declare this
to be my last will and testament in the manner and form following, that is to say. First, I recommend my soul to almighty God
my creator who gave it and my body I desire to be decently intered, and as to such worldly estate as it hath pleased God to
blefs me with, I dispose of the same as follows. In the first
place, I desire all my just debts to be paid as early as practicable. Secondly, I give and bequeath to my beloved wife Sarah
HAIRSTON during her natural life of widowhood all my estate both
real and personal for the use and support of my wife Sarah and
my children. And after the death of my wife Sarah or marriage,
I desire that my property be sold both real and personal and
divided equally between my children, John Speak, Elizabeth Cal-
mes, Sarah Francis, William Peter, and Martha Catharine. Thirdly. Should my wife Sarah deem it best at any time to sell any
part of my personal estate, she may do at public sale, and the
proceeds thereof if not wanted to defray expenses, to be placed
out on interest for the benefit of my estate. And my wife Sarah
may if she thinks proper, as my children arrive of full age, may
make advancement and take their receipt for any money she may
give them, the sums they receive shall be accounted for in the
general settlement of my estate. And lastly, I do nominate,
constitute and appoint my wife Sarah HAIRSTON executrix of this
my last will and testament, hereby revoking and cancelling all
other wills heretofore made by me. In witnefs whereof I have
hereunto set my hand and seal the 20th day of Sept., in the year
of our Lord, one thousand eight hundred and forty four. Signed,
sealed, published, and declared by the above named Peter HAIRSTON
to be his last will and testament. In the presence of us who
have hereunto subscribed our names as witnefses in the presence
of the Testator.

John Whitten   Peter Hairston (L. S.)
John W. Owens
John F. Kern
Recorded in Will Book A, Page 137.   Recorded and proven dates
not available. W. D. Watts, Ordy.   Laurens District.

WILL OF ROBERT TAYLOR

In the name of God, Amen. I Robert TAYLOR of the District of
Lurens and State of South Carolina, being of sound and disposing
mind and memory, but weak in body and calling to mind the uncertainty of life, and being desirous to dispose of all such worldly
estate as it hath pleased God to blefs me with, do make and ordain this my last will in the manner following, that is to say.
I desire that William W. SLOAN be the executor of my estate.
And after my deseas I wish Maragaret to hive mosthy for his and
his hairs, if she his any, if not, after the death of Julius
MARTIN and Margaret his wife, I wish his Marthy and his increase
to return to the neardist hands on his side, and Marthy shall
have Lueasy for his and his heirs. And I wish John to have

Catharine him and his hairs. And I wish James to have Fransis
him and his hairs. And I wish Jane to his Soph for his and his
hairs with the exception of the next child she his is she his
any. If she dus, it goes to William I. TAYLOR of Wm. and his
hairs if he his no hairs at his death it returns to the nearest
hairs in my famaly, and if Soph his any more children then tho
go to Jane. I think that the three negores that the girls gets
is one hundred dollars better then the too the boys gets, and
that I leave them in place of land and thare is a small track of
land of forty acres more or les bounded by land of Robert SLOAN
John TAYLOR, John MOCK, and others. That I wish William I. TAY-
LOR of Wm if he should live to nead it to have if not the land
must be sold to the hiest bedder and the monny to be divided
among the legaleese and then the balance of my property is to be
sold and my just debts paid out of it. And the balance divided
equely among the legatees of this my last will and testament by
me hear to fore made. In testamony where of I have hear unto
set my hand and affixed my seal this third day of April, one
thousand eight hundred and forty three. Signed in the presence
of us.

Taylor Goodwin   Robert Taylor (SEAL)
John Goodwin
James Goodwin
Proven date Sept.26, 1831. W. D. Watts, Ordy. Recorded date
not available. Recorded in Book A, Page 139, Bundle 124, Pkg. 25.

WILL OF WM. GREEN

In the name of God, Amen. I Wm. GREEN of South Carolina Laurens
District, being of sound and disposing mind and memory, blessed
be God do, this 14th of June, in the year of our Lord, one thousand eight hundred and forty seven, make and publish this my
last will and testament in manner following that is to say. 1st.
I give to my daughter Gilly A. PASLAY five dollars to be paid
to her by my executor at the death of my beloved wife Francis.
2nd. I want all the rest of my children namely; Nancy SIMMS, N.
A. GREEN, E. B. GREEN, J. F. GREEN, Wm. W. GREEN, Washington
GREEN, S. R. GREEN, S. C. GREEN, to be made equal in every respect, that is to say, in education and horses, and saddles. It
is also my wish that all my estate both personal and real should
remain in possession of my beloved wife Francis GREEN during her
life or remains my widow with the exception of so much of my
estate that can be best spared to be sold by my executors in
thirty days after my death sufficient to pay all my just debts
ballance of my estate personal and real to remain in possession
of my beloved wife during her life or remains my widow. If she
should marry then to be sold by my executors and equally divided
between my wife Francis GREEN and her children above named. I
want my wife or executor when any of her above named children
should marry or become of age to have any part of property that
can be spared to them at valuation and a record kept of the same
so as to make a fair and equal distribution between all of my

Francis GREEN's children. I appoint no executor to this my last will and testament. This I do ordain to be my last will and testament whereof I have hereunto set my hand and seal, the year and date above written. Signed, sealed, and published by the testator as his last will and testament in the presence of the witnesses who were present as the signing and sealing thereof.

Wm. C. Nickles   Wm. Green (LS)
Willis Dendy
Benjamin M. Wells
Recorded in Will Book A, Page 140. Original will not in files of Probate Judge. W. D. Watts, O. L. D. Proven and recorded dates not available.

WILL OF ELIZABETH S. HITT

In the name of God, Amen. I Elizabeth S. HITT calling to mind the uncertainty of life, that it is appointed once for all to die, being of sound and disposing mind, and being disirous of disposing of all such worldly estate as it hath pleased God to blefs me with, do make and ordain this my last will in manner following: (VIZ) 1st. I resign my soul to God who gave it and my body to the dust from whence it came. 2nd. It my will and desire immediately after my death that my hereinafter named executor, do sell all of my estate both real and personal, consisting of lands, negros and horses, and all property of any kind as accumulated by me since the death of my husband. 3rd. It is my desire that my executor dispose of my clothes by distributing of them amongst my several son's wives. 4th. I will a devise out of the monies arising out of the sales of my estate, that all my just debts be paid, the residue or ballance of the monies to be equally divided, share and share about between my sons Jesse, William, Henry, Benjamin, Martin, and their children. 5th. And lastly, I do constitute and appoint my son William my sole executor of this my last will and testament, revoking all others by me heretofore made, this eighteenth day of June, 1844. Signed, sealed, and published as my last will in presence of.
                                                        her
J. W. H. Johnson   Elizabeth X Hitt (L. S.)
John R. Spearman   mark
H. N. Carter
Recorded in Will Book A, Page 141. Recorded and proven dates not available. W. D. Watts, Ordy. Laurens District. Original will not in files of Probate.

WILL OF HUGH SAXON

In the name of God, Amen. I Hugh SAXON of the District of Laurens and State of South Carolina, being infirm of body, but of sound mind and considering the uncertainties of life, do make and ordain this my last will and testament. First. I give my soul to God, who gave it and my body to the earth from whence it came. Second. I desire that all my just debts and funeral expenses be paid out of the proceeds of the sales of my property. Item, I give to my sister Susan W. THRUSTON one thousand dollars. 2nd. I give to Capt. Samuel BARKSDALE one thousand dollars in trust for the sole benefit of my sister Mary during her life, and after her death equally divided among her children. 3rd. I give to my nephew Hugh SAXON son of Saml. SAXON deceased a good horse saddle, and bridle worth one hundred dollars. 5th. I give to my name sake Hugh SAXON LEWERS a horse, saddle, and bridle worth one hundred dollars. 6th. I give to Mrs. Oney STONE two good milch cows. 7th. To my niece Ruth ARNOLD, I give my buggy and harnefs and five hundred dollars in money. Item 8th. To Hugh SAXON FARLEY son of Wm. R. FARLEY, Esqr. I give a horse, saddle, and briddle worth one hundred dollars. 9th. I desire that the thirteen negroes I received of the estate of Polly HARRIS decd. to wit; Charles and Martha, Hannah, Biddy, Emma, Tom, Eliza and her children, Ben, Louisa, Aury, Anice, Sally and Eliza Ann to be sold as much in families and nighbourhoods as possible, to prevent too great separation, and the proceeds of the sale of these negroes I wish to be applied as follows. First, In refunding to my estate all the moneys I have paid out for the support of Jno. L. HARRIS, Sally HARRIS, and the negores named above, to be found in notes and interest made in my books of accounts. I also desire my executors to pay adebt due by Jno. L. HARRIS and Polly HARRIS decd, to Abner BABB, but now transfered to Capt. Johnathan (Illegeable) and some sents as may be found in my privates a c. book. Also I desire that the debts due by the aforesaid Jno. L. HARRIS and Polly HARRIS, decd. to Dr. Jno. C. SULLIVAN, Joseph SULLIVAN, Geo. W. CANNERS, Wm. FRANKS, Jno. BOLT, esqr., Wm. SIMPSON, and Edward GARRETT, agent of the estate of Stephen GARRETT decd., be paid and should there be any funds left after paying these debts, I desire it to be equally divided between Monima BROOKS, Matilda LITTLE, and Nancy PARKS, these being the children of my Aunt Cynthia WILLIAMS decd. And also Mefs Frances ALLEN and Lucy ARNOLD the childre of my uncle Lyddall ALLEN decd., and also Susan W. THRUSTON, Clarissa DOWNS, and Polly ARNOLD all to share and share alike of the Harris' estate. The ballance of my estate real and personal, I wish to be sold at a convenient day to suit my executors and the proceeds of said sale to be distributed as follows, that is to say. To each of my surviving brothers and sisters share and share alike. And to the surviving children of my deceased brothers and sisters I give the part which their deceased parents should have received had they been living, to be equally divided among the children of such deceased parents. And lastly, I wish my executors to return to my mother her sideboard and my bureau which I give to her. And I would willingly make her one of my legatees, but that it would only be an encumberance to her in her infirm state, but in lieu, I give her all the love and affection of a devoted son. I do hereby constitute and appoint my brother Joshua SAXON and my friend Willis WALLACE my executors to this my last will and testament. In testimony whereof I have hereunto set my hand and affixed my seal this the eleventh day of November, one thousand eight hundred and fifty one. Signed, sealed, published, and declared as the last will and testament of the above named Hugh SAXON in the presence of us who signed in the presence of the testor and in presence of each other.

Geo. W. Canners   H. Saxon (L. S.)
N. Barksdale
Jerimiah Glenn
Recorded in Will Book A, Page 142. Recorded and proven dates not available. W. D. Watts, Ordy. Laurens District. Original will not in files of Probate.

CODICIL

Whereas I, H. SAXON did on yesterday, duly make and constitute the above as my last will and testament, I do hereby further declare and publish this Codicil to the same to have all the force and effect of the said will and testament. In the foregoing will I desire that wherever I have given property to Mary ARNOLD it is my express will and intention that it be conveyed. And I do hereby convey the same to Saml. BARKSDALE in trust for the sole use and benefit of the said Mary ARNOLD during her life. And at her death to be equally divided between her children. I give to my niece Mary SULLIVAN wife of Henry W. SULLIVAN, of Charleston, the sum of five hundred dollars. Signed, sealed, published, and declared by the said H. SAXON as and for a Codicil to be annexed to his last will and testament to be taken as part thereof in presence of us this 12th Novr., 1851.

G. W. Conners   H. Saxon (L. S.)
N. Barksdale
J. Glenn

WILL OF SAMPSON BABB

South Carolina Laurens District. In the name of God, Amen. I Sampson BABB of the District and State aforesaid, being sound, disposing mind, memory, and understanding, do make and ordain my last will and testament in manner and form following, to wit. 1st. I give and bequeath to my son Alston the home tract of land on which I reside on all thereof that his on the north side of the Big Branch, but not to include the part which I bought from Abner, supposed to contain about one hundred and fifty acres. And I further will and direct that my said son Alston shall receive out of the ballance of my estate an amount sufficient to make his share equal to what I have given to my other children beside the said land, to have and to hold the same, his heirs and afsigns forever. 2nd. I give and bequeath to the children of my daughter Polly Ann who married William BOYCE six hundred dollars to have and to hold the same their heirs and afsigns forever, share and share alike. 3rd. I give and bequeath to William BOYCE fifty dollars. 4th. The ballance of my estate both real and personal I will and direct to be equally divided among the whole of my children now living share and share alike to have and to hold, the same their heir forever. 5th. I appoint Martin BABB, Sampson BABB, and Alston BABB, three of my sons executors to this my last will and testament. Witness my hand and seal this 3, Oct., 1847. Signed, sealed, published, and declared in presence of. Test:

his

John Woods   Sampson X B Babb (L. S.)
Hosea Mahaffy   mark
Thomas A. Paden
Recorded in Will Book A, Page 145. Recorded date and proven date not available. W. D. Watts, Ordy, Laurens District.

WILL OF DUKE GOODMAN

South Carolina Laurens District. In the name of God, Amen. I Duke GOODMAN of said state and district, being of sound and disposing mind, do make and ordain this my last will and testament. First, I direct my executor herein after named pay all my just debts and funeral expenses out of my estate and put up suitable head and foot stones to my grave and the graves of my father, mother, brother Bluford, and sister Sally GOODMAN, and all my other brothers and sister heretofore dead, and to pay for the same out of my estate. I then give to Willis WALLACE in trust for the use of my sister Kitty GOODMAN one negro girl named Sarah the daughter of Willy and five hundred dollars in cash with power to invest the money in land or negros as the and the Cistiquea Trust may think best or put the same to int and the int annualy to the said Kitty GOODMAN. And at the death of the said Kitty GOODMAN, I give the same equally amongst her children, but should she die without having a child or children or the child or children of a deceased child, then I direct the same or the remainder thereof to go in equal portions to the children of my sister Rebecca WILLIS the wife of Humphrey WILLS or their children the child or children of a decd. child taking the share their parent would be entitled to if living. All the rest and residue of my estate which I may die possed of real or personal I direct to be sold by executor and the proceed thereof equally divided between the children of sister Rebecca WILLS the child or children of a and child taking the sahre amongst them that their parent would have been entitled to if living. This clause to include money and notes, bonds and C. which are owing to me at my death. Witnefs my hand and seal 25th day of Oct., 1851. In presence of.

Jas. Parks   Duke Goodman (SEAL)
J. J. Atwood
W. D. Watts
Recorded in Will Book A, Page 147, Bundle 113, Pkge. 14. Recorded and Proven dates not availabe. W. D. Watts, Ordy, Laurens District.

WILL OF JOHN FINLEY

In the name of God, Amen. I John FINLEY Senr. of the State of South Carolina Laurens District, being of sound and disposing

125

mind and memory, and knowing that it is appointed unto all men to
die, and not knowing how soon I may be called, and being desirous
to dispose of all such worldly estate as it hath pleased God to
blefs me with, do ordain, make and institute this my last will
and testament, revoking all others hitherto made. First. I bequeath my soul to God, who gave it to me and my body to the dust
from whence it sprand, to be burried in a desent and christian
like manner. After paying all my just debts and funeral expences
I give, demise, and dispon of my property in the following manner
that is to say. I lend to my beloved wife, Polly FINLEY my homestead tract of land whereon I now live, and also all my personal
estate, except what it may take to pay all of my just debts, during her natural lifetime. I wish such things sold to pay my
debts as my wife, Polly FINLEY may think she can spare best. I
give to my son, James FINLEY and the heirs of his body, after
the death of my wife, Polly FINLEY, my homestead tract of land
whereon I now live. I give to my little grand daughter, Mary
Francis FINLEY daughter of my son Hampton FINLEY, two thousand
dollars, to be paid her by my executors, hereinafter named, when
she become of age or married, provided she live to have an ifsne.
If other wise the above amount of two thousand dollars to be
thrown back to my estate, except five hundred dollars which
amount of five hundred dollars, in case of the death of my little
gran daughter Mary Frances FINLEY. I give to her mother Susan
FINLEY, wife of Hampton FINLEY, I have advanced to my daughter
Elizabeth COLEMAN, wife of Larkin COLEMAN, one negro girl. I
charge Larkin COLEMAN for board and schooling of his and my
daughter Elizabeth three children six hundred and fifty dollars,
which amount I give to my grand children, VIZ., Sarah Frances
TYLER, James F. COLEMAN, and Nancy Elizabeth COLEMAN to be equally divided between them. I wish at the death of my wife Polly
FINLEY, the whole of my estate, both real and personal except
what is willed as above to be sold and equally divided between
my son James FINLEY, Margaret MILLER, Jane WALKER, James F. COLE-
MAN, Sarah Frances TYLER, and Nancy Elizabeth COLEMAN are to
have one share divided among them the share that their mother
would have had, and Mary Frances FINLEY is to have an equal share
with my own children. And lastly, I do hereby constitute and appoint my son James FINLEY my executor to this my last will and
testament, by me hereunto made. In case my son James FINLEY
should ie, in that event I then hereby constitute and appoint
Albert MILLER, Azaniah WALKER and James F. COLEMAN executors to
this my last will andtestament, by me hereunto made. In testimony whereof I have hereunto set my hand affixed my seal this
20th Feb., one thousand eight hundred and fifty one. Signed,
sealed, and published and declared as and for the last will and
testament of the above named John FINLEY sen. In presence of.

John Wharton   John Finley Senr. (L. S.)
     his
Moses X Griffin
    mark
J. H. Coleman
Continued on page 127
                              126

Continued from page 126
Recorded in Will Book A, Page 148, Bundle 113, Pkg. 4. Recorded
date not available. Proven date 30th August, 1852. W. D. Watts
Ordy, Laurens District.

WILL OF DAVID LITTLE

South Carolina Laurens District. In the name of God, Amen. I
David LITTLE, of the St. and Dist. above written, being weak in
body, but of sound mind, memory, and understanding, do make this
my last will and testament in manner and form following (VIZ).
First. I give and bequeath unto my wife Sarah LITTLE all my
property of every discription to have and to hold the same to-
gehter with its increase during her natural life. In the event
of her death or marriage, then I desire the whole of my property
sold and divided as follows. Viz: I desire my son George Fran-
ick LITTLE to be made equal with her other children had by John.
Then the residue to be equally divided between all her children
share and share alike. I do hereby nomenate and constitute and
appoint Dr. J. F. DORROH my executor to this will and do hereby
revoke all others by me made. Given under my hand and seal this
23rd day of July, 1850. Signed in presence of us.

W. D. Byrd   David Little (LS)
E. C. Simpson
J. L. Williams
I, J. F. DORROH do hereby relinquish the trust given to me by
the above instrument 13, March, 1852. Witnefs my hand and seal.

                                John F. Dorroh (LS)
Recorded in Will Book A, Page 151, Bdl. 115, Pkge. 8. Proven
and recorded dates not available. W. D. Watts, O. L. D.

WILL OF JOHN GRANT

South Carolina, Laurens Dist, July 24, 1852. I John GRANT, im-
prefsed with the shortnefs of life, and the certainty of death,
on this the twenty fourth day of July, eighteen hundred and fifty two, being in pofsesion of my usual strength of my mind, do
make this my last will and testament. First. I will that all
of my just debts and funeral expenses be paid out of my estate
by my executrix. Second. I will and bequeath to my wife, Mildred, all of my estate consisting of three negroes; Jane, Amy,
and Sob, together with my other pofsefsions to be at her disposal during her widowhood. And if she should marry to have and
retain one third of the property in her pofsefsion at the time
of her marriage, during her life. And I also will to my son,
Milton, the two thirds remaining at her marriage and also the
remaining third at my wife Mildred's death. I also will that if
my son Milton should die without heirs, that the daughters of
Robert WHITEFORD shall fall heirs to my son's part of my estate.
Signed, this 24th July, 1852, in the presence of these witnefses.
Test.

Continued on page 128

Continued from page 127
Henry Whitmire   John Grant (L. S.)
G. D. Smith
Wm. S. Shell
Recorded in Will Book A, Page 151. Recorded date and proven
date not available.

                    WILL OF PATRICK TODD

South Carolina Laurens District. In the name of God, Amen. I
Patrick TODD Senr. of the State and District aforesaid, being of
sound and disposing mind and memory, but calling to mind the uncertainty of life, and being desirous of making a distribution
of such worldly estate as it has pleased Hevin to blefs me with
in this life, do make and ordain this my last will and testament
in the manner following (revoking all others heretofore made).
(viz). First, I loan to my beloved wife Jane TODD during her
natural life, the following property (to wit) all of that portion of my homestead tract of land laying on the No East side of
the big road leading from Springgrow to James C. VAUGHAMS and to
John CHAPPELLS bridge, containing near about three hundred acres
also a tract of eight acres of land I purchased of Charles SNOW
laying on the So. We. side of said big publick road, opposite and
joines the above tract of three hundred acres, on which includes
all of the buildings on that side near said big road, and is
bounded by lands of Drury SCURCY, James C. VAUGHAM, Wesley SMITH
and my other lands not yet disposed of, and which lays on the
same side of said big road, that the above eight acres does,
also nine negroes, Fanny and eight of her children, Jim, Mat,
Ester, Martha, Fanny, Aaron, Anny, and Charles, and the future
issue and increase of the said females and as much of my household furniture and provision and stock of all kinds as she may
wish or thinks she may need. Should my wife at any time conclude, that she had rather, my executors here in after named,
would sell the foregoing tract or tracts of land, loaned to her
and purchefs another tract for my estate to be loaned to her in
the same manner as the one in the fore part of this clause.
Then and in that case, I direct them to do so, that is, to sell
the one willed her and purchefs any other she may wish or select
provided it can, in the judgement of my executors be purchased
upon reasonable terms and as a price not more than they can sell
the one loaned her. At the death of my wife, my will and desire
is that all of the foregoing property loaned her, during her
natural life time remaining; shall revert back to my estate and
be sold by my executors as early as practable, and after paying
her funeral expences and just debts, such as she ought to contract, the ballance to be divided in seven equal parts, between
my five sons, Archa, John, William, Andrew, and Dct. Patrick
TODD, and my daughter Jane MCCALL and the children of my decd.
daughter Ellen M. MCFALL. Should any of my children die before
the division takes place, then my will and desire is for the
children of any ded. child taking amongst themselves such part
as their parent if living would have ben entitled to, when the
foregoing lands loaned to my wife is sold. I wish my executors

                              128

to reserve one half acre around my family grave yard. Secondly I will in trust to my executors for the benefit of my son James TODD and his children, a tract of land where on he now lives, containing fourty two acres more or lefs, and bounded by lands of Abranham HOLLINGSWORTH, Henry MILLER, and John P. WATTS. And six hundred dollars in cash, to be paid out of the proceeds of the sale of that portion of my estate hereafter directed to be sold at my death by my executors. If my son James TODD wishes and my executors think prudent or best, I direct them to purchefs a negro girl, with a portion or with the whole of the six hundred dollars, and for to hold her intrust for the special benafit of my son James TODD and his children. Other wise I direct my executors to pay our annually the lawfull interest on the six hundred dollars to my son James TODD for the special benafit of himself and children, and nothing more unlefs in there judgment thear be an actual necefsaty for them to pay more. Then in that case, I will leave it to there judgement. Should they purchefs a negro girl and there be any money left, I direct my executors to pay it on to my son James TODD, as they might think best, for his interest and the benafit of his children. I give the tract of land of fourty two acres and the six hundred dollars to my executors intrust for my son James TODD in lus of the whole of his interest in my real or in my personal estate, for the benafit of himself and his children forever. Thirdly. I will and desire that my executors do sell as early as practable after my death, the whole of the ballance of my estate both real and personal not heretofore disposed of. And after paying my funeral expenses, and just debts, pay to Mifs Caroline REED, two hundred dollars in cash. The ballance after paying the foregoing bequeaths, Just debts and funeral expences, I wish and direct to be devided in seven equal parts, between my five sons Archa, John William, Andrew, and Doct. Patrick TODD, and my daughter Jane MCCALL and the children of my decd. daughter Ellender M. MCFALL. The child or children of any of my decd. children taking amongst themselves such part of my estate as their parent would be intitled to if living. Fourthly. Should my wife at any time, conclude to give up to my executors any portion of the property loaned to her, I wish and direct them to sell the same and devide the next proced, in seven equal parts as are directed in the first and third clause of this my last will and testament. Fifthly. Should my son John TODD die before my death, or die without a will, then it is my wish that that portion of my estate wiled to him, be equally divided between his two children, his daughter Martha WINN, and his son Patrick TODD the child of the woman he now lives with. Should Patrick die before he arives to the age of twenty one years, then my wish is for his half sister Martha WINN to receive his portion or in o er words the whole of that portion of my estate his father John TODD would be entitled to if living. Lastly. I do hereby nominate, constitute, and appoint my friend John D. WILLIAMS and my son Doct. Patrick TODD, my sole executors of this my last will and testament, revoking all others, hereby giving them all power and authorty. And I do hereby acknowledge this and no other to be my last will and testemony whereof I have hereunto set my hand and affixed my seal this (Anno Domine) the fifteen June, 1852. Witnefs my hand and seal and in the presence of Wesley SMITH

Westley Smith   Patrick TODD (SEAL)
Franis Hill
John H. Goodman
Recorded in Book A, Page 151, Bundle 115, Package 5. Recorded date not available. Proven date Dec. 11, 1852. W. D. Watts Ordy.

WILL OF WILLIS CHEEK

In the name of God, Amen. I Willis CHEEK being of sound mind and memory, and of tolerable good health, but knowing that it is appointed for all men to die, and being desireous to dispose of my worldly goods which it hath been please God to give me, do make this as my last will and testament. First. I give and bequeath to my beloved wife, Eliza CHEEK, one negro man named Zack and his wife named Treecy, together with all their children, being four with all their increase from this time, together with my house and furniture, both household and kitchen, and all my plantation tools, and farming implements, with horses sufficient for tending a farm, together with all my stock of cattle of every description, or so much as she sees proper to keep, with a decent support for one year, or until she has time to make support. And two hundred acres of land to be so laid out us to include the house, during her natural life or widowhood, but if she should marry my will is that the above property should be sold, at public sale and be equally divided between her and her two children, James Wm. CHEEK, and Willis Abram CHEEK, and as to my first wife, Jemima CHEEK's children, Viz: Randal CHEEK, Anna GARRETT, Silas CHEEK, Autsin CHEEK, Rebecca HAMMONDS, Levi RIDDLE, and Ellis CHEEK, I have portioned them all off and debar them from ever receiving any more of my estate, except Rebecca HAMMONDS children, 4 which I give five dollars a piece, and I give my daughter Levi RIDDLE, the tract of land where she now lives, number of acres not remembered during her natural life. Then to return to my estate. The ballance of my whole estate, whether of land or negroes, or whatsoever it may consist, I give and bequeath to my two sons, James William CHEEK and Willia Abram CHEEK, to be equally divided share and share alike. And further, I recommend my soul into the hands of almight God, who gave it me, and my body to the earth from whence it was taken, neatly to be interred at the expense of my executor. And lastly I constitute, nominate, and appoint my friend William M. DOROUGH my sole executor to execute and carrythis (illegeable) belonging to my estate, should become refractory and unmanageable, to expose them to public sale for the use of my said two sons, Viz: J. Wm. and W. Abram. And I do acknowledge this to be my last will and testament. In witnefs I have hereunto set my hand and affixed my seal, this 7th day of November, one thousand eight hundred and forty five. Signed, sealed, and acknowledged as the last will of Willis CHEEK, in presence of us.

Continued on page 131

Continued from page 130
Joseph Sullivan   Willis Cheek (LS)
Hasting Johnson
Andrew McKnight
Recorded in Will Book A, Page 154. Original will not in files
of Probate Judge. Proven and recorded dates not available. W. D.
Watts, O. L. D.

CODICIL

I, Willis CHEEK, of Laurens District, and State of South Carolina
having made and executed my last will, bearing date the 7th November, 1845, do make the following Codicil, and make the same a
part of my said will, that is to say. The land which I have
given to my daughter, Levi RIDDLE, during her life, I hereby give
to Wm. M. DORROH, in trust for the use of my said daughter, during her life. And at her death I direct my executor to sell the
same, and divide the proceeds thereof between my two sons J. W.
and W. A. CHEEK equally between them. And further, the property
willed to my two sons, J. W. and W. A. CHEEK, I direct shall not
be sold, but to be put in two lots and valued by three disinterested men, and made equal. And should they not be of age,
the whole to be kept together and worked in common until they
shall arrive at age. And the lands which I have purchased since
the execution of my aforesaid will, I direct shall also go to
my two sons, in the same way as the other property willed to
them and all monies, notes, and other securities for money. I
give also to my said two sons equally between them. Witnefs
whereof I have hereunto set my hand and seal, this the 1st day
of March, A. D., 1851. In presence of.

Andrew McKnight   Willis Cheek (LS)
Barrington Avary
T. J. Mahon

WILL OF ELISHA WILLIAMSON

In the name of God, Amen. I Elisha WILLIAMSON of the State of
South Carolina Laurens District, being of sound disposing mind
memory and understanding, but weak in body and knowing the uncertainty of life, and being desirous of disposing of all such
worldly estate as it hath pleased God to bless me with, do make
and ordain thismy last will and testament in manner following,
to wit. 1. I will my body to the ground from whence it came an
and my soul to God who gave it. 2. I desire after my death
that my body be decently buried and my funeral expenses and all
my just debts be paid out of my personal property. 3. I devise
give and bequeath to my wife Elmina WILLIAMSON, a tract of land
where on I now live embracing my dwelling and all my houses,
containing two hundred acres more or less beginning at a red oak
corner on the Tumbling Shcal Road running with said road until
it intersects the Aususta Road at a State corner, thence S. 56
W. 19c to a State corner, thence S. 16, W. 20c to a post oak,
thence S. 45 W. 6c tc a Black gum, thence S. 45E8. 35 to an Ash
thence S66.E 13.50 tc a State thence S 82. E 10.75 to a Blk Oak
thence S 4.64 to a State thence S 75. E45 to a State thence N15.

E19.75 to a State in the fork of the branches, thence to the beginning corner to have and to hold the said land during her natural life. 4. I devise, give and bequeath to my wife Elmina
the following property to wit four slaves (viz) Rose and child
Elliek, Valentine and Emiline, with their future increase. Also
all my household and kitchen furniture, plantation tools, black
smith tools, Blacksmith bookes, my waggon and gear, my carry all
and harness, one Rone horse, two mules, one is a black roan, the
other a sorrel, one half of my stock of hogs, half of my stock
of cattle, all my sheep, the whole crop made on my plantation
the year of my death, and three hundred dollars in money. This
I give to my wife absolutely and forever. 5. I devise, give
and bequeath to my daughter Essey BROWN and her children one
hundred acres of land where on she now lives, this land I price
at five dollars per acre, my daughter Essey must account for
this land in the division of the other property the land is
platted and nee (illegeable). 6. The balance of my land belonging to the tract where on I live, after the two hundred acres
which I have given to my wife is taken off. I devise wish and
desire to remain unsold until my grandson Elisha WILLIAMSON who
is now a minor becomes twenty one years old, my wife controlling
it and apying the taxes for it until my grand son becomes of age.
Then I desire the land to be devided into two tracts and sold
and the proceeds equally divided between my daughter Clarrissa
LOVELASS my grand son Elisha WILLIAMSON, and the children of my
daughter Essey BROWN, that is, her children is to have one third.
7. I devise, give, and bequeath to my grand daughter Elizabeth
L. ARNOLD one hundred dollars in money to come out of the proceeds of my personal property. 8. I devise and leave with my
wife Elmina, four negroes (Viz) Hannah, Armstead, Felina, and
Hendrick, that if she my said wife, should have a living child
by me. Then I devise and give to that child the last named four
negroes, and the land that I have willed to my wife, after death
to be the childs, absolutely and forever. And if my wife Elmina
should not have a living child by me, then I devise wish and desire that my wife shall keep the last named four negroes, upon
condition that she pays to my two grand sons (Viz) Elisha WILLIAM-
SON and John LOVELASS, each the sum of six hundred dollars. I a
also wish and desire that if my wife should not have a living
child by me, that after death the tract of land which I have giv-
en to her be sold and the proceeds equally divided between Clarrissa LOVELASS my daughter, Elisha WILLIAMSON my grand son, and
the children of my daughter Essey BROWN. 9. I devise, will and
direct that the following negroes be sold, to wit, Frank, Charity
Squire, Annis, Mariah, and her children, with every other article
of property belonging to my estate either real or personal of
whatever nature or qulity it may be, that is not herein before
porticularly disposed of and after all my just debts is paid.
And three hundred dollars which I have given to my grand daughter
Elizabeth L. ARNOLD is paid. The balance I desire to be equally
divided between my daughter Clarrissa LOVELASS my grand son
Elisha WILLIAMSON and the children of my daughter Essey BROWN.
She first accounting for the land that I have given to her and

her children. And I give the same to them and their children, executors, administrators and assigns forever. Furthermore that this my last will and testament may be fully unterstood, I will go into a detail and recapitulation. 1. It is understood that I have in the 3 article of this my last will devised given and bequeathed to my wife Elmina two hundred acres of land as there in described, to have and to hold the same during her natural life. And in the 4 article I have given and bequeathed to my wife Elmina four negroes, to wit, Rose and her child Elleck, Valentine, and Emaline, with their future increase, all my house hold and kitchen furniture, plantation tools, Black smith tools, Blacksmith books, my waggon and gear, my carry all and harness, one Rone horse, two mules, one half of my stock of hogs, half my stock of cattle, and all my stock of sheep, and the crop made on my plantation the year of my death, and three hundred dollars in money absolutely and forever. And in the 5, I have given and bequeathed to my daughter Essey BROWN and her children one hundred acres of land, she is to account for the same in division of other property. And in the 6, I have devised and directed that the balance of my land remain unsold until my grand son Elish WILLIAMSON comes of age, then the land to be divided into two tracts,a and sold and the proceeds equally divided between my daughter Clarrissa LOVELASS, my grand son Elisha WILLIAMSON, and the children of my daughter Essey BROWN, them and their mother accounting for the land I have given to them. And in the 7th clause, I have given and bequeathed to my grand daughter Elizabeth L. ARNOLD, one hundred dollars in money to be paid out of the proceeds of my personal property. And in the 8 clause, I have devised and left with my wife four negroes (viz) Hannah, Armstead, Pelina and Hendrick, and if she my said wife should have a living child by me, then the four last named negroes and the land that I have given to my wife, I have devised and given to that child absolutely and forever. And if my wife should not have a living child by me, then I have devised and desired that my wife shall keep the four last named negroes upon condition she pays to my grand sons Elisha WILLIAMSON and John LOVELASS, each the sum of six hundred dollars. I also devise and desire taht if my wife should not have a living child by me, that after her death the land that I have given to her be sold and the proceeds equally divided between my daughter Clarrissa LOVELASS my grand son Elisha WILLIAMSON and the children of my daughter Essey BROWN. And in the 9th clause I have directed that certain negroes there in named and all other property that is not particularly disposed of be sold, and after all my just debts and the three hundred dollars which I have given to my wife, and the one hundred which I have given to my grand daughter Elizabeth L. ARNOLD is paid. The balance to be equally divided between my daughter Clarrissa LOVELASS, my grand son Elisha WILLIAMSON, and my daughter Essey BROWN's children, that is they have one share her and there accounting for the land therein named. And I have and do give the same to them and their children for ever. 10. And lastly, I do constitute and appoint my wife Elmina executrix of this my last will andtestament by me heretofore made. In witness whereof I have here unto set my hand and seal this the 7th day of August, in the year of our Lord, one thousand eight hundred and fifty one. Signed, sealed, published, and declared as for the last will and testament of the here in named Elisha WILLIAMSON in his presence and in the presence of each of us, who have subscribed our names as witnesses to the same.

R. L. Stephens   E. Williamson (SEAL)
John K. Suson
Charles Murphy
Recorded in Will Book A, Page 156, Bdle, 120, Pkge. 17. Proven date May 23, 1853. Recorded date not available. W. D. Watts, Ordy, Laurens District.

WILL OF JOHN FELTS

South Carolina Laurens District. In the name of God, Amen. I John FELTS, Senr. of the aforesaid State and District, being of sound and disposing mind and memory, but weak in body and calling to mind, the uncertainty of life, and being desirous of disposing all such worldly estate as it has pleased God to blefs me with, do make and ordain this my last will and testament in manner following, viz. It is my will and desire, that I may be buried in a decent christian like manner, and that my exeuctors, hereinafter appointed shall as early as convenient pay off all my just debts and funeral expenses, out of any monies they have at command, belonging to my estate. I give to my daughter, Mary J. FINLEY, one negro woman Rachael and Patty, and one boy, Wade, together with future increase of the female slaves, to her and her heirs forever. I give unto my son John A. FELTS, one negro man, Moses, one negro woman, Mariah, and her two female children Susan and Carolina, one good beadstead, and furniture, the bay Filley that he now claims, and one thousand dollars in cash, when collected together with the future increase of the said female slaves, to him and his heirs forever. I give to my beloved wife Mary FELTS, one negro woman, Jinney and her two female children, one girl Sarah Dinah and a negro man Anthony, two cows and calves, two sows and pigs, two bed steads, and furniture, all of her own choosing, all the fowls of the yard consisting of turkey, geese, and hens, and two hundred and fifty dollars to purchase provisions for the first year, one buggy and harnefs, and also two thousand dollars to afsist in purchasing a place for her and my son, John A. FELTS, to live on together with the future increase of said female slaves, to her and her heirs forever. I give to William H. HOULDITCH and John F. HOULDITCH, children of my deceased daughter Susanah HOULDITCH, fifteen hundred dollars to be divided equally between them, when they arrive to the age of twenty one years, but should either of them die before that time, leaving no child or children, then the survivor to receive the distributive share of his deceased brother, But should there be a child, or children left, the child or children so left, shall be entitled to and receive the distributive share the parent would have been entitled to if living. The amount willed to

134

the said Will H. and John F. HOULDITCH, to remain in the hands of my executors until they arrive at age, then to be paid over to them or their heirs with lawful interest. Should, however, the said William H. and John F. HOULDITCH die before they arive to the age of twenty one years, leaving no child or children, the amount willed to them to revert back to my estate, and be equally divided between my wife, Mary FELTS, John A. FELTS, and Mary J. FINLEY, to them and their heirs forever. It is further my will and desire that all my estate both real and personal not herein before disposed of shall be sold at public outcry, by my executors, the real estate on a credit of one and two years, interest from date, the personal property on a credit of one year. And out of the monies arising from said sales, all the above bequests to be paid, the ballance to be equally divided between my wife, Mary FELTS, John A. FELTS, and Mary J. FINLEY, to them and their heirs forever. Lastly, I do hereby constitute and appoint my son in law William T. FINLEY, and my son John A. FELTS, executors of this my last will and testament, hereby revoking all other and former wills by me heretofore made. In witnefs, I have hereunto set my hand and seal, this 11th day of December, 1852.

Alsey Fuller   John Felts (LS)
James F. Coleman
        his
Mathew X Bryson
        mark
Recorded in Will Book A, Original Will not in files of Probate Judge. W. D. Watts, O. L. D. Proven and recorded dates not available.

WILL OF JESSEE GARRETT

State of South Carolina Lurens District. In the name of God, Am Amen. I Jefse GARRETT Senr., being of sond and disposing mind and memory, but calling to mind the uncertainty of life and being desirous of making a distribution of such worldly estate as I may have been blefsed with in this life, do make and ordain this my last will and testament as follows. I give and bequeath unto my wife Elizabeth GARRETT, during her natural life and at her death to be sold by my executors here in after named and the money to be disposed of as as I shall herein after direct, the following real and personal estate to wit. The tract of land where on I now live containing two hundred acres more or lefs adjoining lands on Dr. Hugh SAXON the widow GOODJIONS, William LENDLEY, and others, Sam and his wife Hannah, Sarah and her son Henry, Elizabeth and Isaac, together with all my household and kitchen furniture or as much as she may want. I direct further more that upon the death of my said wife Elizabeth all the above mentioned property both real and personal be sold by my executors herein after named and the proceeds of said sale be divided unto seven parts on shares. And that one share be paid to my son John GARRETT to him and his heirs forever. And that one share b be paid to my son Thomas H. GARRETT to him and his heirs forever. And that one share be paid to my son Edward H. GARRETT to him and his heirs forever. And that one share be paid to my son Jefse GARRETT to him and his heirs forever. And that one share to paid to my daughter Polly COOK to her and her heirs forever. And that one share be paid to the children of my deceased daughter Fanny MARTIN to them and their heirs forever. And that one share be paid to my daughter Betsey ASHLEY to her and her heirs forever. I also give and bequeath to my sons Thos. GARRETT and Jefse GARRETT in trust for the use and benefit of my son Stephen GARRETT the tract of land on which he the said Stephen GARRETT now lives containing one hundred acres more or lefs, during his life time and at his death the same to belong to his wife Polly during her natural life. If she should be the longest surviven and at their death the said tract of land to be sold by my executors herein after (illegeable). forever. I also give and bequeath to the said Thoams GARRETT and Jefse GARRETT in trust for the use and benefit of my son Stephen GARRETT and his wife Polly during their life, a negro man named Alexandria and at their death the said negro to be sold and the money divided equally among heirs by my executors. I consider that that makes Stephen equal with the rest of my children. I hereby direct my executors to sell a negro girl Marildar and divide the proceeds of the sale among the children of my deceased daughter Fanny MARTIN to be paid to them as they arrive to alwful age or marry. I also will and bequeath unto my son William H. GARRETT the notes which I hold on him which I consider will make him equal with the rest of my children. I further more direct my executors to sell a negro man named Martin together with all the remainder of my property not herein specially disposed of on a reasonable credit after my death and that the proceeds of siad sale after payment of my just debts and funeral expences be divided and paid out precisely in the same manner as is directed for the property herein before directed to be sold at my death with this exception that my wife must first take a third part of the proceeds of said sale. And after her death to make the same disposition of her portion an her thirds as is done with the forgiving named property. Lastly, I nominate, constitute, and appoint my sons Thos. GARRETT and Jefse GARRETT executors of this my last will and testament. Signed, sealed, and acknowledged by Jefse GARRETT Senr. as and for his last will and testament in whose presence and at whose request we have wifnessed and in the presence of each other subscirbed our names as witnefses to the due executors of the same this the twenty second day of September, one thousand eight hundred and forty seven. Attest:

Willis Wallace   Jefsee Garrett Senr. (SEAL)
William Clardy
Calvin A. Crombie
Recorded in will Book A, Page 161, Bundle 132, Pkg. 10. Recorded date not available. Proven date 3th day of October, A. D., 1853.

WILL OF DAVIS WILLIAMS

The State of South Carolina Laurens District. I Davis WILLIAMS of the District and State aforesaid, do make, publish, and declare this to be my last will and testament in manner and form following. 1st. I will and desire my just debts and funeral expenses first to be paid out of the proceeds of the sale of my property hereinafter auction to be made by my executors. 2nd. It is my will that all my property both real and personal that may belong to me at my death (except a negro girl Emma now in the pofsefsion of my daughter Elizbeth A. MILLER, which said negro girl I hereby give to my said daughter) be sold by my executors, the real estate on a credit of one and two years from the day of sale. I include within the provisions of this clause as part of my estate such negroes as I may have loaned to my daughters hereinafter named, or may hereafter lend to them as well as the increase of said negroes since they have been in their pofsefsion and the increase they may have after the date of this will. 3d. It is my will that after the payment of my debts and funeral expenses, the proceeds of the sale of my property as above directed together with all monies which may be arriving to my estate from any source whatsoever, be equally divided share and share alike among my following named sons and daughters to wit, Samuel M. WILLIAMS, Henry R. WILLIAMS, Joseph H. WILLIAMS, Leonard WILLIAMS, Robert H. WILLIAMS, Ephraim WILLIAMS, William A. WILLIAMS, James H. WILLIAMS, Elizabeth A. MILLER Frances CLARY, and Mary METTS. Provided however, that in said division my son Samuel M. be charged with having already received seven hundred dollars, the value of negro girl Harriet, I have already given to him. Also my son Henry R. with eight hundred dollars, the value of negro boy Lewis, I have heretofore given to him, Also my son Joseph H. with nine hundred dollars I have paid him in cash. Also my son Leonard with one thousand dollars which I set down against him for the expences of his collegiate education. Also my son Ephraim with six hundred dollars which I set down for his expences at college. Also my son William A. with six hundred dollars which I set down for expences which I will have in and upon his completion of his course at the Citadel Academy. Also my son James H. with twelve hundred dollars which I set down as the expences I will have incured for his collegiate and medical education when completed. My intention is that my above named sons against whom I have made the above charges, shall in the division of my estate above directed, account to my others sons and daughters for said sums, and stand back until my said other sons and daughters are made equal with them. 4th. In the event of my death before my son James H. has completed his course of medical lectures, wherefore my son William A. has been graduated at the Citadel Academy, it is my will that my executors retain in their hands a sufficiency of funds to defray their expences for that purpose, charging them however in the said division only with the sums I have above set down against them. 5th. The legacies to which my above named sons are respectively entitled under this will I give to them absolutely and forever. 6th. The legacy hereinbefore given to my daughter Elizabeth A. MILLER, including the girl Emma, I give to my son Henry R. WILLIAMS, in trust for the sole and separate use of the said Elizabeth A. during her life, free from the control and subject to the contracts of her present or any husband she may hereafter have. And at her death to the ifsue of her body then living in such proportion as they would take if the property were her own under the statute of distributions. 7th. The legacies given hereinbefore to my two daughters Frances CLARY and Mary METTS respectively, I give to my son Leonard WILLIAMS in trust for the sole and separate use of the said Frances and the said Mary during their respective lives, free from the control and not subject ot the contracts of their present or any husbands they may hereafter have and at their death to the ifsue of their bodies then living respectively, in such proportions as they would take if the said property belonged to the said Frances and Mary in their own right absolutely, under the statute of distributions. 8th. It is my will that the trustees herein before appointed do invert the trust funds given to them respectively in such property as my daughters may respectively choose and direct. And I also vest the said trustees with the power to sell my property is purchased by them and to reinvest the proceeds in other property under the advice and direction of my said daughters. And if either of the said trustees should die or decline to serve, it is my will that the court of Equity shall appoint another in the place of the one so dying or declining to serve, to be vested with the same powers, and to hold the trust property upon the same trusts terms and limitations hereinbefore contained. 9th. In the event of the death of either of the above named legatees under this my will leaving a child or children, it is my will that such child or children shall take the share or shares to which his her or their parent would have been entitled to take if living. 10th. I hereby nominate, constitute, and appoint my two sons Henry R. WILLIAMS and Leonard WILLIAMS executors of this my last will and testament hereby revoking all former wills by me made. In witnefs whereof I have hereunto set my hand and seal this 26 day of March, Anno Domini, 1853. Signed,. sealed, published, and declared, by the said Davis WILLIAMS as his last will and testament in the presence of us, who in the presence of each other and in his presence have subscirbed our names as witnefses thereto.

W. J. Witmire   Davis Williams (LS)
R. C. Cannon
A. C. Garlington
Recorded in Will Book A, Page 163, Bdl. 117, Pkge. 5. Proven Oct. 11. 1853. Recorded date not available. W. D. Watts, O.L.D.

WILL OF ABNER JONES

The State of South Carolina, Laurens District. In the name of God, Amen. I Abner JONES of the district and state aforesaid, being of sound and disposing mind, memory, and discretion, but

weak of body, and calling to mind the uncertainty of life, do
make and ordain this for my last will and testament, touching
all such worldly estate as it has pleased God to blefs me with.
First, I give and bequeath to Oliver H. P. JONES, a negro woman
Firsly at my death. And at the death of my wife, I also give
and bequeath to the said Oliver H. P. JONES a negro girl Harret
daughter of Ferrisly (not including however any income that Fer-
rily my have in my lifetime nor any income that Harriet may have
either in my lifetime or that of my wife) and the sum of one
hundred dollars in cash, all in trust for the sole and separate
one of my daughter Alethia HARRIS wife of A. W. HARRIS, during
her life. And at her death I give and bequeath the said slaves
and money with any increase of said slaves whist in the enjoyment of my said daughter to such children as she may leave share
and share alike, the child or children of any deceased child taking the share which the deceased parent would take if living.
And I authorise the said trustee to vist the aforesaid fund of
one hundred dollars in such property as may in his judgement,
best suit my said daughter subject to the trust and limitation
aforesaid as if such investment should not be deemed advisable.
Then to put said fund to interest and pay her the interest thing
annually during her life, and also to see that the property
aforesaid is faithfully applied to the uses and purposes aforesaid. Secondly. As I have hereto fore settled on my daughter
Mary Carolina COOLY and otherwise given her a full share of my
estate I make no further provision for her. Thirdly. I settled
on my daughter Sarah D. WESTMORELAND a negro girl Grace, before
her marriage, and I give and bequeath to my son Wm. R. JONES at
the death of my wife a negro girl Julia, without any increase,
upon condition that he has the said Julia appraised at the period
aforesaid or as soon thereafter as conveniently there disinterested men and advances one half the appraised value of said
slave in cash and vest the same in suitable property for my said
daughter Mary WESTMORELAND to be held by him in trust for the
sole and separate use of the said Sarah D. WESTMORELAND during
her life. And at her death to deliver over the same in per smple
to such children as she may leave including the child or children
of my deceased child who will take the share the deceased parent
would be intitled to if living. Fourthly. At my death I give
and bequeath to O. H. P. JCNES, a negro girl Sarah not including
any increase that she may have in my lifetime and at the death
of my wife, I give and bequeath to him a negro woman Rhoda but
not her increase, all in trust for the sole and separate use of
my daughter Eliza JONES during her life. And at her death I
give and bequeath the aforesaid slaves, with any increase they
or either of them my have after they go into her pofsefsion, to
such children as she may leave, the child or children of any deceased child taking the share the deceased parent would be entitled to if living. And I further give and bequeath to the
said O. H. P. JONES upon the trust and limitation aforesaid one
feather bed, bedstead, and furniture and one cow and calf. Fifthly. I give and devise to my son Oliver H. O. JONES the tract
of land upon which he now lives containing one hudnred and thirty

acres and also one other tract of land on the opposite side of
the road from his residence containing ninety or ninety five
acres called the Sloan tract. And further give and bequeath at
the death of my wife, to the said O. H..P. JONES a negro fellow
called Ned. Sixth. At the death of my wife, I give and bequeath
to my son R. A. JONES a negro boy named Prince and to my son J.
M. JONES a negro boy called Jeff. Seventh. I give and devise
to my two sons R. A. JONES and J. M. JONES a tract of land on
Durbins Creek containing one hundred and twenty one acres with
the Mills and Machinery hereon, also about fifty acres of land
to be laid off from my homestead tract beginning on a Hicory corner on the line dividing the mill tract and the lands of Mary
Frances HOLCOMB, thence south running in a straight line through
my field to the crop fence, then east in a direct line across
the spring branch and through the plantation to the branch that
divides my lands from the said Frances HOLCOMB's thence down
said branch to the corner between me and the said Frances, thence
along the line between me and the said Frances to the Mill tract
then with the mill tract to the hickory corner at the beginning.
But the said devise is made subject to the condition that the
said divisions and the survivor of them shall grind the grain of
my wife dureing her life use of any toll, and I give and devise
to my said two sons the privilege of getting such timber off of
my homestead tract of land as may be necefsary to keep the said
mills in repair during the life of my said wife. Eighth. The
balance of my homestead tract of land supposed to contain over
five hundred acres after deducting the prices that or otherwise
disposed of. I give and devise to my beloved wife Ester L.
JONES during her life, but if my sons W. R. JONES and John H.
HONES or either of them should see proper to live with their
mother and attend to her busness, I give them or either of them
the right to do so, and to settle upon as cultivale such portions
of siad land as they or either of them and their mother may
agree upon, during her life. And I make this devise to my said
wife expense subject to the right and privilege aforesaid of my
two sons. And at the death of my wife, I give and devise to W.
R. JONES so much of said land as is included within the following boundaries, to wit, that lying west of the road leading from
my residence to Greenville court Haven begining on said road at
the Patton field, thence along the road a short distance South,
then South West along the road leading around the bottom out to
Step's old field, then along said road through the old field by
an orchard to the Stone corner at the mouth of Clary whites line
then with my line to the begining corner making about two hundred
acres. The residue of siad homestead tract, at the death of my
wife not otherwise disposed of, supposed to contain probably
four hundred acres I give and devise to my son John H. JONES in
per simple. Ninth. At the death of my wife, I give and bequeath
to my son W. R. JONES one negro Solomon. And at the same period
before stated I give and bequeath to my son John H. JONES two
negro boys named Lewis and Perry. Tenth. I give and bequeath
to my said wife duringher life the following slaves, Ned, Solomon
Prince, Jeff, Harriet, Lewis, Perry, Sarah, and Julia and at her

death, to be disposed of according to the provisions of this will. And I give and bequeath all the balance of my household and kitchen furniture of my description and plantation tools to my said wife absolutely. But I expect her of course, to give such of my children as have not married such household furniture and stock as even given to my other children as they severally married. This clause is intended to untrace my live stock of my discreption. Eleventh. Whenever my daughter Eliza JONES leaves her mother to live elsewhere I give and bequeath to her a negro called Rose, but should she remain with her mother until the death of the latter, then I give her the said slave Rose. The said slave is to be enjoyed by my wife until one or the other of the contingencies before mentioned shall happen. And I also give Eliza at her mother's death another slave Sarah without any increase. Twelfth. I will and direct that my executors herein after appointed by my funeral expenses and other debts out of my money and choses in action, I may leave on hand at my death. But should mon be necefsary for that purpose I authorise said executors to will such of the property willed to my wife as she can best spare to answer that purpose. Thirteenth. I will, devise, and bequeath that all the residue of my estate whether in pofsefsion, remainder or reversion of what even kind or description it may be, not otherwise disposed be said by my executors and the proceeds thereof equally divided amongst all of my children except, Mary C. COLLY, Alethia HARRIS, and Sarah D. WESTMORELAND who an provided for otherwise as for as I expect to do. Fourteenth. Should any of my said daughters who are provided for by this will die without leaving a child or children or a grand child or grand children, then I give, devise, and bequeath the interst and estate given them or such of them as may so die to their surviving borther s and sisters, the children of any deceased brother or sister taking the share which such deceased parent would take if living. Fifteenth. In the event that my said wife should not survive me, then I will and devise that the devises and legacius which even to take off at and be enjoyed in remainder or otherwise at her death shall take off at and be carried into execution at my death should I survive her. Sixteenth. I appoint my sons O. H. P. JONES and W. R. JONES executors of this my last will and testament covering this and the proceeding sheet. In testimony whereof I have hereunto set my hand and seal this 12th day of November, in the year of our Lord, one thousand eight hundred and fifty two, and in the seventy seventh year of American Independence. In presence of us.

John Jones   Abner Jones (SEAL)
Richard H. Vaughan
C. P. Sullivan
Recorded in Book A, Page 166, Bundle 117, Package 14. Proven date Nov. 15, 1853. W. D. Watts, Ordy. Recorded date not available.

WILL OF SALLY MCNEES

State of South Carolian Laurens District. In the name of God, Amen. I Sally MCNEES of the District and State aforesaid, being of sound and disposing mind and memory, do make, ordain, publish and declare this to be my last will and testament, Viz. 1st. A After the payment of all my just debts, it is my will and desire that my executors hereinafter named, procure a marble slab or head stone with appropriate inscription, and have the same placed on or near the grave of my deceased husband, Lewis SAXON, one for the grave of my infant son, Lewis, and one for my own grave. 2nd. I give to my executor the sum of three hundred dollars in trust for the separate use and benefit of Elizabeth ARNOLD, (wife of Lewis ARNOLD, of the State of Alabama) and I hereby authorise him to purchase a negro girl with the same, and to execute a deed of trust to some suitable person, securing the use and pofsefsion of said negro to the said Elizabeth, during her natural life, and at her death to the lawful heirs of her body. 3rd. I give to my daughters, Clarifsa DOWNS, Polly ARNOLD and Susan THRUSTON, all my wearing apparel and to Clarifsa DOWNS my family Bible. 4th. I give to my grand daughter Ruthy ARNOLD daughter of Polly ARNOLD and Ira ARNOLD, my negro boy named Mark Anthony, about 3 years old. 5th. I give my grand daughter Sally ARNOLD, one bed and furniture. 6th. I give to my grand son Robert Lewis CLEVELAND, son of Benjamin F. and Tabitha CLEVELAND my small Bible, a negro boy Bob, and negro girl Nancy, the children of my negro woman, Esther. The said negroes to be appraised to him as a part of his distributive share of my estate as the representative of his mother, my daughter Tabithas. 7th. I give to my son Hugh SAXON a negro girl Rhoda, about 20 years of age, to be appraised to him as a part of his distributive share of my estate. 8th. I give to my daughter Susan THRUSTON, two hundred and fifty dollars to remunerate her in part for the lofs of a negro woman, Seyly, given her some years ago. 9th. It is my will that all my children receive an equal share of my estate (with the exception of the little negro given to Ruthy ARNOLD, who is a cripple, and the children of those who are dead, to receive the share their parents would have received if living. And as I have made advancements to my sons Joshua SAXON, and Lydall P. SAXON, and to my daughters, Polly ARNOLD, Susan THRUSTON, and Clarifsa DOWNS, and to my grand daughter Isabella WEATHERALL, the daughter of my son, Allen SAXON, decd., it is my will that the property so advanced be appraised to them as so much of their distributive shares of my estate. And that all who have received money, account for the same with interest to the time of final settlement of my estate. But no advancement of money be taken into the settlement or accounted for, where the amount received is below twenty dollars at any one time. 10th. It is my will that all my negroes not before disposed of, be valued after my death, by three disinterested persons, and taken at valuation by such of my children as may be willing to do so. And account to the others for their equal distributive shares of the same. But if two or more make choice of the same negro, and cannot agree, then the negro must be sold as directed in the next clause of this my will. It is also my wish that my land be valued in the same manner, and taken by some one of my children at valuation, and account to the others for the same. 11th. It is my will and desire that all my property not hereinbefore disposed of, be sold by my executor, and in the event of my children refusing or neglecting to take the negroes and land at valuation as above, then it is my will that my executor sell my land and negroes, together with all the resid of my estate, and distribute the smae as before directed. 12th. It is my will and desire that the distributive share of my estate, to which my daughter Clarifsa DOWNS, may be entitled, be given in trust, and I hereby give the same to W. R. FARLEY, in trust for her sole and separate use and benefit during her natural life, and at her death to be equally divided between her four children. 13th. Lastly, I appoint my son Hugh SAXON, my executor to carry this my last will and testament into effect. Signed, sealed, and published, this 17th June, 1846. In presence of.

```
     her
Eliza X Coker                          Sally McNees (L. S.)
     mark
Wm. Leak
James McNinch
```

Recorded in Will Book A, Page 175. Recorded and proven date not available. Box 149-17. W. D. Watts, Ordy, Laurens District

CODICIL TO MY WILL

1st. It is my will that the distributive share of my estate to which my daughter Polly ARNOLD, may be entitled be secured in trust and I hereby give the same to Sameul BARKSDALE and my son Joshua SAXON, in trust for her sole and separate use and benefit during her natural life. And at her death, it is my will that the said share, or what may be remaining in their (the trustees above named,) be equally divided between her children. It is my wish that my son Joshua SAXON, act as co- executor of my estate with my son Hugh SAXON and I hereby appoint him one of my executors. Signed and sealed, this 25th day of November, 1847. In presence of.

```
Wm. Leak                               Sally McNees (L. S.)
James McNinch
George Saxon
```

WILL OF JEREMIAH BALL

South Carolina Laurens District. In the name of God, Amen. I Jeremiah BALL of the District of Laurens do make and ordain this my last will and testament in manner following to wit. I gave to my wife Polly BALL all my plantation, house goods and chattles also my servant Jake, during my wife's life time and then he is to go to his wife at praise value. I charge my sone Stephen BALL three dollars per acre for one hundred and twenty eight acres of land. I charge my sone Harriss BALL three hundred dollars for one hundred and twenty five acres of land. I charge my son John BALL three dollars per acre for one hundred and eighteen acres of land. I charged my son Minyard BALL three dollars per acre for one hundred acres of land. I charged my son Young F. BALL three dollars per acre for one hundred and forty seven acres of land. I charge my daughter Elisabeth GARRETT three hundred dollars for a negro girl name Lid and other Sundris. I charged my daughter Nancy ABERCRUMBIA children three hundred dollars for a negro girl name Sall and other sundris. I charged my daughter Francis OWENS children three hundred dollars for a negro girl name Cinda and other sundris. My servant Limus and all my land, stock, and plantation tool, household and kitchen furniture is to be sold and equaly divided among the heirs after our funeral expencis is paid. And know I nominate, ordain and appoint my son John BALL to be my lawful executor. Witnes my hand and seal this 18 day of Nov., 1850. Codacil with the exception of grave yard.

S. Knight   Jeremiah Ball (LS)
Z. C. Garrett
James A. McDawal
Recorded in Will Book A, Page 180, Bdl. 143, Pkg. 2. Proven March 8, 1856. Recorded date not available. W. H. Langston, O. L. D.

WILL OF EDMOND RAGSDALE

In the name of God, Amen. I Edmond RAGSDALE of the State of South Carolina and District of Greenville, being of sound and disposing mind and memory, but weak in body, and cawling to mind the uncertainty of life, and being desireous to dispose of all such worldly estate as it hath pleased God to blefs me with, do make and ordain this my last will in manner following that is to say. I desire that after my death, that my body be decently buried my funeral expences paid, and all my just debts paid. I desire that my executors hereinafter named, may sell the whole o of my estate both personal and real, after payment of my debts and funeral expences. I give to my wife Sarah RAGSDALE, an equal share with all of my children, except the heirs of my son John which I intend to draw one half share with my wife. And the rest of my children, as I have already given unto my son Peter, John William and my daughter Marinda. Two hundred and sixty dollars each. I desire in the first place that the same amount which I have given to my son Peter John William and Marina, be given to my daughter Ann and Jane ($260) and two hundred dollars ($200) to my son Edward C. with interest thereon from first of August last (1848). I desire that the half share which I have given to Johns heirs shall be given exclusively to his two sons, Thomas and Robert, after making up the above amount of two hundred and sixty dollars. To my daughter's Ann and Jane with interest and two hundred dollars to my son Edward C. with interest. I desire that my wife Sarah and all of my children be made equal as above specified, except the children of my son John who are to draw one half share with the rest.

The children of my son John are both together unty to have one half as much as the rest of my children. And lastly, I do constitute and appoint my son Edward C. RAGSDALE executor of this my last will and testament by me heretofore made. In testimony whereof I have hereunto set my hand and affixed my seal, this the ninth day of November, and in the year of our Lord, 1848. Signed, sealed, published, and declared as and for the last will and testament of the above named Edmond RAGSDALE in the presents of us.

William Bolt   Edmond Ragsdale (SEAL)
Sarah C. Saxon
Thomas J. Sullivan
Recorded in Book A, Page 181, Bundle 120, Package 13. Recorded date not available. Proven date March 6, 1836. W. N. Langston O. L. D.
South Carolina Laurens District. Personally appeared before me William BOLT, who beina sworn made oath that he saw Edmond RAGSDALE execute the within instrument as his last will and that he together with Sarah C. SAXON and Thomas J. SULLIVAN in the presence of each other and in the presence of the testator subscribed as witnefses to the same that he saw the testator sign the will and also each of the other witnefses sign and they saw him and the testator sign swoan to before me March 6th, 1836.

W. N. Langston O. L. D.   William Bolt

WILL OF SALLY CUNNINGHAM

State of South Carolina Laurens District. Last will and testament of Mifs Sarah CUNNINGHAM. In the name of God, Amen. I Sarah CUNNINGHAM being of sound and disposing mind and memory, but weak in body and calling to mind the uncertainty of life, and being desirous to dispose of all such worldly estate as it hath pleased God to blefs me with, do make and ordain this my last will in manner following that is to say. I bequeath to my brother Elihue CUNNINGHAM two hundred dollars. To my mother I bequeath fifty dollars in case of my brother Elihue CUNNINGHAM to my sister Jane, I bequeath fifty dollars in case of Elihue CUNNINGHAM to be paid to her as she needs it without interest. To my brother Jacob, I bequeath two hundred dollars which I desire him to purchase land with. To my sister Margaret NORRIS children, I bequeath one hundred and fifty dollars to be divided equally between them. To my sister Francis HUDGINS, I bequeath one hundred dollars with a request that you give Mrs. Elizabeth BOYD twenty dollars and Mrs. Allison twenty dollars and the balance to be equally divided amoungest your other children to my sister Anna BOLT I bequeath one hundred dollars with a request that you divide it equally between your eight daughters. William and yourself. To my nepheu Franklin CUNNINGHAM, I bequeath ten dollars. To my sister Elizabeth D. CUNNINGHAM, I bequeath my bed and bedsteads and all the rest of the things belonging to me. The balance of the money I wish to be appropriat-

ed to the prepairing of min and sister Mary's graves after the
payments of my debts and funeral expences, my notes are worth at
the present time to the amount of nine hundred dollars or nearly
so. And lastly, I do appoint my brother Elihue CUNNINGHAM and
my nepheu James HUDGINS executors of this my last will and testament by me heretofore made. In testimony whereof I have hereunto set my hand and affixed my seal. Signed, sealed, and delivered as and for the last will and testament of the above named
Sarah CUNNINGHAM in the presence of us. Witnefs.

M. Madden   Sally Cunningham (L. S.)
Benjamin Yeargin
Sarah C. Ray
Recorded in Will Book A, Page 184. Recorded date not available.
Proven date 30th day of Jan., 1855. W. D. Watts, Ordy. Laurens
District.

WILL OF THOMAS F. FARROW

South Carolina Laurens District. I Thomas F. FARROW of the District and State aforesaid, being of sound disposing mind and in
good health do make this my last will and testament. Item. It
is my will that as soon after my death as it is convenient that
all my just debts and funeral expenses be paid out of such of my
personal estate as my wife may think can be best spared for that
purpose. I then give to my wife Sophia W. FARROW, all the ballance of my estate, real and personal, which I may die pofsefsed
of during her life. And at her death it is my will that all
that remains of my estate real and personal, be sold by my executor and after paying the expenses of said sale, the ballance to
be divided equally between my children, the child or children of
a deceased child to take among them the share the parent would
take if living. I appoint my wife Sophia W. FARROW my executrix
to this my last will and testament. Witnefs my hand and seal
this the 2nd day of March, 1852. In the presence of Attest:

J. H. Thomson   Ths. F. Farrow (L. S.)
John R. Lyons
W. H. Langston
Recorded in Will Book A, Page 185, Bdl. 122, Pkge. 1. Recorded
date not available. Proven date Jan. 23, 1855. W. D. Watts,
Ordy, Laurens District.

WILL OF JEREMIAH LEAKE

In the name of God, Amen. I Jeremiah LEAKE of the District of
Laurens and State of South Carolina, being of sound and disposing mind and memory, calling to mind the uncertainty of life,
and being desirous to dispose of such worldly estate as it hath
pleased God to blefs me with, do make, constitute and ordain
this my last will and testament in manner and form following,
that is to say. First. It is my will and desire that all my
just debts, funeral expenses, and the expenses of my last illness

be paid as soon after my death as practicable. Second. I give and bequeath to my beloved wife Jane LEAKE, during her natural life the following property, to wit, one half of the tract of land whereon I now live, and one half of my tract of land on Bush River and my negroes John, Pompy, Milton, Wesly, Moses, Lewdy, Nancy, Marte, and Samuel, and their future increase. And I also give to her absolutely, to be disposed of as she pleases my slaves Winny and Adeline and their future increase. Third. I have given to my daughter Margaret L. BONDS, five negroes, to wit, Matilda, Caroline, Marthena, Madison, and Cecily, which I confirm by this my last will. Fourth. I give to my son Jeremiah LEAKE, in trust for the use of my daughter Rachel B. LEAKE during her natural life the following slaves to wit. Anna, Lucretia Henry, Bedford, and Betty, with their future increase. And at her death to such child and children as she may leave surviving her, but should my said daughter die leaving no child or children, then the said negroes and their increase are to be equally divided amongst her brothers and sisters of the whole blood. Fifth. I give to my son Jeremiah LEAKE in trust for the use and benefit of my daughter Lucinda B. LEAKE during her natural life, the following slaves to wit, Randel, Tabetha, Loicy, Elliott, Martha, and Louisa, with their future increase. And at her death to such child or children as she may leave surviving her, but should my said daughter die leaving no child or children surviving her, the aforesaid (Illegeable) her brothers and sisters of the whole blood. Sixth. I give to my son Jeremiah LEAKE in trust for the use and benefit of my daughter Jane Emiline LEAKE during her natural life the following slaves, to wit, Polly, Elizabeth, Calvin and Wyatt, with their future increase. And at her death to such child or children as she may leave surviving her, but should my said daughter die without leaving a child or children, the aforesaid slaves are to be equally divided amongst her brothers and sisters of the whole blood. Seventh. I give to my son Jeremiah LEAKE in trust for the use and benefit of my daughter Isabella P. LEAKE during her natural life the following slaves, to wit, Dinah, Catherine, Louisa, and Amanda, and their future increase. And at her death to such child or children as she may leave surviving her, but if my said daughter should die leaving no child or children, the aforesaid slaves with their increase shall be equally divided amongst her brother and sisters of the whole blood. Eighth. I give to my son Jeremiah LEAKE one half of my plantation and tract of land on Bush River adjoining lands of Mason YOUNG, Hickerson, Barksdale, and others and the following slaves, to wit, Jacob, Jane, and Lucretia, with their future increase, but should my said son die, leaving no child or children surviving him, the aforesaid property with the increase of the slaves to be equally divided amongst his brothers and sisters of the whole blood. Tenth. At the death of my wife, I give and bequeath to my son Jeremiah LEAKE the remaining half of my tract of land on Bush River. To my son William J. LEAKE the remaining half of the tract of land whereon I now live and the slave Milton, to my daughter Rachel B. LEAKE the slave Mose, to my daughter Lucinda B. LEAKE the slave

Pompy, to my daughter Jane (Illegeable) the slave Lindy, to be
held subject to the same trusts and limitations herein before
provided as to the property given to them respectively. Eleventh.
I give and bequeath to my wife Jane LEAKE during her natural
life all the balance of my estate of every description not herein before disposed of. Twelfth. After the death of my wife, it
is my will that my executors hereinafter named, do raise from
that portion of my estate given to her for life, exclusive of
the land negroes, the sum of one thousand dollars which is to be
placed by them at interest as an accumulating fund untill the
income shall amount to three hundred dollars, which sum of three
hundred dollars I give to my grand daughter Jane Emeline BONDS,
and the principal sum of one thousand dollars to to be held by
my executors for the sole and separate use of my daughter Margarett L. BONDS during her natural life. And at her death to be
equally divided amongst her children, and if she should leave no
child or children the sum is to be equally divided amongst her
brothers and sisters of the whole blood. And should my said
grand daughter Jane Emeline BONDS die leaving no child or children then the fund above given to her shall be equally divided
amongst my children by my present wife. Thirteenth. After the
death of my wife all the balance of the negroes herein given to
her for life is to be equally divided amongst her four youngest
daughters. Fourteenth. It is my will and desire that in all
cases where property is limited by this my will to my children
for life, with remainder of their children, and in the event of
their leaving no child or children surviving them, then to the
brothers and sisters that the grand children of a deceased child
of any one of my children shall represent their parent and be
entitled to whatever their parent would have been entitled to
(have they survived their father or mother) under this my will.
Lastly. I do nominate, constitute and appoint my son Jeremiah
LEAKE executor of this my last will and testament, and in the
event of his (Illegeable) former wills by me heretofore made.
In testimony whereof I have hereunto subscribed by name and affixed my seal this fourth day of July, one thousand eight hundred and fifty one. Signed, sealed, published, and declared as
and for the last will and testament of the said Jeremiah LEAKE
in presence of.

                                        his
H. C. Young   Jeremiah X Leake (SEAL)
B. R. Campbell   mark
Wm. Mills Jr.
Recorded in Will Book A, Page 189, Bundle 120, Pkge. 8. Record-
ed date not available. Proven date Mar. 4, 1853. W. D. Watts,
Ordy, Laurens District.
I desire it to be destinctly understood that altho I have quoli-
fied as executor, I renounce the appointment of trustee in the
different clauses of the within will. Jany. 31st, 1856.

                        J. F. Leak

WILL OF THOMAS POTTER

South Carolina Laurens District. In the name of God, Amen. I Thomas G. POTTER of Laurens District and State aforesaid, being weak of body but of scund mind, memory, and understanding and knowing that it is appointed for man once to die, and after that the judgement I commet my soul into the hands of almighty God who gave it and my body to be decently intered at the discretion of my friends and as to my worldly estate I make and ordain this my last will and testament in maner and form following, hereby revoking all other wills made by me. First. I will and desire that all my just debts and burial expense be paid out of any money of my estate. Secondly. I will and desire that all my property both real and personal be sold on a credit of twelve months and be equally divided between my children Weymen H. POTTER, Thomas C. POTTER, Francis A. POTTER, Allen T. POTTER, George W. POTTER, Moses POTTER. And I give in trust to my son Allen T. POTTER the share of my daughter Nancy H. KENNEDY now living in the State of Georgia to be laid out in any property that the said trustee may think best ofr the benefit of my daughter Nancy H. KENNDY and her children. I also give in trust to my son Francis A. POTTER the share of my daughter Elizabeth H. POTTER now living with me to be laid out in any property that the said trustee may think best for the benefit of my daughter Elizabeth H. POTTER and her children. Thirdly. I will and desire that each of my children, on the final settlement of my estate shall account for what they have received from me in my life time. Lastly. I constitute and appoint my son Weynam H. POTTER sole executor of this my last will and testament. In witnefs whereof I hereunto set my hand seal this third day of February, one thousand eight hundred and fifty two. Signed, sealed, and delivered in the presence of us ot be his last will and testament who in the presence of the testator and each other have subscribed our names as witnefses.

William Young   Thomas G. Potter (SEAL)
Thos. Wier
John H. Kern

Recorded in Book A, Page 193, Bundle 115, Package 25. Proven date Feb. 16, 1852. W. D. Watts, Ordy. Recorded date not available.

South Carolina Laurens District. Personally came before me William YOUNG and upon being sworn, made oath that he saw the within named Thomas POTTER execute the within paper as his last will and that he together with Thomas WILL and I. F. KERN in the presence of each other and in the presence of the testator subscribed as witnefs to the law sworn to before me the 16th day of Feby., 1852.   William Young   W. D. Watts, Ody.

WILL OF WILLIAM COOK

South Carolina Laurens District. In the name of God, Amen. I William COOK of the aforesaid State District, being of sound and disposing mind and memory, but calling to mind the uncertainty of life and being desirous of disposing of all such worldly estate as it hath pleased God to blefs me with, do make and ordain this my last will and testament in manner following, VIZ. 1st. I bequeath my body to the dust and my soul to God that gave it. 2nd. It is my will and desire that as early after my decease as may be convenient that all my just debts and funeral expencs be paid. 3rd. I give to my beloved wife Jamima COOK during her natural life all my estate both real and personal of whatever natur or quality so ever to receive use and enjoy all the rents, profits, or imoluments arising from the sue of the same. And after her death one half of all the estate both real and personal to be disposed of as she may wish or desire. The other half of the estate to be equally divided among all the children of my sister Ann FULLER. VIZ: Franklin G. FULLER, Anthoney C. FULLER, Mary Cmanda now SMITH, Edny now RICHARDSON, Augustus A. FULLER, Malefsa J. FULLER, John C. FULLER, and Edward P. FULLER share and share alike to them and their heirs forever. Should any of the above mentioned children die before they arrive of age or die without ifsue their distribution shares to be equally divided among the surviving children. Lastly, I constitute, nominate and appoint my beloved wife Jamima COOK my executrix of this my last will and testament, hereby revoking all other former wills by me heretofore made. In witnefs whereof I have hereunto set my hand and affixed my seal this 19th day of May, 1850. In presence of.

Henry W. Paslay   Wm. Cook (L. S.)
Duke Goodman
Jones Loyd

CODICIL

Whereas I have made this my last will and testament, being the same deate, I do further will and desire that a half acre of land be resirved at the old burying ground on east side for my mortal body and my wife Jamima. If it should be her wish to be buryed by my side, and that the said be walled in or so much as is necesary with rock in a good and substanchel manner, this the same date May 19th, 1850. Signed in the presence of

Herny W. Paslay   Wm. Cook (L. S.)
Duke Goodman
Jones Loyd

Recorded date not available. Recorded in Will Book A, Page 197, Bundle 123, Pkg. 12. Proven date 4th day of October, 1853. W. D. Watts, Ordy, Laruens District.

WILL OF JAMES MCDOWELL

South Carolina Laurens District. In the name of God, Amen. I of the District and State aforesaid, being in ordinary health and sound and disposing mind and memory, but calling to mind the uncertainty of life, and being desirous to dispose of all such worldly estate, as it has pleased God to blefs me with, do make

and ordain this my last will and testament in manner and form
following, that is to say. I desire that immediately after my
decease or as early thereafter as convenient so much of my personal estate, not otherwise disposed, as may be nefsery to pay
my funeral expenses and just debts, be sold for cash by my executors hereinafter appointed or on such credit as they may think
most expedient. After payment of my funeral expenses and debts
aforesaid, I give and bequeath to my beloved wife Jane one negro fellow named Stefeny, two good horses, to be selected by her
out of my stock on hand at my death, two beds and furniture and
so much of the kitchen furniture and utensils as may be deemed
necifsary for her comfort, two cows and calves, a reasonable
portion of the hogs, provisions on hand, farming utensils and
my wagon during her natural life. And I also give and devise
to my said wife during the term of her natural life all that
portion of the tract of land whereon I reside, including my
residence, that lies east cf the following line to be marked
out by me in my lifetime, to wit, commencing at a corner between
me and J. H. IRBY near a hollow north west of my house, thence
in a direct line southwardly until it reaches near the house of
my son James, then to be curved so as to leave four or five
acres of land on the east side of his house. Thence in a
straight line to a dogwood on the line between me and Wm. TEMPLE-
TON. And at the death of my wife, I will and desire that the
aforesaid property both real and personal, in which I have given
her a life estate, be sold on a reasonable credit by my said
executors and the proceeds thereof equally divided amongst the
following children to wit, Permelia HOLLANDSWORTH, Elizabeth
CANNADY, Telitha BRYSON, Jam TAYLOR, and Isabella MARTIN after
first giving my son James one hundred dollars out of said proceeds, which sum I will and bequeath to him. But he shares of
Jane TAYLOR and Isabella, I give and bequeath to them severally
during their respective life. And at the death of each I give
and bequeath their respective shares to such children as they
may leave living at their deaths. Furthermore, I give and devise
all the balance of my said homestead tract west of the line before designated to my son James MCDOWAL Jr. and his heirs forever, which balance I suppose contains about one hundred and
sixty acres of land. And upon reflection I give and bequeath to
my said son James at the death of my wife the wagon in which I
have given her a life estate. Again, I give and devise the
tract of land whereon the widow Jane MCDOWAL now lives to her
the said Jane MCDOWAL during her natural life, as a home for her
and her children. And at her death I will and desire that the
said tract of land, which I suppose contains about eighty four
acres, be sold by my executors and the proceeds thereof I give
and bequeath in equal shares to such children as the said Jane
now has living. And I also direct my executors at my death to
sell my negro fellow Jim and the balance of my estate not other
wise herein disposed of and after payment of my debts and funeral
expenses to divide the balance of the proceeds equally amongst
the following children, to wit, Permelia HOLLANDSWORTH, Elizabeth
CANNADY, Telitha BRYSON, Jane TAYLOR, Isabella MARTIN, and James

MCDOWAL Jr. Lastly, I do constitute and appoint my friend C. P. SULLIVAN and my son James MCDOWAL executors of this my last will and testament hereby revoking all wills by me heretofore made. In testimony whereof I have hereunto set my hand and seal this 20th day of February, anno Domini, one thousand eight hundred and fifty. Signed, sealed, published, and declared as and for the last will and testament of James MCDOWAL Senr. in the presence of us who witnefs the same at the request of the testator in his presence and in the presence of each other.

Edward Anderson   James McDowal (LS)
T. W. Anderson
B. R. Campbell
Recorded in Will Book A, Page 203, Bdl. 119, Pkge. 13. Proven 6th day of Jany., 1855, W. D. Watts Ordy. Laurens District. Recorded date not available.

WILL OF JOHN RIDDLE

In the name of God, Amen. I John RIDDLE of Laurens District and State of South of Carolina, being of sound and disposing mind and memory, but weak in body and calling to mind the uncertainty of life, being desirous to dispose of all such wordy estate as it has pleased God to blefs me with, do make and ordain this my last will and   following that is to say. I desire that my wife Mary shall have all of my estate both personal and real during her natural life time or widowhood except so much thereof as will pay my just debts and funeral expences which I desire my executors immediately after my death to sell so much of my personal estate and pay said debts. If there should not be money on hand to pay the same and desire that after the death of my wife Mary RIDDLE that all of my estate both personal and real be sold by my executors herein after named and the proceeds or moneys arising there from be equally divided between my children hereinafter named. My son Harris RIDDLE, my son Newton RIDDLE, my son Melmoth RIDDLE, my son Berry RIDDLE, my daughter Catharine GARNER, my daughter Elizabeth, the wife of Elihu GARRETT, my daughter Mary, the wife of John CANNARY, my daughter Matilda Caroline RIDDLE, who is not married. And I do hereby give to my son Berry RIDDLE whom I hereby make and appoint trustee for my son Fealden RIDDLE in this my last will to receive for the benefit of the children of my son Fealding an equal shear of my estate with the rest of my children herein before mentioned and named. And I desire that the said shear as above willed and given to my son Berry RIDDLE for the benefit of the children of Fealden RIDDLE taken at no time for the payment of my debts that my son Fealding RIDDLE may owe at the time of my death, no that he may hereafter contract. And it is also my desire and intention that the said shear of my son Fealding shall not be taken no liable to be taken for any debts that my son Berry may owe or may hereafter contract, but be appointed to the sole use and benefit of the children of my son Fealding as said trustee may think best. And lastly, I do constitute and appoint my son Berry

RIDDLE and my friend Wm. POWER executors of this my last will
and testament by me heretofore made. In testimony where of I
have hereunto set my hand and affixed my seal this 19th day of
August, 1850. Signed, sealed, published, and delivered as and
for the last will and testament of John RIDDLE as above named in
the presents of us.

Fountain Martin
Rubin Martin
Jeremiah Martin
Benjamin Martin

                              his
                       John X Riddle
                          mark

Recorded in Will Book A, Page 209. Recorded date not available.
Proven date July 6, 1855. Original will not in files of Probate
W. D. Watts, Ordy, Laurens District.

WILL OF NANCY THOMASON

South Carolina. In the name of God, Amen. I Nancy THOMASON of
the District of Laurens and state aforesaid widow, being sick
and weak in body, but of sound mind and memory, praised be God
for the same do make and declare this my last will and testament
in manner and form following. First. I give desire and bequeath
unto my son James Dunlap THOMASON and Caty Prend THOMASON my
youngest daughter and to the heirs of her body their executors,
administrators afsignes all my house and tenament, land hereda-
taments with the appertinance situated lying and being in the
aforesaid state and district of Laurens to be sold at the discretion of my executcr a mority of the proceeds to be paid over
to my son James D. THOMERSON on his arriving at the age of twenty
one years and the half to be vested in specific property by my
executor for the benefit cf my daughter Cary P. THOMORSON to
descend in perpituity unlefs she may chose to have her portion
in money upon arriving at full age or after marriage. And also
to James D. THOMERSON one chesnut colered horse, a saddle, bridle to kept by my executor untill her arrives at full age if
thought exssedient by him otherwise to be sold and proceeds applied to his the said James's benefit, one rifle gun, 1 falling
aser sow and pigs, bed and furniture, second choice all the crop
that may be grown or produced on the plantation where on I now
reside except as much thereof as has been tended for the present
year. 2nd. Also I give, devise and bequeath farther to my daughter Caty P. THOMASON one bed and furniture, first choice one pine
chest, big spinning wheel, side saddle, and half of the rent
that may acrue to me from thr portion of plantation which is now
in the tinure and occupation of Martha GAUNT leased for one year.
3rd. To my step daughter Nancy THOMERSON I give devise and bequeath the other half of the rent or the value thereof which
accrue or arrise from the said portion of my lands now in the
tenure and acception of Martin GAUNT leased for one year, also
one big spinning wheel. 4th. All the rest rendue and remainder
of my estate and effects of what nature or kind soever I direct
and desire to be sold by my executor and equally divided among
my five children to wit, Polly THOMASON and Caty P. THOMERSON or

so much thereof as may remain after settling my just debts paying funeral expences probate of this will. Provided never the lefs if the real estate herein mentioned should not legally pay according to my will and bequest to James and Caty above named them and in the case it is my will that they receive the whole of my personal affects or estate in equal portions. And I do hereby nominate, constitute, and appoint my son in law William THOMASON executor of this my last will and testament hereby revoking and making will all former wills and testaments at any time heretofore by me made. And do desire this to me my last will and testament. In witnefs whereof I the said Nancy THOMERSON have hereunto set my hand and seal this 27th day of May in the year of our Lord, one thousand eight hundred thirty seven. Signed, sealed, declared and published by the above named Nancy THOMASON as and for last will and testament in the presence have subscribed our names as under

	her
Gidun Thomason	Nancy X Thomason (SEAL)
M. P. Evins	mark
Wm. Studdard	

Recorded date not available. Recorded in Will Book A, Page 211.
Proven date not available.

WILL OF MARTIN KINARD

The State of South Carolina Newberry District. The last will and testament of Martin KINARD. In the name of God, Amen. I Martin KINARD, being of sound and disposing mind and memory, do make and ordain this my last will and testament in manner following that is to say. First. It is my will that all my just debts be paid out of the proceeds of the sale of such of my personal property as my wife may wish sold for the purpose and if not sufficient then out of any money or choses in action, I may have on hand at the time of my death. Second. I give and bequeath all my estate both real and personal to my wife during the time of her widowhood and no longer, but should my wife, at any time during her widowhood be desirous to have the whole of the estate sold or disposed of, and for that purpose shall give her consent in writing to my executor then and in that case, I direct the same to be sold by my executor upon such terms and upon such credits as he may desire advisable, and in lieu and place of what I have herein given my wife. I give and bequeath unto her during her widowhood and no longer, two hundred and fifty acres of land to be selected by herself out of the tract hereon I now reside, so as to include the homestead, or else out of any other loands of which I may die seized and pofsefsed. Also the following negroes to wit; Peter, Alsey, Caroline, Soloman, Patsey, and her child with their future increase, also stock of every description, provisions, household and kitchen furniture, plantation tools so as my executors may think she needs he to be the sole judge. If however my said wife should think proper to manage, then and in that case, I will and devise to her during her natural life and no longer the following negro slaves to wit: Peter and Caroline my Burrouch and Harnefs this last mentioned property to be in lieu of and in place of the above mentioned property and is after her death to go and be disposed of, as is herein after directed. The several provisions herein made by this clause of my will for my wife is to be in lieu and for of all her claim and right of dower. Third. I give and devise the whole of my lands (including the interest herein before given to my wife, after her termination of her interest in them) to my three sons H. H. KINARD, M. T. KINARD, and J. P. KINARD, on the following terms and conditions to wit. Three men are to be chosen by my friend Mr. WILSON Esq. Ordinary, for Newberry District, or his succefsor in office and duly sworn to make a true appraisement of the lands. And after they shall have appraised the same, the sum of fifteen hundred dollars shall be deducted from the said appraisement and my said three sons shall then take the land at that price, to have and to hold the same to them, their heirs and afsigns forever. The fifteen hundred dollars above to be deducted from the appraise value of my lands is not to be considered as an advancement to my three sons as it is my intention to give them that much more out of my land, over and above the rest of my children. But the price at which my three sons shall take the land, after the deduction of the aforesaid fifteen hundred dollars, is to be accounted for as is herein after directed. Fourth. All the rest, residue and remainder of my estate of what a nature or kind so ever, U ordain and direct shall be sold by my executor, at such times and upon such terms and conditions as he may think proper, and after the whole is collected, it is to be added to the sum, or price at which my three sons are to take the lands, and the whole amount is then to be divided in to seven equal parts. One part is to be allotted to each one of my following named children, after deducting from the part allotted to each child the following advancements, to wit. From the part allotted to my daughter Catherine the sum of five hundred and fifty dollars. From the part allotted to my daughter Elizabeth SUMMER nine hundred dollars. From the part allotted to my daughter Martha GAREE five hundred dollars. From the part allotted to my daughter Sarah GLYRUPH four hundred and fifty dollars. From the part allotted to my son H. H. KINARD four hundred and ten dollars. From the part allotted to my son J. P. KINARD five hundred and fifty dollars. From the part allotted to my son M. T. KINARD nothing, as I have not advanced him anything. After all these deductions are made on account of advancements and they are all the advancements that I intend shall be made against any of my aforesaid children, I give and bequeath the one seventh part allotted as aforesaid to each one of my said children, to them and their heirs and afsigns absolutely and forever. Except the part allotted to my daughter Elizabeth SUMMER which I ordain and direct shall be laid out in young negroes by my executor, and settled on her to her sole and separate use during her life, and after her death to the lawful ifsue of her body. Fifth. For the purpose of carrying into effect the intention of this will and to have the property herein contimplated to be settled on my daughter Elizabeth SUMMER and her ifsue, I do here by nominate and appoint my executor, trustee for that purpose, and do hereby direct and authorize him to institute such proceedings in the Court of Chauncery, as may be necefsary to carry this my intention fully into effect. Sixth. Whereas by deed executed by me on the second day of January, in the year of our Lord, one thousand eight hundred and forty three, I conveyed to H. H. KINARD two negro slaves, to wit; Harriet and Sarah, with their future increase in trust, for the use of my daughter Huldah M. HENSON, during her natural life, and after her death to and for the use of her child or children. All of which will more fully appear by reference being had to the aforesaid deed. Which I direct shall be considered as a part of this my will, and where as the said Huldah M. HENSON has since died, leaving one child now therefore in accordance with the aforesaid deed, I do hereby give and bequeath to the said child the aforesaid two negroes, to have and to hold the same according to the terms and conditions of the aforesaid deed. Seventh. The rest residue and remainder of my property given to my wife, by the second clause of my will, not otherwise disposed of after the termination of her estate therein I direct shall go and be disposed of in the same manner, and to the same persons as is directed by the fourth clause of my will. Eighth. It is my further will and desire that the probate and recording of this my will, and all the other proceedings that may be had thereon shall be at Newberry Court House, and all the proceedings that may be had on my estate shall be in Newberry District as for as may be. And it is my exprefs will and desire that upon my executor as trustee or agent as aforesaid investing the funds for Elizabeth SUMMER and her ifsue, as herein directed and delivering over the property to her, and making areturn thereof to the Court of Chancey for Newberry District, that he shall for with be released from all further responsibility. Ninth. I do hereby nominate, constitute and appoint my son H. H. KINARD executor of this my last will and testament, but in case of his death or refusal to qualify, then and in that case, I constitute nominate and appoint my son M. T. KINARD, and in case of his death or refusal to qualify, then and in that case, I constitute, nominate, and appoint my son J. P. KINARD hereby revoking all former will by me heretofore made, and declaring this to be my last will and testament. In witnefs whereof I have hereunto set my hand and affixed my seal this fourteenth day of June in the year of our Lord, one thousand eight hundred and forty nine. Signed, sealed, published, and declared by the testator as his last will and testament in our presence, who at his request, and in his presence, other witnefsed the deu executrix thereof.

Jacob L. Eichelburger   Martin Kinard (L. S.)
R. R. Pratt
Jacob Kiblers
Recorded in Will Book A, Page 222, Bundle 122, Pkg. 7. Recorded date not available. Proven date 30th day of August, 1854. W. D. Watts, Ordy., Laurens District.

CODICIL

Whereas I the said Martin KINARD have made and executed my last will and testament bearing date the 14 day of June, 1849, when said will I do hereby republish and confirm in all its parts and provenores except as are herein after attened and reformed by this Codicil. That is to say. I do hereby give and bequeath to my grand son Henry Oliver HENSON (in addition to what I have given him in the sixth clause of my will) one eigth part of my estate, which is intended to make him take an equal share with either of my children, and which will leave them each one eighth instead of one seventh of my estate as provided for in my said will. The property which I gave his mother by deed, and as specified in my said will, to be considered as an advancement to him and to be deducted from his share, which I estimate as twelve hundred and fifty dollars. This legacy to be in lieu and for of all claim, which he the said Henry O. HENSON shall or may have for the hire or service of the negro girl named Hamiet which I have, or may have in my pofsefsion belonging to him. It is the exprefsed condition of the above legacy, given the said Henry O. HENSON that in the event of his dying without leaving ifsue, living at the time of his death. The said legacy shall revent to my issue living at the time of his death, and shall be equally distributed amoungst them according to the provisions of the State of Distribution of Intestate, estates. Each of my children then living (should there be any) to take one share, and the issue of a deceased child to represent his or their parents per Stirpies. Secondly. I further will and direct that my said will be so modified as to restrict my wife in the event of her marriage, to take the girl Ninty and no others part or portion of my estate. In testimony whereof I have hereunto subscribed my name this sixteenth day of October, in the year of our Lord, one thousand eight hundred and fifty two. Signed and published as a codicil (Illegeable) the said Martin KINARD in presence of us, who have hereunto subscribed our names, in presence of the said testator.

Whitfield Walker
Mos. W. Thompson
John Coats
Book A, Page 227.

Martin Kinard (L. S.)

WILL OF LAVAINA TUCKER

State of South Carolina Laurens District. In the name of God, Amen. I Lavina TUCKER of the State and District aforesaid, being of sound and disposing mind and memory, do make and ordain this my last will and testament in manner and form following, to wit. First, I desire that all my just debts and funeral expenses be paid by my executors herein after named out of my estate. 2nd. It is my will that my sister Haney and my brother in law James B. HIGGINS who is the husband of said sister Haney shall have my land if they chose at the price of thirty five hundred dollars and after deducting their full share of my estate from the price

of the land if they take it at the price specified they are to
pay to the children of my decd. brother James HIGGINS to be equally divided amongst them the sum of two hundred dollars and to
pay the like sum of two hundred dollars to the children of my
sister Lavina MOFS to be equally divided amongst them. The above
amounts to be paid in twelve months after my decease or to carry
intrust from and after twelve months from my deceased and if not
all paid at the same time the payments to be made equal, to each
family of children above named. But should they not think proper to take my land at the price above mentioned then I desire
that the land be sold by my executors upon such credits as they
think proper and out of the proceeds thereof to pay the four
hundred dollars aforementioned and for the balance to be assets
in the hands of my executors to be disposed of as hereafter directed. Be it understood that nothing herein is to be so construed as to give to Haney and James B. HIGGINS more than one share
of the remaining of my estate. 3rd. I give to my nephew Benjamin B. HIGGINS one negro boy, Silas and seven hundred dollars
to be paid out of my estate. 4th. All the balance of my estate
real and personal mony choses in action and etc. I will to be
equally divided between my brothers and sisters and the share
that William HIGGINS decd. would have been entitled to be equally divided amongst his children after deducting one fourth part
then from which is to be divided amongst (Illegeable) brothers
and sisters under the fourth clause of this my will Savina MOFSS
children and the children of my decd. brother James HIGGINS, being provided for an excluded in the division in the fourth clause
And I also exclude William FOWLER, son of my sister Nancey FOWLER
intirely in my will, he is to have no share of my estate in any
way. The shares of my estate that are going to my surviving
brothers and sisters, I will to them during their lives and then
to the heirs of their bodies respectively, share and share alike
Except William FOWLER who is already excluded. And further the
share of my estate that is going to Elizabeth FRENCH the wife of
James FRENCH, I will to James B. HIGGINS and Benjamin B. HIGGINS
in trust for the separate use of the said Elizabeth FRENCH during her life, and direct that she receive the interest or him
from the trustees annually and that thy pay to her only for her
own use. And that it is not liable to said FRENCHES debts or
contracts and at her death that it be equally divided amongst
her brothers and sisters as my estate agreeable to this clause
of my will. And further it is my desire that the share of my
brother Ezekiel HIGGINS which he is to recive under this clause
of my will be paid over to my brother David HIGGINS in trust and
for the said David HIGGINS to have the use of said property as
compensation for taking care of the said Ezekiel HIGGINS during
his life. And should the said Ezekiel out live the trustee David
HIGGINS, I then direct that my executors hereinafter named shall
have charge of the estate of Ezekiel and on it in manner above
denoted and at the death of the said Ezekiel HIGGINS I direct
that what ever remains shall be divided amongst his brothers and
sisters agreeable to the meaning of this clause of my will to
wit. To be equally divided between the heirs of his body. And

it is further my will that if either of my brothers or sisters
should die leaving no child or children or child or children of
decd. child that their share shall return my estate and be equally divided amongst the surviving brothers and sisters agreeable
to this clause of my will. Further it is my desire that my estate may be divided without a sale but should it become necessary
to sell my slaves or any part of them, I impower my executors
hereafter to be named to sell them at private sale if they think
proper so to do at the valuation of three disinterested persons
who shall be deem judges of the price of property and otherwise
respectable. 5th. I direct that one hundred dollars be taken
from the share of my sister Elizabeth FRENCH or from the share
of James B. and Benjamin B. HIGGINS in trust for Elizabeth FRENCH
and thrown in to my estate and divided agreeable to the fourth
clause of my will. I do this because I have paid a high interest
to her or her husband on money heretofore. Lastly, I do hereby
nominate, constitute and appoint James B. HIGGINS and Benjamin
B. HIGGINS my brother in law and nephew executors of this my
last will and testament, and in lieu of commission I give them
the sum of three hundred dollars each out of my estate for man-
aging my estate and if either of my executors heretofore named
should die or refuse to act, I direct that who ever manages my
estate shall receive for his or their services the same of six
hundred dollars in lieu of commissions. And I do hereby revoke
all other former wills by me heretofore made. In witnefs where
of I have hereunto set my hand and seal this 17th day of December, in the year of our Lord, one thousand eight hundred and
forty two. Signed, sealed, published, and declared to be the
last will of the said Lavina TUCKER in the presence of us. (The
five words on third page) (12 lines from bottom crofsed out before signing).

L. Meredith   Levina Tucker (SEAL)
Reubin Estes
Meredith Fowler
Joseph Prior
Recorded in Will Book A, Page 230, Bdl. 120, Pkg. 16. Proven
and recorded date not available. W. D. Watts, O. L. D.

                         Codicil
South Carolina Laurens District. Whereas I Lavina TUCKER of the
sd. State and District have heretofore made and executed my last
will and testament bearing date the 17th day of December, 1842
by the third clause of which will I give to my nephew Benjamin
B. HIGGINS, a negro boy Silas, and seven hundred dollars to be
paid out of my estate. And whereas the said Benjamin B. HIGGINS
is since dead. Now that clause of my will is revoked and I give
to his widow and children the said negro boy Silas, which is now
in their possession and the seven hundred dollars aforesaid, but
the seven hundred dollars is to be paid out of my land by laying
off one hundred acres round the improvements that the said Benjamin B. HIGGINS had possession of in his lifetime in such manner
as will be most to the advantage of his family, and the remainder
of my land to do the least injury to either party. And for the

widow and children to have and enjoy the same both land and services of the negro so long as she remains his widow and is disposed to stay on the land. But so soon as she marries or leaves the said land then it is to belong exclusively to his children in equal share and whereas I have in said will allowed my brother in law James B. HIGGINS to take all my land at valuation, I now allow him to take the balance after the one hundred acres above named is tied off upon the same conditions this to interfire with nothing else in my will. And I further direct that whereas the said James B. HIGGINS has recently moved to my house at my request, I wish him at my death to call in three disinterested men and if they think he has sustained injury by so doing they are to assess the amount of injury to the said James B. HIGGINS and I direct the same to be paid to him out of my estate. And I do hereby direct that this codicil be and is a part of my will as fully to all interest and purposes as it it had been executed at the time the said will was executed. In witnefs where of I have hereunto set my hand and seal this the 24th day of December, 1845. In presence of us.

Joseph Prior   Lavina Tucker (SEAL)
Joseph Terry
Thomas P. Gray
Wallace Thompson

The matter of proveing the will of Lavina TUCKER in due form of law. March 14th, 1837 Joseph PRIOR swoan. Says he saw Mrs. TUCKER sign the will and that Saml. MEREDITH and K. ESTICT saw the same that it was signed at B. HIGGINS house he does not know who wrote it and that there was no conversation about the writing thereof in his presence. And that the will was not read to Mrs. TUCKER at the time she signed it. And that she walked over to Benjamins the morning she signed and after she came Benjamin requested her to sign says he saw her Mrs. TUCKER signd two other wills or codacils and that they were all executed at the same place. And that he was not well acquainted with the old lady and that he thinks used a great deal of Laudnum saw a great many bials and the old lady took a dram of Spirits after she signd the will. Mrs. TUCKER lived about 100 yards from Benjamine and Benjamin managed the old ladys businefs looked like a very old lady and weekly. B. HIGGINS is now dead, died in the year 45 says he saw Wm. TUCKER sign a codacil and that Joseph TERRY, Thomas E. GRAY and Wallace THOMPSON the subscribers to the codicil saw the same in the presence of each other and also in the presence of the testors. And he thinks she signed at the regurst of Jos. B. HIGGINS. It was signed at the old ladys own house and that Jas. B. produced the Codicil for the afsignment. And that it was not read to the old lady in his presence and thus she was in bed and had to be proped up to sign. She signd in the room and the witnefs signd at the Brereau in the adjoining room from the old ladys does not know whether she was capable of making a will or not. J. B. HIGGINS took the codacil after signing and that she was a woman of good sence as he thought and never saw her at any time that she was not capable of doing her own

businefs says that Eliy FOWLER was living with the old lady at
the time the codacil was signd. Saml Meredith swoarn says that
the witnefs and the will and that M. FOWLER, X. ESTICT, and
Joseph PRIOR all signd in the presence of the old lady and she
signd also in the presence of each others. It was signed at
Benjamin HIGGINS house and Benjamin brought it from the beureau
that it was not read in her presence at the time of signing.
After signing B. HIGGINS took it and put it up on in or on the
said HIGGINS sent for Juin when he went the old lady was there
and told him that she had a will she wanted him to (Illegeable)
saw her sign other will at the same place says that she was 65
or 70 years of age. 3. HIGGINS at that time attended to her
businefs saw the old lady often never at any time when she was
not compted to make a will. Joseph TERRY swears that he saw Mrs.
TUCKER sign the Codacil and that he together with Joseph PRIORS,
Thos. GRAY, and Wallace THOMPSON all signed the same in the presence of each other and in the presence of testators. And that
he saw Mrs. TUCKER sign the will also, and said at the time she
wanted to amend her will the resin was that Benjamin HIGGINS was
dead and she wanted his children to have his part already willed
to him in his lifetime signed the codacil sitting in the bed
says the witnefses signed on the beureau in the other room thinks
in plain view of the old lady says he never saw her but what she
was capable of making a will. James HIGGINS was living with the
her at the time and took charge of the whole plantation after
the witnefses signed the codacil they handed it back to Mrs.
TUCKER to let her see it. She then give it to Mr. Jas. HIGGINS
and he fastened it to the will with a seal he thinks says he has
seen her drink Laudrum and that she was a very weekly old lady
about 70 years of age. Jas HIGGINS lived with her untill her
death in August, 1855. Wallace THOMPSON on oath says he saw
Lavina TUCKER sign the codacil and that Joseph PRIOR and Joseph
TERRY saw the same. They signd in the presence of each other,
that Mrs. TUCKER was in the bed when she signd after she signed
they took the codacil in the adjoining room to a Beureau or a
table, he is not certain which, and that Mrs. TUCKER might of
seen then signs but does not know whither or not, thinks her not
capable of making a will. And that the codacil was not read to
her in his presence nor nothing said about it only signd and
handed back. Saw Mrs. TUCKER take laudrumeh and a great many
vials about her house lookd vary old at the time does not know
her age. Jas HIGGINS and Mrs. E. FOWLER lived with her at that
time hered her say often that she was half distracted. Dr. M.
M. HUNTER swoarn says he lived in about 3 miles of Mrs. Lavina
TUCKER was at her house and herd he say she had to use Laudrum
for her healthlooked old a decrepted bot vials from some boys
labeld Laudrum pr bushel at a time and he thinks that she might
of bine influence by a (Illegeable) friend at the time he saw
her. R. G. BALL swoarn says he knew Mrs. TUCKER ever since he
was a small boy lived with in Genl. TUCKERS in his lifetime
conversed with her about a will in 1841. Benjamin HIGGINS asked
him to write a codacil to the old ladys will and he don so after
they had got done writing Benjamin looked at it and said if he

161

was her he would not make it that way the old lady replyed then
write it the way Benjamin says. He then began to write another
codacil and Benjamin dicated for him in the first part and Mrs.
TUCKER the last part in 1835 he kept store and sold her a great
many vials of Laudrum thinks she used as much as a vial pr day
from 42 to 45 he dos not think her compted to make a will was
vary old when she did died in July, 1855 could read and write
well. Ely SLOAN swoarn says she lived with Mrs. TUCKER from
1845 untill her death and thinks Mrs. TUCKER used a much as a
vial of Laudrum pr day and it would cause her to sleep nearly
all day some days she slep in the room with her and waited on
her. James HIGGINS attended to Mrs. TUCKERS businefs that she
lay in bed nearly all the time had often to be proped up in bed
had vary poor legs said she took Laudrum to ease the pain. Was
about 74 years old when she died at our time asked her to go out
of the room and stay about one hour before she came in, and she
did so said she was a going to take back the property that she
had given Benjamin as he was then dead that she haited to die
quarelling and that she would alter things from what they were
at now. That Benjamin has spent moore then he ought to of done
that she had bins rouged out of about $2000.00 that the old lady
had 4 or 5 negro when she went then to live, and only 2 when
she died. They worked with Jas HIGGINS hands for there vituals
and clothes when HIGGINS moved to Mrs. TUCKER he brot 15 or sixteen negores with him all worked the old ladys plantation that 1
doz. vials of Laudruam would not do her 2 weeks would have a half
bushels of veals at a time. And that her mind was good enough
at times at other times would be fretful and childish that her
mother Mrs. FOWLER got 2 negroes and Mrs. GARRET 2 negroes. Mrs.
TUCKER was very much afflicteted with pain took Laudum to eas
then one person had no more influence over her than another when
I told her any thing she would always agree to it when speaking
of her land said it was two good to lie idol and that Jas. HIG-
GINS said he would take Henney off unlefs she wiled to her the
land had hedd Mrs. TUCKER say this often says that Mrs. TUCKER
could of seen the Beureau from where she was lying if she had of
lookd. Wm. FOWLER swoarn says Mrs. TUCKER was in a lowe state
of health from 42 to 45 in 1850 he saw her again and she steill
was in the condition in 1850 when he saw her he conversed with
and she appeard not to have good recollection would conmence
talking about one thing and the ould quit that subject and talf
of another he went then to see something concerning a land warrant but could not get her to talk long enough about it to gain
any information about it says Jas HIGGINS and B. HIGGINS had
considerable influence over Mrs. TUCKER, herd B. HIGGINS say that
he intended to make his Jack that was often he went to live with
Mrs. TUCKER thinks he himself went to Mrs. TUCKER to live in
1837 and left in 1839 says Mrs. TUCKER used a great deal of Bait-
man drop during the time he lived with her saw her taking something out of vials and they told him it was Lauduam. Saw Mr.
TUCKER vary much excited times especially when she went towards
general TUCKERS grave would hollow and slap her hands. When she
return to the house would take a drink of drops would hollow and

162

slaps her hands sometime in the house says that B. HIGGINS kept
spirits for his friens saw Mrs. TUCKER drink spirits at Benjamin
house. Benjamin sold 2 of Mrs. TUCKER negroes to George BOBE for
$1200 interest from date this was done after he said he was going
to make his Jack. Benjamin sold other negroes belonging to Mrs.
TUCKER to R. G. BALL thinks it was a girl and boy sold then all
after he moved to Mr. HIGGINS says he saw Benjam sign the old
ladys name to different papers thinks he sold negroes to Nesbitt
and some to Thomas FARROW. X did not say that the old ladys was
not capable of transacting her businefs. Says that the notes
given for the negroes sold by Benjamin was made payable to Mrs.
TUCKER does not know who got the money for them. Never saw nothing wrong as regards the old ladys mind only she would commend
talkin on one subject and quit that commence another says Mrs.
TUCKER give Mrs GARRET a negro Mrs. FOWLER a negroe and Mrs.
SLOAN one and that they had to account for them to her estate.
Benjamin sign Mrs. TUCKER name to notes signd Lavina TUCKER by
B. HIGGINS sold spirits to Benjamin for himself and some for Mrs.
TUCKER that he knew Mrs. TUCKER well never saw her intoxicated
nor never saw any thing wrong about her. W. D. WATTS swoarn say
that he wrote Mrs. TUCKER will and codicil never saw Mrs. TUCKER
as he recollects that Benjamin HIGGINS applyed to him to get the
will written and Jas B. HIGGINS applyed to get the Codicil the
will was taken from as memorandrun does not know whether it was
executed or not. Saml. MILLS swoarn in reply. Says he lived in
1 pr mile of Mrs. TUCKER knew her from about 1834 her mind was
good at his first acquaintence and continud so untill her death
she was weaker from age he had conversd with her on worldly and
religious matters all right. X Says he was only on visits friend-
ly calls, talked on businefs matters saw vials in her room saw
Mrs. SLOAN give her drops dont know how much dont know anything
about the management of the property statement made was about
right 75 or 80 years old at death. Wm. POWERS swoarn says that
he was acquainted with Mrs. TUCKER thinks the last busenefs
transaction he had with her was in 1855, he went to deposition
for the p .pose of procuring Bourty land she sent more then once
before he could go said Mrs. TUCKER observed when he went she
had sent for him frequentyly and wanted some person to go this
money but supposed they did not go says he went to her house in
1837. She ofred to sell him negroes she owed him and wanted to
sell him silver spoons to pay him, did no purchase saw her in
1851 or 52 took deposition for land warrant she was tational and
competed to transact businefs. Examind. X Says he went when in
1848 with E. H. GARRETT for the purpose of executing a covenant
Got the information respecting the affadavit respecting land
warrant, gave him the information herself. She only proved he
marreage and that she was the widow of houe Starling TUCKER.
Always wrote her name when he executed papers for her in 1852 or
53 he was again at Mrs. TUCKERS for the purpose of witnefsing
the transfer of a land warrant she said she had given the land
warrant to her nephew who resides in Mifsifsippi. Said there
was public land near when her nephew resided and he would locate
said land. When he went with Mr. GARRET in 1845 the covenant

about the negro was executed after some conversation about the forms and C. She was rather inclind to intail the negro upon her sister Mrs. GARRETT but was waived. The was then competent to execute papers. O. RICHARDSON swoarn says he traded with Mrs. TUCKER in 1844 and 45 sold her goods she gave him a note or notes regarded her competent to transact businefs he was pealing sold her some of the goods in her own house and some was sent from Scuffletown x thinks the amt was $14 in 45 some of the goods was for herself and some for Mf E. FOWLER now sloan he was several times in 1844 and 45 says Mrs. TUCKER selected her own goods when at her own house reply says he never saw any defect in her mind. <u>Closed</u>.

Joseph Higgins Vs James Higgins
Laurens in the matter of the last will and testament of Levenia TUCKER decd. After hereing the evadurce in the above stated case, it is ordered and decred that the said will and codacil be admitted to probate. Given uner my hand and seal.

W. H. Langston, Ordy. <u>Evadence</u>

WILL OF ANNA DALRYMPLE

In the name of God, Amen. I Anna DALRYMPLE of the State of South Carolina and Laurens District, being of sound and disposing mind and memory, but weak in body, and calling to mind the uncertainty of life, and being desirious to dispose of all such worldly estate as it hath pleased God to blefs me with, do make and ordain this my last will in manner following, that is to say. I desire that all my land be immediately sold after my decease upon a credit of one and two years, and out of the monies arising there from all my just debts and funeral expenses be paid. Again my will is that my son Benjm. C. DALRYMPLE have seventy dollars in money out of the sale of my property. I also will and bequeath unto my said son two cows and calves and one bed and furniture. Again I give and bequeath unto my grand daughter Anna BENJAMIN, one bed and furniture now in her pofsefsion. I further will and bequeath unto my grand daughter Susanna I. HITT one bed and furniture, now in her pofsefsion. Also one white and red heifer, and my side saddle. It is further my will and desire that the balance of my personalty estate of what kind soever, that has not been disposed of by will be sold on a credit of twelve months Again it is my will and desire that after the payment of all my debts and funeral expenses that all of my children Viz; my daughter Susanna JONES, Ephraim DALRYMPLE, Mahala BENJAMIN, John DALRYMPLE, the legal representatives of my daughter Lucinda HITT decd, the legal hiers of my daughter Lucretia JONES decd. Benj. C. DALRYMPLE, and Henry H. DALRYMPLE have equally (after the payment of those specific legacies) in the nett balance of my estate. Allowing it to be expectly understood that the representatives of my decd. daughter shall jointly receive that portion which their mothers would have received if they had survived. And lastly, I do constitute and appoint Lewis D. JONES executor of this my last will and testament by me heretofore made. In testemony whereof I have hereunto set my hand and affixed my seal this third day of Feby., one thousand eight hundred and forty six. Signed, sealed, published, and declared as and for the last will and testament of the above named Anna DALRYMPLE in the presence of us.

John Jones
Thomas W. Dalrymple
Thomas Dalrymple

                         her
            Anna (X) Dalrymple (SEAL)
               mark

Recorded in Book A, Page 246, Bundle 123, Package 16. roven date Nov. 15, 1852. Recorded date not available. W. D. Watts, Ordy.

WILL OF MARY ANN STARNS

The State of South Carolina Laurens District. In the name of God, Amen. I Mary Ann STARNS of the District and state aforesaid being of sound and disposing mind and memory, but weak in body, and calling to mind the uncertainty of life and being desirous to dispose of all such worldly estate as it has pleased God to blefs me with, do make and ordain this my last will and in manner following. I desire fust that the whole of my estate both real and personal after my decease be sold by my executor hereinafter named, on a credit of twelve months and out of the monies arising therefrom all my just debts and funeral expences be paid. Secondly. After the payment of my debts and funeral expences aforesaid, I give and bequeath the ballance of my estate one eighth part to such of the children of my deceased daughter Ann SHERBY as may be living at my death and also the sum of four hundred and twenty six dollars and sixty cents over and above : said sums are to be distributed amongst them equally to such of the children of my disease son John STARNS as may be living at my death. I give and bequeath one eighth part of my estate lacking one hundred and sixty nine dollars twenty four cents. And the balance of my estate I give and bequeath as follows. To my son Moses STARNS one eighth part of my estate lacking fifty five dollars. To my daughter Rebecca GRAVES wife of Lewis GRAVES, one eighth part of my estate wanting thirty three dollars and forty two cents. To Susan SHERBY wife of Berryman SHERBY one eighth part of my estate to Mary COBB wife of Willi COBB one eighth part of my estate. To Elizabeth HILL, wife Aaron HILL one eighth part of my estate and to Sarah EDINGS wife of Isaac EDING one eighth part of my estate wanting one hundred and sixty nine dollars and twenty four cents. All the rest of my estate both real and personal of what nature or quality soever it may not be herein particularly disposed of. I desire may be divided into eight equal parts amoungst my several children herein before named the children of Ann SHERBY to take one share amoungst them and the children of John STARNS to take one share amoungst them, their heirs executors administrators and afsigns forever. And lastly, I constitute my friend Martin SHAW sole exeuctors of this my last will and testament. In testimony whereof I have hereunto set my hand and affixed my seal this twentyeth day of May, in the year of our Lord, one thousand eight hundred and forty three and in the sixty seventieth year of the Independence of the United States of America. Signed, sealed published, and declared as and for the last will andtestament of the above named Mary Ann STARNS in the presence of us and subscribed by us in the presence of the testatrix and at her request.

Joel L. Anderson

Asa Fogy

James McPherson

her

Mary Ann X Starns

mark

Recorded in will Book A, Page 256. Original will not in files of Probate Judge. W. D. Watts, O. L. D. Proven and recorded dates not available.

CODICIL

I Mary Ann STARNS do hereby alter the aforesaid will as follow to wit. So much of said willas given a share of my estate Mary COBB wife of Wm. COBB I revoke and give and bequeath the legacy give by said will to her to such children as the said Mary COBB surviving now, shear and sheare alike to be paid to them when they respectively arive at the age of twenty one years of age by my executor. And I further alter said will so far as it gives a legacy to my grand son Joel SHERBY as one of the children of my deceased daughter Ann SHERBY as followes to wit. I revoke the legacy and intrest give the said Joel SHERBY as aforesaid and give and bequeath the said legacy and intrest to Mary BERRY the sisters of the said Joel and one of the children of the said Ann SHERBY deceasd. This I give her the said Mary BERRY in addition to the share which she will take under said will as one of the children of the said Ann decd. Given under my hand and seal this 28th day of Jan., A. D., 1851. In presence of

Joel L. Anderson

Asa Fogy

James McPherson

her

Mary X Starns

mark

WILL OF WILLIAM R. SMITH

S. Carolina Laurens District. I William R. SMITH do make and ordain this my last will and testament following. Item. I desire all my just debts and funeral expences be paid. Item. It further my will that all the estate both real and personal of which I may die seized and pofsefsed be sold by my executors herein after named on a credit of one and two years. The real estate in such lots or parcels may be advisable by my executors. And one sixth part of the proceeds thereof be paid over to my intended wife Ursula. The remainder to be equally divided amongst all my children share and share alike. The child or children of any deceased child to take the same share that their parents would have taken if living. It is here understood that the children of my deceased son Marshall all to take out of my estate five hundred dollars each which is all I give to them. I do here by appoint my sons Hazel SMITH and Archabald SMITH executors to this my last will and testament. I witnefs whereof I have here set my hand Sept. 24th, 1850. Signed, sealed and acknowledged in the presence of.

J. H. Irby   William R. Smith (SEAL)
C. C. Higgins
W. B. Henderson
Recorded in Will Book A, Page 271. Recorded date not available.
Proven date April 7, 1857. W. H. Langston, Ordy. Laurens Dist.

WILL OF JOHN MILAM

South Carolina Laurens District. In the name of God, Amen. I John MILAM being of sound and disposing mind and memory, and calling to mind the uncertainty of life, and being desirous of disposing of such worldly estate as it hath pleased God to blefs me with, do make and ordain this my last will and testament. In the words following to wit. It is my will anddesire that all my estate both real and personal of whatever kind or nature it may be   sold as soon as convenient after my decease, and that my executor after first paying all my just debts divide the ballance between my children, Barlet MILAM, Isam MILAM, William A. MILAM, Betsey BRADDOCK, Patsey BRYSON, Polley BRYSON, Catherine MAY, Jimmey BRYSON, Henry MILAM, John MILAM, Nansey BRYSON, Milton MILAM, Ferrie MILAM, Leander I. MILAM, equally to each one except those who have had a portion given to them before now. Each child shall render in what they have had and let it be deducted out of the estate. It is further my desire that the part of my estate which would of been Betsey BRADDOCKS fall in to the hands of Feral MILAM to keep for her children and to be paid to them when they come of age. And lastly, I do hereby constitute and appoint Feral MILAM and Leander I. MILAM executor of this my last will and testament. In testimony whereof I have hereunto set my hand and seal this 13th day of January, 1857. Signed, sealed and delivered as the last will and testament of the with in John MILAM in presents of us.

                                              his
William Bailey   John X Milam (S. L.)
Joseph Vance   mark
Robert Bryson
Recorded in Will Book A, Page 272, Bdle. 127, Pkge 12. Recorded date not available. Proven date April 21, 1857.

WILL OF JAMES DORROH

In the name of God, Amen. I James HOLLIDAY, otherwise called James DORROH, being of sound and disposing mind and memory do make and constitute this my last will and testament in manner and form following that is to say. First. It is my will and desire that all my just debts and funeral expenses and the expenses of my last illnefs be paid. Second. I give and devise all the residue of my estate, both real and personal after the payment of my debts to my beloved wife Martha DORROH, to her her

heirs, executors, administrators, and afsigns, absolutely forever.
Thirdly. I nominate and appoint my said wife Martha DORROH sole
executrix of this my last will and testament hereby revoking all
other will by me heretofore made. In testimony whereof I have
hereunto set my hand and seal this seventeenth day of October,
one thousand eight hundred and fifty. Signed, sealed, published
and acknowledged in the presence of.

W. D. Simpson   James Dorroh (SEAL)
Alexander McCarley
H. M. Young
Recorded in Will Book A, Page 288, Bdl. 129, Pkge 5. Proven
Oct. 6, 1857. Recorded date not available. W. H. Langston,
O. L. D.

WILL OF ANTHONY F. GOLDING

South Carolina Laurens District. In the name of God, Amen. I
Anthony F. GOLDING of the district and state aforesaid being of
sound and disposing mind, memory, and discretion and in ordinary
health, but calling to mind the uncertainty of life and being
diserous of disposing of all such worldly estate as it has pleased God to blefs me with, do make and ordain this my last will
and testament in manner and form following, Viz. First. I
authorize my executors hereinafter appointed as soon after my
death as convenient to sell so much of my personal estate as
they my think necefsary to pay all my just debts and funeral expenses, unlefs I should leave on hand a sufficient amount of
cash and available debts due me to answer that purpose. Second.
After payment of debts as aforesaid, I give, devise and bequeath
the whole of my estate both real and personal to my beloved wife
dureing her natural life, and after her death I will and devise
that the whole of said estate be sold by my executors on such
credit as they my deem most expedeint and the proceeds thereof
distribute as hereinafter provided. Third. I give and bequeath
out of the proceeds of said sole the sume of one thousand dollars
to Dr. R. E. CAMPBELL and A. G. CAMPBELL in trust for the sole
and separate one of my daughter Caroline Matilda Elizabeth GOLD-
ING during her life. And at her death I give and bequeath the
same to such child or children as she my leave surviving her,
including the child or children of any deceased child, to whom
I give and bequeath the portion to which the deceased parent
would be entitled of living, under this clause of my will. Fourth. I give and bequeath out of the proceeds of said sole the
further sum of one thousand dollars to Dr. R. E. CAMPBELL and A.
G. CAMPBELL in trust for the sole and separate on of my daughter
Pamela Cunningham GOLDING during her life and at her death I give
and bequeath the same to such child or children as she may leave
surviving her, including the child or children of any deceased
child to whom I give and bequeath the portion to which the deceased parent would be entitled, of living under this clause of
my will. Fifth. I give and bequeath out of the proceeds of said
sale the sum of one thousand dollars to my son John Brown GOLDING

during his life, and at his death I give and bequeath the same
to such child or children as he may leave surviving him, including the child or children of my deceased child to whom I give and
bequeath the portion to which the deceased parent would be entitled if living under this clause of my will. These three last
legacies aforesaid are intended to put said two daughters and
son upon an equality with my elder children who have heretofore
been advanced. Sixth. I will and desire that the residue of the
proceeds of said sale including all the balance of my estate of
every discription be divided into six equal parts or shares to
be disposed of as hereinafter directed and provided. Seventh.
I give and bequeath one of the shares arising under the said
last clause of my will to Dr. R. E. CAMPBELL and A. G. CAMPBELL
in trust for the exclusion use and benefit of the children of my
deceased son Anthony R. GOLDING for and during the term of their
respective lives and at the death of any one of them, I give and
bequeath the share of such deceased child to such child or children as he or she may leave surviving him or her. And in the
event that any one of my said grand children should die without
leaving a child or children, then I give and bequeath the share
of such deceased grand child to such of my said grand children
as may be then living. But should all my said grand children
die without leaving a child or children, then I give and bequeath
the aforesaid share arising under this clause to my surviving
children, including the child or children of any deceased child,
who will take the share of the decd. parent. Eighth. I give and
bequeath one other of said shares arising under the said sixth
clause of my will to Dr. R. E. CAMPBELL and A. G. CAMPBELL in
trust for the sole and separate one of my daughter Clementine B.
PHILIPS, wife of Dr. Wm. PHILIPS, during her life, and at her
death I give and bequeath the same to such child or children as
she may leave surviving, including the child or children of any
deceased child, to whom I give and bequeath the portion to which
the deceased parent would be entitled if living under this clause
of my will. (Illegeable) the said sixth clause of my will, to
Dr. R. E. CAMPBELL and A. G. CAMPBELL in trust for the use of my
grand son Calvin FOSTER during his life and at his death I give
and bequeath the same to such child or children as he may leave
surviving him, including the child or children of any deceased
child, to whom I give and bequeath the portion to which the deceased parent would be entitled, if living, under this clause of
my will. And should my said grand son Calvin FOSTER die without
leaving a child or children or the child or children of a deceased child, in that event it is my will and desire that the
legacy given to my said grand son Calvin FOSTER should revert
back to my estate and be distributed amongst my surviving children, including the child or children of any deceased child, who
will take the share of such deceased parent, under the same trust
and limitations as on herein contained and are applicable to them
respectively. Tenth. I give and bequeath one other of said
share arising under the said sixth clause of my will to my son
John Brown GOLDING during his life and at his death, I give and
bequeath the same to such child or children as he may leave

surviving him, including the child or children of any deceased
child, to whom I give and bequeath the portion to which the deceased parent would be entitled if living, under this clause of
my will. Eleventh. I give and bequeath on other share arising
under the said sixth clause of my will to Dr. R. E. CAMPBELL and
A. G. CAMPBELL in trust for the sole and separate use of my
daughter Caroline Matilda Elizabeth GOLDING during her life, and
at her death I give and bequeath the same to such child or children as she may leave surviving her, including the child or children of any deceased child, to whom I give and bequeath the portion to which the deceased parent would be entitled, if living,
under this clause of my will. Twelfth. I give and bequeath the
remaining share arising under the said sixth clause of my will
to Dr. R. E. CAMPBELL and A. G. CAMPBELL in trust for the sole
and separate use of my daughter Pamela Cunningham GOLDING during
her life, and at her death I give and bequeath the same to such
child or children as she may leave surviving her, including the
children or children of any deceased child to whom I give and
bequeath the portion to which the deceased parent would be entitled, if living, under this clause of my will. Thirteenth.
Should any of my said children die without leaving a child or
children or the child or children of a deceased child, then and
in that event I give and bequeath the legacy or legacies of such
child under this will to my surviving children and my grand son
Calvin FOSTER and the children of my deceased son Anthony R.
GOLDING the latter taking among them the share of their decd.
parent, and also to the child or children of any deceased child
who will take among them the portion to which the deceased parent
would be entitled if living. This clause to include likewise
the child or children of the said Calvin FOSTER should he die
leaving such. But if he should not leave a child or children
then the portion to which he may be intitled under this clause
shall be distributed at his death as his other legacy is directed to be. Fourteenth. I hereby rest the aforesaid trustees of
my said daughters and grand children, and each and every of them
with full power to approfnate the leagacies given them for my
said daughters and gran children respectively, faithfully and
truly according to the trusts to which they an subject and to
invest and reinvest the said legacies as any portion thereof in
such property real and persoanl as they or any of them may deem
most advantageous for my said daughters and my said grand children as any one of them, to be held by said trustees respectively
subject to the same, trusts and limitations as the assigned legacies are held. Lastly. I constitute and appoint my nephew B.
R. CAMPBELL exq. and A. G. CAMPBELL executors and my wife Caroline Matilda executrix of this my last will and testament with
full power and authority to carry it into complete execution.
In witnefs whereof I have hereunto set my hand and seal this the
27th day of September, in the year of our Lord, one thousand
eight hundred and fifty three and of American Independence the
seventy eight. In presence of us.

H. G. Dean   A. F. Golding (SEAL)
Continued on page 171
                           170

Continued from page 170
Pro. O. P. Vernon
E. I. Henry
Recorded in Book A, Page 303. Recorded date not available.
Proven date April 23rd, 1858. W. H. Langston, Ordy. Bundle 129,
Package 13.

CODICIL

Whereas I Anthony F. GOLDING have heretofore made and duly executed my last will and testament in writing hearing date the
twenty seventh day of September Anno Domini eighteen hundred and
fifty three and therby directed clause fifth that my executors
should advance to my son John Brown GOLDING the sum of one thousand dollars for the purpose therein named and whereas since the
execution of said instrument I have made cash advances to my
said son to the amount of five hundred dollars. Now therfore I
do hereby modify the said fifth clause by substituting the sum
of five hundred dollars instead of one thousand. And I do here
by further modify the said fifth clause by bequeathing this legacy to my son in law Dr. Wm. PHILIPS in trust for the sole and
separate use of my said son during his life. And at his death
for the child or children of my said son as mentioned and provided for in the said fifth clause. And I do hereby also modify
the tenth clause of said justment which gives to my said son a
further legacy by directing that the legacy provided for in the
said tenth clause shall also be to my son in law Dr. Wm. PHILIPS
in trust for the sole and separate use of my said son during his
life, and at this death to go as directed in the said tenth
clause. And I do also hereby modify the last clause of said instrument so far as to constitute my nephew Dr. Robert E. CAMPBELL
as one of my executors in place of A. G. CAMPBELL who has died
since the execution of said justment. In witnefs whereof I have
here unto set my hand and afixed my seal this thirtieth day of
October, A. D., 1857. In presence of us.

Jas Farrow   A. F. Golding (SEAL)
Lewis Camp
Thos Stobo Farrow

WILL OF DR. E. M. BOBO

South Carolina Laurens District. I E. M. BOBO of the State and
District aforesaid to make and ordain this as my last will and
testament. 1st. I will and bequeath to my beloved wife all my
property both real and personal her lifetime and at her death to
be equally divided between my son C. D. BOBO, Mary Ann BOBO, and
Susen Jane SPRINGS, C. D. BOBO accounting for what I have given
him which is thirty five hundred dollars (my old house and lot
in union and the negro boy Carter). 2nd. I nominate and appoint
Dr. C. D. BOBO and my son in law R. A. SPRINGS executor to this
my last will and testament hereby revoking setting aside all former wills by me made and acknowledging this as my last will and
testament. Witnefs my hand and seal this 23rd day of Mary, 1853.
Signed, sealed and acknowledged in the presence of us who at the
request of the testator and in the presence of each other have

subscribed our names as witnefs thereto.

Tho. W. Holloway   E. M. Bobo (SEAL)
Drayton Nance
Jams. A. Graham
Recorded in Will Book A, Page 313.   Recorded date not available.
Proven date not available.

WILL OF MARGARETT BOYD

In the name of God, Amen. I Margaret BOYD of Laurens District
So. Carolina, being of sound and disposing mind and memory, and
calling to mind the uncertainty of life, do make and ordain this
my last will in manner following, that is to say. I desire that
all my just debts and funeral expences be paid out of the monies
due me, also that my executor procure and pay for out of the
same fund, a marble slab tomb stone. The remainder of my estate
consisting of monies due me by bonds, notes, or otherwise, together with my negro woman Sarah and her daughter Mary Anne and
their future increase, as well as all other property of which I
may be pofsefsed at my deat I give to my son in law Samuel R.
TODD in trust to and for the use and benefit of my daughter Jane
TODD during her natural life, the interest of the monies at
interest to be paid to her annually to be desposed of by her at
her pleasure. And at her death the whole of my estate to be
equally divided between her children. Lastly, I do constitute
and appoint the said Saml. R. TODD my son in law executor of
this my last will and testament. In testimony whereof I have
hereunto set my hand and affixed my seal this fourth day of November, 1843. Signed and sealed in the presence of.

Jno. W. Simpson   Margaret Boyd (SEAL)
S. D. Simpson
W. L. Templeton
Recorded in Will Book A, Page 329, Bundle 145, Pkg. 5. Recorded
date not available. Proven date 3rd April, 1860. W. H. Langston
Ordy., Laurens District.

WILL OF JOHN BURTON

South Carolina Laurens District. John BURTON of said District
do make this my last will and testament. First. It is my will
that all my just debts and funeral expenses be paid out of my
estate. And for that purpose I direct all my estate both real
and personal be sold by my executors hereinafter named upon the
usual credits and after the payment of debts and expenses as
above stated, I give the children of my decd. daughter Edny WELLS
one hundred dollars each and to the survivors or survivor of
them. The balance of my estate I give to my children equally
amongst them and if any of be dead haveing a child or children
they are to take their parents share amongst them. The share of
my daughter Susanah HARDY the wife of Wiley HARDY, I give to
James HENDERSON my son in law in trust for the use of my daughter

Susanah HARDY during her life, and her death to her children
equally between them. Allowing the trustee to invest the money
in property for her use if he thinks best or to loan it out and
pay her the interest annually. The children of my daughter Edney
to have no more than the three hundred dollars amongst. I appoint my son in law James HENDERSON my executor. Witnefs my
hand and seal this 19th Decr., 1853. In presence of.

<pre>
                                                   his
W. D. Watts   John X Burton (SEAL)
H. R. Shell   mark
J. M. Rose
</pre>

Recorded in Will Book A, Page 344, Bdl. 141, Pkge. 5. W. H.
Langston, O. L. D. Recorded and proven dates not available.

WILL OF ALEXANDER ABERCROMBIE

State of South Carolina Laurens District. In the name of God,
Amen. I Alexander ABERCROMBIE of the State and District aforesaid, being sick and weak in body, but of sound and disposing
mind, memory, and understanding praised be God for the same, do
make and declare this my last will and testament in manner and
form following that is to say. After the payment of funeral and
medecal expences and payment likewise of all my just debts, I
will and direct that my house or tenement, land and heredate-
ments with the appurtenances setuate lying and being in the
state and district aforesaid now in my own tenure and accupation
be sold upon such credit or credits as my executors may think
most proper. I likewise direct that all my personal property,
goods, chattels and so forth be sold by my executors (except my
beds and furniture and my chests which I reserve for my five
daughters Eliza, Martha Jane, Susannah Sarah, Elizabeth, and
Lucretia, giving to my three oldest daughters that portion which
they now claim of said goods and to my two youngest the remainder in equal share each), and to be part and parcel equally
devided among my nine children. (Viz): Richard A, Hugh, Robert,
and Winfield SCOTT my four sons and my five daughters before
named. After allowing to Rich'd A. the house which is now in
his right and possession to Hugh a young mare which he now claims
named Kit. And to my two youngest sons Robert and Winfield
SCOT each the sum of fifty ($50) on their arrival severally at
the age of twenty one years. And I do hereby nominate constitute
and appoint John WOODS and my son Richard Alexe. ABERCROMBIE
executors of this my last will and testament, hereby revoking
and making void all former wills and testaments at any time here
tofore by me made. And do declare this to be my last will and
testament. In witness whereof I the said Alexander ABERCROMBIE
have hereunto set my hand and seal this the 28th day of April,
in the year of our Lord, one thousand eight (Illegeable). Signed
sealed, declared and published by the above named Alexander ABER-
CROMBIE as and for his last will and testament in the presence
of us. Who at his request and in his presence have subscribed
our names as witnesses thereunto.

Continued from page 173
M. P. Evins   A. Abercrombie (SEAL)
Arther Rodgers
Thos. A. Saden
Recorded book and date not available. Bdle, 119, Pkge. 2. Prov-
en date Mar. 25, 1853. W. H. Langston, Ordy., Laurens District.

177